mat. We weren't to retrieve the cat as that would likely be impossible, but if we could leave some cat food inside the door, it would be much appreciated. Those were my very instructions. It was almost humorous as I jotted them all down. I was sure whoever would read them the following day would be elated at the tedious manner in which I had spelled out this particular rescue attempt.

About six o' clock each morning, crews would line up convoy style to receive their instructions for the day. Each crew would be assigned to an area based on information we had gathered from the previous day's calls and reconnaissance. We would go from cab to cab of each pickup, trailer in tow, and give each driver a master list of all the rescues, with his own responsibilities marked in bold letters. As the drivers looked down the sheet, scanning the information, they would figure out the materials needed and gather what was necessary from our now-awesome stock of donated supplies. Some areas were heavily flooded and would require canoes or waders or both. Often crews would need to deliver hay and supplies to farms along the way.

As the crew headed to Chalmette read through its list with my information, they didn't think twice. They marched over to the small-animal rescue barn and asked for a bag of cat food.

"Forget why or how; in fact, don't ask us anything about what we're doing. We just need some cat food."

They threw the bag into the back of the truck along with halters, ropes, and waders, and off they went. It was almost comical, venturing off into the unknown with very little idea of whether we could even access these areas. We had so little in-

stable or from stables nearby, was found on the levee that was the only dry land separating Lake Pontchartrain from the lake that was now New Orleans. There he was, though nobody at the time knew it was him.

I was not present on the levee that day. Dr. Shannon Gonsoulin, along with other LSU team members and a slew of volunteers, finally had made his way onto Haynes Boulevard on day ten. Duncan was simply one horse among a group of horses gathered up that day in the LSU net. After being housed at Lamar-Dixon for a few days, his sun-bleached coat no longer matched the photos Kristin had e-mailed to Dr. Rusty Moore. But his markings and the distinctive scar on his forehead matched the description closely enough to cause us to take a second look. It was Duncan, sure enough.

A phone call informed Kristin and her father. Probably through tears, lingering doubts, fear of another disappointment, and an underlying hint of "please, God, let it be him," she came to be reunited with her horse. Exactly how he survived, we will never know; but Duncan made it, and he was headed home to Oregon.

To see things come full circle is a rare opportunity. Often during the mayhem of daily operations, it is easy to lose sight of the real reason for a given task. To be honest, in many instances our efforts seemed incredibly futile. To think that jotting down the requests, descriptions, and directions of a horse owner now hundreds of miles away was going to make any sense once we got down into New Orleans was truly difficult to believe. Particularly when the city had been turned upside down and covered in water.

Depending on whether there was cell phone service, rescue teams would occasionally update us throughout the day. Often, however, we wouldn't know a rescue attempt's outcome until the teams returned at nightfall. The information would be compiled in a report so that by the following day everyone knew where everything stood. It was a great time of day when those rescue reports came in. Manning the phones for hours, we could easily lose that connection with the realities occurring just an hour south of us. Hearing the results and seeing the fruits of our labors, so to speak, were something all of us looked forward to.

Like most other callers, a woman I spoke to one evening went into great detail about the location of her horses, their breeding, size, and color, along with a description of her home in Chalmette. As usual, I wrote down exactly what she said.

Like so many others before, this woman had evacuated, leaving enough feed and water for her horses to get by for a few days. Three days, to be exact. She then learned that the area in which she lived had flooded and it might be months before she could return to what was left of her home. As she described her horses, her address, her house color, and the multiple methods of entry into her neighborhood, she paused for a second and then said, "Do you all only go after horses, or can you help small animals as well?"

I told her that our primary focus was horses but we had assisted with small-animal efforts, depending on the circumstances and our ability to help.

"Well, I have this cat," she said. "You can't catch him or any-

thing, but I wondered if you might leave him some food?"

My eyes started to roll. It would be a miracle if her hou was even accessible, much less that her horses would still where she left them, and even more so a miracle if we were ab to locate a feral cat that supposedly lived somewhere on tl premises.

"OK," I continued. "Tell me about the cat."

The cat lived pretty much wherever he wanted, and the wom; had kind of adopted him over the years. He came and went he pleased, and she had never actually caught him, but he us ally lived in the storage room at the top of her house. It was ; old apartment she had turned into a makeshift workshop ar storage area. There was a staircase alongside the house, right b tween the horses' paddock and her home. It was a white stairca; and white house. The stairs went up to the workshop entranc and the cat often could be found inside.

"I think if it has flooded, he'll most likely be there," she said

I jotted down the information in barely legible format, nc ing the information on the horses and then included the sto about the cat.

I don't know if I had become overly doubtful simply due the nonstop bad news we kept hearing about the situation New Orleans or if ten straight hours of answering phone ca had left me less than enthusiastic, but I had my doubts abo these horses, and I would have bet money we couldn't check (this cat.

I wrote it all down anyway. The cat was supposed to be in tl apartment; the key was at the top of the stairs under the do(

formation about the actual circumstances we would encounter when we arrived. We learned to go with the information we had and do the best we could once we got there.

About three o' clock that afternoon a crackly voice came back over the Nextel radio.

"We got those two horses out of Chalmette."

I couldn't believe it. "I thought it was flooded," I said.

"No, the area where she lived was pretty bad, but the horses were still there, and they were actually in pretty good shape. We've got them loaded, and we're taking them back to Lamar-Dixon right now."

A brief silence followed: "Oh, and we fed the cat."

I called the woman and reported the news. "We have your horses," I said.

She immediately began to cry. "Oh, thank God," she said. "You all are so wonderful."

We talked for a few minutes, and I almost forgot to tell her, "Oh, by the way, we also fed the cat."

She was speechless. It was nothing, really. Somebody walked up some stairs, reached under a mat, retrieved a key, opened a door, and dumped a bag of cat food on the floor. Not exactly the work of a superhero. But it meant something to her, and I would have to say it probably meant the world to the cat.

Chapter 12

Helping Hands

From the beginning, we were flooded with volunteers. They came from throughout Louisiana and from across the nation. In pickups, campers, and cars, they showed up at Lamar-Dixon wanting to help. Usually this was a blessing, and it was particularly a blessing when they had animal-rescue experience and a vague idea of what they were getting into.

Such was the case when representatives from Lone Star Equine Rescue contacted us. Based in Texas, the group conducts rescue operations all over the country and takes in displaced animals. And as luck would have it, two of their more prominent members happened to have recently relocated to Louisiana.

The first time I met Terry and R.T. Fitch, I was struck by their quiet manner. Completely unassuming and good-natured, they followed LSU crews for weeks into the deluge of New Orleans, providing their own truck and trailer to the cause, paying for their own fuel, and rarely saying a word.

Each day they showed up bright and early, got in line behind an LSU rescue team, took their list of rescue orders, stocked their vehicle with supplies, and off they went. They brought their own food and shared it with everyone. They had equipment, ropes, leads, and a lot more. Sometimes they even had a cooler with a few cold beers to pass around. Because they said very little, often they went unnoticed, until it mattered, and then they were everywhere. What we didn't realize at first was that the Fitches were no strangers to the horse-rescue game. They had contacts, resources, and a passion for helping animals that stretched back decades.

With silver-white hair and a "Fu Manchu" mustache to match, R.T. Fitch stepped out each morning sporting his old cowboy hat, faded jeans, and his usual light blue "Lone Star" T-shirt. Terry Fitch would be at his side, dressed in a similar style but with a bit of a bohemian twist.

The pair had met working for the same offshore oil company, and six weeks after their wedding they were shipped to Brazil.

"There was not much to do there if you don't speak the language so several of my friends and I thought it would be fun to own horses," Terry Fitch said.

One day while riding through the Brazilian countryside, they found a stranded horse tangled in a barbed wire fence. After rescuing it and being unable to locate its owner, they adopted the animal and nursed it back to health. On other occasions they found unclaimed, starving horses, so they took them under their wing as well.

"We rescued horses on a small scale down there, and when

we moved back [to the United States] we realized that it was needed here," she said. "In 2000 we started working with Lone Star Rescue."

Having thrown their names into the volunteer hat via our hotline, the Fitches were called by Dr. Becky McConnico to join our horse-rescue effort. And not only did they have their own equipment, they also had the attention of their organization. They immediately sent out a press release to the other members of Lone Star Equine Rescue, informing them of the plight in Louisiana and the need for supplies.

"We had an overwhelming response," Terry Fitch said. "The first day we got over one hundred responses. There was no way we could have kept up with it. From there we just kept bringing in trailer loads of stuff that was needed."

Each day as the troops met in the morning, the Fitches would take into account what tools, equipment, and supplies the group still needed. As they drove along rescuing horses throughout the day, they would contact their organization headquarters and let them know of any new needs. The necessary equipment often arrived within days.

Even when the rescue days had come to an end, as if their efforts weren't enough, R.T. Fitch hopped out of the truck at the end of a rescue one day and handed me a check for $10,000.

"This is from our organization to help with the rebuilding and to assist the equine victims," he said.

Other animal-rescue groups from around the country pitched in to help, sometimes without our knowledge. This often complicated things because some areas would be visited more than necessary by search groups while other areas were forgotten. Maintaining a handle on the situation was an ongoing battle.

The week after Katrina hit, a volunteer group contacted our hotline, reporting they were in New Orleans and had gathered a small herd of horses, put them in a trailer, and wanted LSU to come and get the animals. As they hadn't coordinated their activities through us prior to their rescue efforts, we had no idea who they were or whether their information was reliable. However, we had to give them the benefit of the doubt. One of our crews ventured southward to transfer the horses to our own trailer and bring them out of the city.

Arriving at the predetermined location, our rescue group found nobody. For hours they waited; still nothing. Long after nightfall our team returned empty-handed only to learn the first group had decided not to make the transfer but were bringing the horses to Lamar-Dixon themselves. The crew had lost nearly an entire day that could have been spent constructively. It was maddening. This example of wasted time resulting from a lack of communication was a lesson we were taught repeatedly throughout the process. Whether it was an actual rescue, volunteer coordination, or donated supplies being distributed through the appropriate channels, time and time again we learned nothing can take the place of clear communication and coordination.

On another occasion our team came upon a group of horse owners determined to haul their own horses out of New Orleans. Usually, this was not a problem, provided they had the necessary equipment. In this particular case, however, the horse owners did not have a trailer and were scouring the neighborhood in search of adequate transportation. Members of our team offered to help, informing the group that we would be happy to bring in horse trailers later that day and transport all of the horses to Lamar-Dixon. Our offers were refused. A member of the group of horse owners arrived shortly thereafter with a horse trailer "commandeered" from a neighbor's property. Declining any assistance or intervention, the group loaded their horses into their "borrowed" trailer and set sail for Lamar-Dixon.

Having sat in the salty floodwaters of New Orleans for nearly a week, the trailer was in terrible shape. The tires were parched, the metal was rusting, and the floorboards had become weak. As the group sped along Interstate 10, just south of the Huey Long Bridge in New Orleans, the waterlogged flooring failed. The boards crashed through the trailer's metal frame. The horses fell to the pavement. We soon received a call asking us to transport the horses to Lamar-Dixon and to tend to the injured horses. Surprisingly, only one horse was seriously injured.

Still, it was an absolute mess when we arrived. For more than an hour, in the middle of an interstate, the team worked to load the horses into our trailer. It took ropes and pulling and coaxing and trickery. It took consideration and patience when those wells had long since run dry. Ultimately, the horses were safely secured and transported to Lamar-Dixon. The seriously injured horse was taken in another trailer to LSU's vet school where he underwent surgery and eventually recovered.

Chapter *13*

Horse Doctors

Along with Bonnie Clark, and with the help of his wife, Nina, Dr. Denny French oversaw the care of the horses under his watch. Daily assignments were handed out to the crews. Stalls needed cleaning, fresh water had to be distributed, and horses needed to be fed. And then there was the actual veterinary work: treating sick horses, changing bandages, taking temperatures, and making decisions on diet and exercise. For nearly four hundred horses, it was an effort of epic proportions.

On the Tuesday after Labor Day, most of the LSU vet students had gone back to school except the handful of fourth-year vet students originally on field rotation with Dr. French. The number of volunteers also had waned as the initial air of emergency wore off. On this particular morning, without the multitude of students and volunteers available, things had fallen a bit behind. Only a few people were milling around the barn area, and at nearly ten o'clock many of the horses still had not been fed.

Without the usual level of customary manpower, Dr. French was frantically trying to feed all the horses and get things on track so that he could begin his veterinary rounds on them.

Horses like a routine and actually depend on one; otherwise, they can get a bit fussy and can even physically decline if they remain off of a schedule. As stewards of animals, we recognize this and usually stick to a given pattern. We feed at a particular time of day; we ride at various times during the week. Water and bedding are always available, and so goes the life of a horse. These are the things a horse recognizes and counts on from day to day.

As Dr. French rushed through the barn trying to get feed and water to four hundred horses, he noticed one mare beginning to show some discomfort. He kept checking on her, and around noon he saw signs of colic. There are numerous types and causes for colic, but the one commonality is that the condition can become extremely painful. Horses aren't capable of vomiting. Their physiological makeup makes it impossible for them to reflux anything at all. Without this ability, the pressure of fluid and gas caused by any abdominal condition can become unbearable and sometimes even fatal.

The mare was in minimal pain, but Dr. French saw "she just wasn't right." He gave her some Banamine (similar to aspirin for horses) and administered routine field colic treatment. She seemed to feel OK once the drugs took effect, but at about four in the afternoon she showed signs of pain again. Dr. Ann Davidson, who had been on the grounds for a couple of days, assisted Dr. French with the mare. To relieve the pressure, a plastic tube was inserted through the mare's nostril into her stomach to siphon fluid from her stomach. About seven that evening the mare began to show signs of dehydration, a possible side effect of the procedure.

Dealing with dehydration in a horse is a simple problem in an equine hospital. In a dirty stall in the middle of nowhere, with very few ambulatory resources, it is a different story. The necessary fluids were on hand, but administering them was an issue. In a hospital, hooks would be overhead to hang the bags of fluid. Sterile IV needles and coil tubes would be at already in place. Everything would be perfect.

But this was not a normal hospital. This was a small metal stall in a covered arena in the middle of a field. It was hot, dirty, and getting dark. While the lighting permitted typical horse activities such as brushing a horse down and throwing a bale of hay into a stall, it was far from ideal for administering an IV.

Looking overhead, Dr. French decided to try to throw a rope over the metal rafters of the barn and hang the fluids that way. As the rafters were well out of reach, a forklift was brought in. Standing on the forks of the lift, Dr. French was raised as high as the hydraulics would allow. With one hand on the forklift for balance and the other holding a lasso, he began tossing the rope at the rafters. After a few tries the rope was in place, bags were hung, and fluids began to flow through the veins of the dehydrated mare.

Having sterile equipment for intensive-care use was a challenge. It was a field hospital at best, and it was understood that if any of the horses came down with a severe case of something, they would be rushed to LSU's veterinary hospital. However, liability was an issue. Of the nearly four hundred horses under our care at that time, the owners of only forty or fifty of them had been identified.

The mare was still holding her own and seemed fairly upbeat, considering her condition. She was a bit scraggly and somewhat underweight. Her brown coat wasn't in the best shape, and as she lay in her stall, constantly moving to get comfortable, the hay and straw of her bedding continually became entangled in her hair, making her look a lot worse off than she truly was. As the fluids were being administered on the hour to keep her comfortable, Dr. Davidson watched the mare closely. The diagnosis at that point was an ileal compaction.

The mare would reflux a little gas through her nasal tube but not any fluids. She was stable while medicated, but as soon as the drugs would wear off, her condition would worsen.

Dr. Davidson turned to Dr. French. "Doc, I don't know. I don't like the way this horse is looking; we probably need to send her to the school."

Dr. French thought for a bit and replied, "I don't know. We don't have an owner for her; I simply can't authorize sending her to surgery right now."

The mare's condition continued to deteriorate, her labored breathing making it obvious she was in considerable pain. Without the necessary protocol in place to send her to surgery, euthanasia would most likely be the next step.

Things were looking grim for the mare, but Dr. Davidson wasn't quite ready to give up on her. Euthanasia was again discussed, as it was clearly the most humane option at the time.

About this time, a *Los Angeles Times* reporter showed up demanding to know what was going on. He saw the syringe in Dr. French's hand and asked what it was.

"Well," Dr. French replied honestly, "this is euthanasia solution. We have a mare that has been in severe pain for a long time now, and if she doesn't turn around soon, we're going to have to exercise the only humane option we have and that is to put her to sleep."

"What does that mean?" asked the reporter.

"I might have to euthanize her," replied Dr. French.

"What does that mean?" the reporter continued.

"I might have to kill her," Dr. French said."

"Oh," the reporter thought for a moment. "Can I watch?"

"You really don't want to," Dr. French replied softly.

"No, but I owe it to my readers," he said.

He was allowed to stay.

Dr. Davidson was intent on keeping the mare going. Several more bales of straw were brought in to prop up the mare on her side to help keep her more comfortable. Dr. French went to find the local law enforcement to let them know what was most likely to occur and to procure their assistance in finding a decent location to carry out the euthanasia in the most private and dignified setting possible.

As Dr. French rode back to the barn with the officer, Dr. Davidson met them at the entrance.

"What if we allow her to get painful again?" she asked Dr. French.

"I'll medicate her one more time, and then we'll see where she's at," he told her.

It was now 1:30 in the morning. He walked back to the mare's stall and examined the horse once again. Her heart rate was fairly normal, and she seemed to be quieting down. Dr. French looked at the mare and she looked right back as if to say, "Well, I might be alright, and I might not." He resolved to leave her in Dr. Davidson's care, to go home and get some sleep, and to see how she progressed through the night.

Dr. Davidson stayed at the mare's side throughout the night, monitoring her vital signs, administering one final dose of medication when the mare had pain again, and waiting. She hoped, she prayed, and she clung to the mare's chances. She stayed by her side until 5:30 a.m.

Thirty minutes later Dr. French arrived. With four solid hours of sleep under his belt, it was a new day, and he was determined to see things went right and according to schedule. As he bounced along feeding the horses and checking all of their water buckets, he was so focused on feeding that he nearly forgot all about the sick mare until he passed her stall. He glanced at the stall door; a sign noted, "Stopped fluids at 5:30, when somebody comes in, please start fluids again." He glanced inside the stall. The mare looked back at him. Perfect, he thought, the mare might make it after all. He went along feeding the rest of the herd when it hit him. Wait a minute, he thought. *I'm* somebody! I could change those fluids. He nearly laughed at himself as he swapped empty bags for fresh IV fluids. He reattached her catheter and made sure she was comfortable. These were the last fluids the mare would need. She recovered fully.

With so many rescue agencies having set up camp at Lamar-Dixon, it wasn't uncommon to have a straggler or two wander into the equine complex, examine the situation, and give advice on how things ought to be done. These well-intentioned newcomers, however, were not always familiar with veterinary procedures and could easily misinterpret situations they weren't yet familiar with.

On one occasion a woman from the Humane Society of the United States ambled over, took a walk down the shed row of the barn, and immediately demanded to know why we were housing a dead horse in one of the stalls.

"I don't know who is in charge around here, but I am assuming leadership of this operation and that dead horse must be removed immediately," she declared.

"We don't have a dead horse," Nina French replied.

"Yes, you do; you've got it right down here in this stall, and this is unacceptable."

Nina French followed the stranger down the shed row quietly chuckling. She nearly laughed out loud when they arrived at a stall she was very familiar with and realized the reason for the woman's concern.

Days before, one of the volunteers had insisted on staying with the horses day and night. His name was Jeffrey, but he was an old codger with a teasing personality, and he took a fair bit of razzing himself. He slept in an empty stall at night. The other volunteers had jokingly placed the nameplate "Aged Stallion" on his stall door. This was the stall Nina French and the humane society representative now stood in front of.

"There is no dead horse in that stall," Nina French said. "I can assure you of that."

Glancing through the bars on the stall door, she could see an old tarp lying on the floor covering Jeffrey's sleeping bag and belongings.

"Well, it says 'Aged Stallion' on the door, and I can see that you've got its body covered up with a tarp," said the woman.

"Ma'am, there's no dead horse under that tarp," Nina French replied, entering the stall and bending down to remove the plastic covering.

"Oh, God, I don't want to see it!" exclaimed the woman as Nina pulled up the tarp, only to reveal a rumpled sleeping bag and a few personal belongings carefully assembled on the stall floor.

We frequently had to deal with onlookers. Whether it was reporters trying to get an interview, photographers, or hurricane evacuees looking for something to do, a small crowd usually followed as the students and vets made their daily rounds.

On one occasion, Dr. David Pugh, a volunteer veterinarian and board-certified theriogenologist (equine reproductive expert), was treating a stallion's genital area for an infection. Glancing at Dr. Pugh, who often wore old overalls and had no aversion to picking up a shovel or rake when necessary, one would be hard pressed to guess he is one of the most respected veterinarians in his field. His friends will say he kind of prefers it that way.

As he entered the stall to treat the horse, a few onlookers happened by. They were representatives from the animal-rights

Lesbian Passion

Loving Ourselves And Each Other

ALSO BY THE AUTHOR:

Lesbian Sex (Spinsters/Aunt Lute)

Period (Volcano Press)

Lesbian Passion

Loving Ourselves And Each Other

JoAnn Loulan

with
Mariah Burton Nelson

spinsters | *aunt lute*
SAN FRANCISCO

First Edition
10-9-8-7-6-5-4-3-2

Spinsters/Aunt Lute Book Company
P.O. Box 410687
San Francisco, CA 94141

Cover and Text Design: Pamela Wilson Design Studio
Cover Art: Pamela Wilson
Typesetting: Grace Harwood and Comp-Type, Fort Bragg, CA
Production: Martha Davis   Lorraine Grassano
                   Debra DeBondt   Kathleen Wilkinson
                   Rosana Francescato   Joey Xanders

Spinsters/Aunt Lute is an educational project of the Capp Street Foundation.

Publication of this book was made possible through the crucial generosity and support of Roberta Brockschmidt, Sharon Gilligan, and Womanspace.

Printed in the U.S.A.

Library of Congress Catalog Card Number: 87-060781

ISBN: 0-933216-29-7

Dedication

*T*his book is dedicated to lesbians everywhere. As we enter another era, the fight for our rights seems unending. We must band together in our clan—our clan of women who feel passion for women, of women who feel passion for human rights. We must band together in our clan to remind the world that we are here. We are never wavering. We must make our voices heard and join the goddess in healing planet earth.

Acknowledgements

I forgot what it was like writing a book. Honest. Now as I enter the last phase of writing this book, I remember how burned out, cranky, let's face it, near psychosis I was the last time. But by the time three years had passed, it seemed like the right time to begin another.

We need a book about our passions. The heat is on. The increasing oppression of lesbians and gay men everywhere is mounting. The AIDS crisis has pushed the planet into overdrive. Everyone is scared and most of us are mourning. I felt we needed a book about our living. We needed a book about opening and healing our hearts. We needed a book that talked about our self-hatred and self-love.

For the last few years, I have been traveling to big and small cities talking with lesbians all across the United States and Canada. We all seem to be working towards the same ends. We are meditating. We are healing with crystals. We are working in factories. We are going to school. We are raising children. We are caring for our brothers dying of AIDS. We are afraid. We are laughing. We are crying. We are dancing. We are having a great time being lesbians. We are everywhere.

This book emerged from all the women I have talked, loved, cried and laughed with throughout the years since I first came out. These lesbians are the reason I wrote this book. I wanted to give back some of what I have been given. The lesbian community is essential to my well-being and to my ability to love my lesbian self. I thank all the lesbians out there who have welcomed me into 'the life.'

There have been many people involved in the writing of this book, which began with talks with the lesbians in my immediate circle. My friend Barbara Austin came up with this brilliant suggestion that I give a series of lectures at the Women's Building in San Francisco, tape each lecture and create a book. She even contributed the word *passion* for the title. She gave me great love and totally enthusiastic support for this whole project. Since I love to talk, and writing is really arduous for me, the process seemed perfect.

Where would I be without Denise Notzon, the best manager a lesbian ever had? In about thirty minutes she had the room rented, the taper hired, the nights organized and had started hounding me for the chapter titles so she could make a flyer. She has held my hand, listened to me cry, encouraged me and loved me through this process. (She and her girlfriend had a baby during this time too!) She takes my calls from airports around the country, listens patiently to my suggestions, and then runs my entire life without any qualms. I love this woman.

Elaine Jacobs came on the scene with a million wires, silver boxes, levers and buttons, reels of tape, microphones, duct tape and her black pants with lots of zippers. She taped my lectures, then painstakingly edited out all the uh's, ah's, sneezes, and buses outside the window, creating a series of audio tapes of these lectures that are also available. She was dedicated and worked under lots of deadlines, including spending time in a motel in Alaska on her summer camping trip to finish on time.

The Women's Building lecture series was filled with lesbians from the San Francisco Bay Area community, many of whom have supported my work for years; I looked from one loving face to another and felt a sense of community, of sisterhood, that we lesbians love so much. To the women in my own town, I truly love being part of this energy we create together.

Mariah Burton Nelson came into my life and became an integral part of this project. She is an excellent writer and a talented and special editor. She gave professionally and endlessly of her time. This book was produced on an insane schedule, and Mariah kept it moving. When she said she would have a chapter to me for my revisions, she wasn't kidding. When she told me of changes she thought I should make, she was loving and specific at the same time. She rarely backed down on her stance, which was perfect, since I am such an opinionated big mouth. Her ideas were always stimulating, and we talked constantly during the process. Late night, early morning, middle of the day. Sometimes arguing, sometimes laughing, sometimes debating the true essence of lesbianism to the point of exhaustion. "Passion, JoAnn, what has this book got to do with passion?" She asked me over and over until I thought I would have to send her a telegram explaining myself. She got her results, though, making me think all the time.

You know, Mariah and I are so different. She's six feet tall; I'm five foot three. She has black, straight hair; I have curly brown hair. She's an athlete; I'm a cheerleader. She's organized; I'm not always wrapped too tight. But when we had differences about what should be written and how, we always seemed to get through it somehow. The bond we felt through this book was intense, her writing and editing skills awesome. This book would have never been readable without her. I am grateful for her constant support, loving energy and wonderful self. (And I still feel fingers in vaginas at restaurants is okay, M.)

Then there is Sherry Thomas, my publisher. Sherry and I worked closely on my last book, *Lesbian Sex*. That experience was so wonderful (except for my being overwhelmed and inhuman by the end), that I had no second thoughts about going with Spinsters/Aunt Lute for this book. Sherry devoted long hours, much creative energy and great love to this book. Whenever I called her tape machine at midnight and rambled on about how much I hated what I was doing and how sure I was that it was worthless, she called me back (at a normal hour) to reassure me that all was well. She has been absolutely invaluable in rewriting and giving me suggestions for additions (although I hated doing more and endlessly more to make each sentence work).

Working with Spinsters/Aunt Lute, embodied in the persons of Sherry Thomas and Joan Pinkvoss, has been a great experience. Martha Davis and Debra DeBondt have also given much of their time and energy to this process. In the initial contract negotiations, Sherry, Joan and I were alternately angry, happy, scared and sad, as we embarked on this feminist undertaking. We reached a settlement, none of us getting all of what we wanted, but assured of each other's personal integrity. I feel honored that I was in on the process, and that we were willing to be so honest.

Mary Alvord, the statistician on this project, was largely responsible for the research included in this book. She helped me prepare the questionnaire, told me what trends were emerging, put the numbers into a huge computer, made miles of printouts, and wrote up preliminary reports. She explained to me what all the numbers meant. She coordinated the coding women, Teri LaRue and Cathy Kirksena. She helped me overcome my fear of numbers and learn how to communicate this material in a way that lesbians everywhere can use. Although she is undyingly humble about her role, I believe that her contribution to the lesbian community has been immeasurable, and I deeply respect and appreciate her efforts.

Amazing Grace Harwood, now that girl can take a picture, type a page, whip up some poetry, write brilliantly and tell a joke all at the same time. She's a true Renaissance woman. We laughed a lot as she transcribed the tapes from the series. Although they went on forever, she never complained, only seemed to enjoy the process. She was a great boost to this writer's crashing self-esteem and I appreciate her insights and middle of the night thoughts.

At the center of every project is a home. Well, in mine was my son Gardner, who is now five and a half and has been through every stage of this book with me. "Mom, don't get so stressed out," was his most calming comment. The most telling was, "Are you going to be done with this book this summer, or the rest of your life?" It has seemed that long to all of us. He is a gentle soul and I suppose the goddess sent me this dear boy to shake up my belief system. He is my greatest love, teaching me always how to open my heart wider and wider.

Peppermint and Julie Cones run my home, take care of my son, make sure I eat and generally give me a sense of loving that is invaluable. These sisters, with their Diet Pepsi and Pepsi ever present in their respective hands, have worked many hours allowing me more time to write. They are ever present in my life and I am grateful beyond words.

Marcia Quackenbush, as in most of my projects, was once again an important part of this one. Not only did she give me unending support as a friend, she also shared her considerable expertise on AIDS, rewriting the chapter after I gave it to her for comments. I was grateful for her energy.

Cheri Pies also was integral in the AIDS chapter, giving me specific information and editorial comments as well. Her work in the AIDS community in San Francisco is important, and I was pleased to have her be a part of this book.

Then there are the women who supported the project financially. Lesbians are not supposed to talk about money, much less ask for it. It was hard enough for me to ask, but for those who gave, I will honor the secret code and not name you. I appreciate your belief in me and your willingness to put your money where your thoughts are, and I send thanks from me personally and from the community as a whole.

My friends are always the reason I'm still alive at the end of a long project like this. They loved and nurtured me. Amy Tzon lent me her computer (what is it we did before computers?) and never complained even though I returned it to her a month late. Sylvia Villarreal gave me information and lots of support. Judy Mullins, my sister, constantly listened to my fears and loved me. Juanita Malouf, my sister-in-law, listened to Judy and me talk about this book till our lips fell off. Margie Adam told me incessantly how important my work was. Linda Reuther kept telling me I was just a scared kid and that was okay. Marny Hall was, of course, my mentor in theory, writing, application and melancholy. Other friends let me freak out with them and still loved me. All these friends supported me through this project and through what was a very hard time in my personal life. Without all of you, I would never be able to do what I do in my life. Thank you so for your loving kindness.

Thanks to Linda, Azalia and the Sonoma County dykes, Peggy, Eva, Sari, Hrieth, Brenda Starr, Laurie, Bridget and Cindie for proofreading during the Harmonic Convergence—wow! Then there's Carla who has brought me great love, healing and joy. Water in the desert.

I could not have done any of this without a strong spiritual belief. This belief has grown from the gentle process of opening to a program of recovery. I grew up in an alcoholic home and learned to depend only upon myself. In recovery, I have learned that I can depend on the universal energy that holds us in its love. I can also depend upon the support of those who love me. I cannot express fully my appreciation for the people in this program of recovery. I no longer have to take care of everyone I meet or have to please others to feel worthwhile. I am so relieved. I now have a life filled with joy and serenity. Namaste.

JoAnn Loulan

On Pretending To Be JoAnn Loulan While Simultaneously Trying Not to Let Her Get Carried Away
by Mariah Burton Nelson

Working together can be almost as intimate as sleeping together, so when JoAnn asked me to help her write *Lesbian Passion*, I considered the offer as carefully as I would a proposal for sex. I noted that JoAnn's professional reputation is impeccable, and I remembered having laughed until I cried at several lectures of hers. Knowing that I would be dealing with, at the very least, an excellent therapist with a remarkable sense of humor, I accepted the job.

As I suspected, a witty therapist makes a good collaborator. JoAnn listened compassionately when I got frustrated, communicated her ideas clearly, admitted her mistakes, forgave me for mine, and, true to form and on a regular basis, cracked me up.

I worked from transcripts of JoAnn's lectures, from written material of JoAnn's, and from long discussions we had late at night, after her son had gone to bed. Sometimes we were insightful and profound; other times we were exhausted, inarticulate and giddy. Always it was interesting; usually it was fun.

Ghostwriting is a bit like acting; one must immerse oneself in the character, learning to see the world from her point of view. I had to think as JoAnn thinks, voice JoAnn's concerns, offer JoAnn's advice, tell JoAnn's jokes. After working on the book all day, I found myself expressing enthusiasm to my friends with such JoAnnisms as, "Coolness. Unbelievable coolness."

Cool though she is, JoAnn is not perfect, and though it was not in my job description, I took on the additional task of challenging her when, in my humble opinion, she was wrong. I found myself in the unusual position of being the more conservative one in our duo. Here's a typical conversation: "JoAnn, I don't know about this suggestion of yours that couples go to a restaurant and have sex under the tablecloth."

"Why?" JoAnn asks innocently. "It could be fun."

"What if other people are watching?" I argue. "Don't people have a right to eat dinner without having the women at the table next to them sticking their fingers up each other's vaginas?"

"Be discreet."

"Isn't it illegal?" I plead, grasping at straws now.

"Mariah, in many states, lesbianism is illegal!"

"I still disagree."

"Too bad." (JoAnn wins that round.)

Here's another example: "JoAnn, the title is okay, but I don't like this subtitle."

"Which one?"

"'Opening Our Hearts and Our Legs.'"

"Why not? I think it sums it up perfectly."

"It's just too far out, JoAnn, please trust me." (One for me.)

The most difficult part of writing the book was telling family, strangers and acquaintances what I was doing. Friends were no problem. "*Lesbian Passion*? That's perfect for you, Mariah," my friend Kimberly said. But how to tell my father? And the people I happened to meet in laundromats? And the publisher of another book I have planned?

The problem is, *Lesbian Passion* sounds like lesbian sex, only more so. Who knows what images straight people come up with when they hear "lesbian passion," but the term can be pretty disturbing. Or so I feared.

I confess: To a few people, I said, "It's a book about how lesbians can develop and maintain self-esteem in a homophobic world." Which is true. But as the months went on, it became increasingly painful to avoid saying the name of the book. If I can't say *Lesbian Passion*, I thought, who can? And if people are embarrassed by the concept of lesbian passion, it's certainly not going to help them get over that embarrassment for me not to talk about it. Nor would staying silent help me get beyond my own homophobia. So I started saying, "I'm working on a book called *Lesbian Passion*." Then I tried not to defend it, not to explain it, not to soften it by adding that it's actually about all kinds of passions, not just sex. I was challenged to come out not only as a lesbian, but as a passionate one, passionate enough to collaborate on this book, and honest enough to admit it.

Now that the book is finished, I have begun working on a book of my own, tentatively entitled *Passion Plays: Women Athletes Who Compete for Love or Money*. Like JoAnn's book, it will be about passion and pain, humor and courage. Like JoAnn's book, it will, in part, be about lesbians. Unlike JoAnn's book: no restaurant sex.

Table of Contents

Lesbian Passion

Loving Ourselves And Each Other

Lesbian Passion: An Introduction

What is love without passion? A garden without flowers, a hat without feathers, tobogganing without snow.

—JENNIE JEROME CHURCHILL

Lesbians are passionate people. We are passionate about our friendships, our children, our lovers. We are passionate about sex, community politics, lesbian rights. We are passionate about issues of race, class, disability, healing, spiritual pursuits, and sports. I can't think of anything lesbians are not passionate about.

Yet as women, we have been taught to keep a lid on this natural passion. We have been told not to talk too loud, not to laugh too loud, not to be angry, not to be exuberant. We have been taught that women's passions are stupid or insignificant. Devotion to ourselves, we have been told, is narcissistic. We have been taught that our passions are worthless.

As lesbians, our passion has been even more taboo. We're not supposed to love women in the first place. Once we do, if we touch our lover in public, we're being 'blatant.' We could avoid much discrimination by pretending we don't love women—but we do. It is because of this strong passion for women that, in the face of homophobia, we continue to express our lesbian love.

Fortunately, more and more of us are allowing our passions to emerge, and not only in the privacy of our own bedrooms. More women than at any other point in history are openly lesbian. We have generated our own lesbian culture that includes musicians, poets, writers and artists of all sorts. We have coffeehouses, conferences, festivals. All of these emerge from our passion.

Nevertheless, sometimes we do not recognize or accept our own passion. Many of us feel ashamed of our passions, and we keep them secret. To make love, or have a conversation, or work with an unabashedly passionate person can be frightening; we may feel dull by comparison, or inadequate. Yet we each express our passions in unique ways.

Even after decades of feminism, we haven't come close to understanding the oppression of women, and the effects it has on our feelings and thoughts. We can't know how passionate we might become, and how we might express this passion, if this world made room for women. The more we free ourselves from the chains of homophobia, the more our passion will come forth.

Passion is a source of greatness within each of us. This is true of great works of art, great deeds of service and the ordinary greatness required to love ourselves and other people on a daily basis. We begin to glimpse the power of our passion when we march in a Take Back The Night rally; express our own form of spirituality; or assert our rights to inseminate, give birth and raise children as we choose. "What has passion to do with choosing an art form?" Gertrude Stein once asked. "Everything!"

The dictionary (Random House Unabridged, 1981) defines passion as: 1) any emotion or feeling as love, desire, anger, hate, fear, grief, joy, hope, etc.; especially when of a powerful or compelling nature. 2) strong amorous need or desire; love. 3) strong sexual desire; lust. 4) a strong or extravagant fondness, enthusiasm for anything.

This is what I was thinking about as I conceived of this book: passion is not only about sex, but about the life force that energizes us. The chapters in this book describe some of the passions of lesbians, and offer suggestions for removing the barriers that keep us from living fully and from truly loving ourselves.

The best way to begin allowing our passion free reign is by healing the little child within. Whether or not we had happy childhoods, each of us has within us a 'child' who needs to be loved. This child often emerges when we feel angry, scared, or jealous. By getting to know her and learning how to take care of her, we make room for more joy in our lives. This process requires a deep commitment to loving and healing ourselves. After that, we can begin to heal the world.

As we heal the child within, our self-esteem grows. But given the realities of homophobia, it's more complicated than that. Only in the past few decades have we begun to be open about who we are. We have fought for freedom for gays; we have marched in parades celebrating our lesbianism; we have admitted to ourselves and sometimes to our families that we are lesbians. We have created a culture of artists, poets, sports teams, musicians, writers, business women, lawyers, dancers, actors, craftswomen and health care providers who are openly lesbian. We have done all of this with great passion. Yet many of us continue to suffer from internalized homophobia. Only when we begin to love ourselves can we truly love each other.

Like all women, lesbians are vulnerable to intense cultural pressure to reject our bodies. Whatever size or shape we are, we probably hate our bodies. Many of us also believe that if we are disabled, old, or in any other way in the cultural minority, we are not attractive. Our choices of food, exercise and clothing are often based on an intense desire to be artificially thin. These feelings can be redirected into self-love.

Can lesbians be celibate and still be passionate? Of course. We can be passionate about celibacy, or self-love, or even about sex. Celibate periods can be times to begin a love affair with ourselves and to build a strength and serenity that will change the quality of our interactions in the world.

Probably the most intense relationships in the lesbian community are those between friends. Passionate friendships are what sustain us through illnesses, child-raising, deaths, jobs, lovers and political upheavals. We become mother, daughter, crone, healer, mentor and angel for each other. Friends often become families and create room for each other to play and grow.

Friends also come in handy when we are summoning the nerve to ask someone to join us in that magical comedy of errors known as the lesbian date. Clearly, sexual and emotional passions drive us to date each other—and sometimes those passions are also our undoing. Could we be passionate and honest at the same time? Could we directly ask someone for sex instead of spending the evening wondering about it? Lesbian dates provide us with great titillation, great fear, and often, right after the first date, a great (or not-so-great) relationship.

A discussion of sex toys is included in this book to encourage all of us to be more playful and inventive. Sex toys are simply toys—playthings that can enhance pleasure and aid in the expression of sexual passion. This chapter describes some of the many sex toys available, and how to use them. If you don't like them, that's fine. But if you might like them, why not give them a try? Despite what our parents taught us, taking risks can be fun.

I expect the chapter on how long-term couples can keep their sex lives exciting will be one of the most popular chapters in this book. Passionate though we are, we can lose sight of our sexual passion after living together and sharing food, clothes, movies, bathrooms and even sometimes jobs with our lovers. Our first task is to admit that the fire has gone down to a glowing ember. After that, we must assess how, if at all, we want things to change. Then, if we can team up with our partners rather than playing the yes/no game, exciting and satisfying sex can become an ongoing part of our lives.

I've included a chapter on what lesbians need to know about AIDS because it elicits our deepest fears and threatens our passions. Everyone is eager for information about AIDS. Lesbians are not immune to this disease, and there are specific ways we can protect ourselves. This information may seem exhaustive, but I feel strongly that our passion for survival must take precedence over anything else.

Many lesbians are recovering from substance abuse, which touches every lesbian's life in some way or other. As we recover from chemical dependence, sexual addiction, eating disorders, or co-dependence, we find that many passions, some pleasant and some unpleasant, are unleashed. We have feelings we never thought possible. We have goals we never thought we could pursue. We have fears we never knew we had. This chapter is about making our lives in recovery rich in intimacy and joy.

Since two out of five women were sexually abused as children, many of us are struggling to integrate our natural passions with the wreckage of our past. Those of us who are incest survivors often vacillate between self-hatred and hatred of the perpetrator. A passion for healing, and for healthy, respectful relationships, is what carries incest survivors forward when the pain becomes overwhelming.

Partners of incest survivors often inadvertently find themselves in the role of helping their partners to heal. Concerns for your partner tend to outweigh concerns for yourself. In this chapter, I suggest turning that compassionate energy into passion for your own healing. Rather than becoming consumed by your partner's pain or her healing process, you can contribute most to the relationship by taking care of yourself.

Researching what lesbians do in bed and other interesting facts is one passion of mine: finding out who lesbians are, how we feel, and what we do. I am not a professional researcher—nosy would be a better word. I wanted to know what we did with each other's and our own bodies. I wanted to know what our backgrounds were like. I wanted to be able to say to women who were suffering from feelings of inadequacy that they are not alone or so different. As I've considered the results of my survey of more than 1500 lesbians, I have felt love, desire, anger, hate, fear, grief, joy, hope. I am grateful to be able to pass on to you this information about our lives, the passions of 1566 lesbians.

This book is a call to lesbian passion. It is an entreaty to expand our awareness of our own passion, to love ourselves and each other more and more. Regardless of numerous political and social attempts to deny us our rights to live and love, lesbians are passionate people. I think it's high time we explored just how passionate we can be.

Healing the Child Within

We are whole beings. We know this some- where in a part of ourselves that feels like memory.

—SUSAN GRIFFIN

Once we reach the age of 21, we're supposed to be grown up. We're supposed to pay our bills, take out the trash, sit around having conversations about world politics. We're not supposed to be needy, sad, or, worst of all, scared. We all wear these grown-up facades. We act like we know what we're doing. We dress appropriately; we say polite things to people in the grocery store; we watch carefully when we are crossing the street.

Then we have conversations with our parents that make us feel ready to run straight to our therapist's office. We have an argument with a lover and feel inadequate beyond description. We get mad at our children and start saying things our parents said when we were growing up, things we swore we would never say. What has happened?

We are so surprised to find ourselves acting irrationally. We suddenly feel foolish. We don't want anyone to see us like this. Sometimes we try to fake it so no one will catch on. We cover up the fear that paralyzes us. We just keep working like we're supposed to, when what we feel like doing is staying home all day. We feel like calling up our friends and telling them to forget it, there's no way we can help them move this Saturday. We feel like crying for no real reason. We don't know what to do or how to do it. We fear any minute now our kids will realize that the rules we are trying to enforce make no sense even to us. We don't believe any more than they do that they have to go to bed. We feel alone even in a room full of people.

These are just some of the feelings that signal that the little child who resides in these grown-up, rational bodies of ours is alive and still directing many of our feelings. This child may be many ages, both sexes and have many different temperaments. She may be a fetus, an infant, a toddler, a young girl, or a teenager. For some women, she may be represented by no more than a vague feeling. Other women have a vivid picture of what this little girl looks like, how old she is, and even what she wears. Sometimes we also have a little boy within, or a tomboy who liked to play baseball and do what the boys were doing. Often, we have more than one of these little beings operating within us at the same time. We can feel like we're running an internal daycare center on those days when feelings change frequently.

Most of us were raised by people who felt very tiny at times themselves. Usually our parents were ill-trained to raise children. It's not that they intentionally tried to hurt us or keep us from growing up to feel positive about ourselves. They just didn't have information about self-esteem. Small children are totally at the mercy of the adult's view of the world. Most children are told such things as: "I'll give you something to cry about." "Don't act like that; don't talk like that." "Why don't you act your age?" Adults don't realize that even innocent comments can hurt children.

Each of us has a little girl within who had her heart broken at an early age. You did not need to have a traumatic, abusive childhood to have your heart broken. Even in the best of homes, little children receive deep scars and later they still feel that pain. Our little children are not gone just because we have adult bodies now.

Many of us did grow up in dysfunctional homes. By dysfunctional, I mean they did not function at a level that supported the emotional health and growth of all the members. This can be measured on a continuum. Some families actually physically abuse their children. Thirty-eight percent of female children are sexually abused by the time they are eighteen. (Russell, Diana. *The Secret Trauma: Incest in the Lives of Girls and Women.* New York: Basic Books, 1986.) These homes are severely dysfunctional. In many families that do not physically abuse, emotional abuse is common. Many families have alcohol and drug abuse as a central factor. Other families are abused by the culture at large—families that are poor or have no access to health care. Frustration and lack of resources can create a cycle of abuse from without that is carried out from within. Other families are abusive with standards of achievement that result in children feeling they can never measure up. This is reflected in today's expectations that children learn to read before they are even in school, that they go to the right nursery school so they can get into the right college. This kind of pressure on children is a form of abuse.

Many of us were never able to be children. We had to be grown-up beyond our years. We had to be quiet when children ought to have the right to be loud. We had to do jobs that adults should do. We were never little kids. We were young, but we weren't allowed to act like children. This is especially true for girls. The oldest daughter in a dysfunctional home often has to parent the younger kids, even when she has older brothers, and even when she herself is very young. She also often has to parent her parents by making sure the home runs smoothly, or offering them advice. Many of us have a long history of denying our child selves. Even in our childhoods it was not okay to be childlike!

Unless you have little children around you now, it's hard to understand how tender they are. I remember when I brought my son home from the hospital. His fingers were teensy and, like most newborns, he had very long fingernails. I was too freaked out to cut them. I said to a friend of mine, "You almost went to medical school. You have to cut his fingernails." (She has had to do a lot of things because she almost went to medical school!) So she trimmed those tiny nails. Now my son is five years old, and he's still tiny. He's average size for his age, but he's very innocent; his heart is very open, and he's very vulnerable.

Children's brains are also little. That's why they can relate to Winnie the Pooh, the Bear of Little Brain. Children don't think like adults do and they can't even understand several key concepts of adult life, such as the concept of time. They don't understand the concept of yesterday or tomorrow. Recently my son had a party for his fifth birthday. Three days later he asked, "When's my next birthday?" He had no idea how long ago his party had been and couldn't conceptualize that his next birthday was a whole year away.

Kids act like they understand what is going on when they really don't.

When a child looks up at an adult and asks what is happening, she really has no choice but to take part in whatever happens. She can't get a job; she can't get an apartment of her own. She can only do what she is told.

If you thought you were really big when you were five or three or one, you weren't. You were young and innocent and should have been receiving nurturance and protection. You shouldn't have had to worry about paying bills, or keeping the younger kids quiet, or settling disputes between your parents. It isn't a child's responsibility to make her parents happy. It is the parents' responsibility to make the child feel welcome in the world.

Some women reading this will insist that the very notion of an inner child with a broken heart is hogwash. Maybe you feel like you're too hip to have a little child inside. Maybe the idea of having the kind of feelings a little child has seems too silly.

But women who are too hip to have a broken-hearted child within still really do have one. The facade they present to the world—the "I'm too hip to have feelings" facade—is just another way the child with the broken heart expresses herself. She's afraid to show her vulnerability. The too-hip woman often finds a girlfriend who wears her feelings on her sleeve, and sees through the facade. In fact, the too-hip woman's girlfriend is usually a therapy junkie. The therapy junkie says to the too-hip woman, "This is exactly what I was talking about. You need to get in touch with your little kid, and then you wouldn't be so mean. This is why you should be in therapy."

The too-hip woman shouldn't necessarily be in therapy, but she probably does have a little girl inside who could use some attention. We all do.

Some people can't understand the concept of having within them a child with a broken heart because they had a happy childhood. They can't remember having had their heart broken. These people say to me, "But I had a wonderful home life. I had kind parents, and a really happy home, and a good extended family."

I think that's incredible, and I think those people ought to write about the experience so the rest of us can marvel at it. But in raising my child, I've found that the tiniest things break his heart. It doesn't have to be a major trauma.

This is a story that I don't like to tell, but I think it's indicative of how easily children's hearts are broken. One day my son and I were getting ready to go to school and work, and we were late. I said to him, "I want you to go get your clothes on. We're leaving. We have to get out of here." If you're a mother, you know how this goes. I had told him about fifteen times. He was three and a half then, so if he was even listening at all, he was probably thinking, "We're late. What's that mean?"

Eventually I said to him, "If you're not ready, I will leave anyway."

From the other room I heard him crying, then his small voice said, "Mommy, even if you leave me I will still love you."

Ahhhhh. That broke *my* heart. So I put another hundred dollars in his therapy fund. I also felt very bad, because I realized that he didn't care if we were late. He didn't even care if we never went where we were supposed to go. It just wasn't part of his reality.

I sat down with him and said, "I didn't mean that. I wouldn't leave you."

But even that relatively minor expression of my impatience scared him. Scaring him only made him feel bad, and reinforced his inability to control his own world. These kinds of experiences build on one another and help to create a child's view of herself as inadequate. Over and over, a child's tender heart is disregarded and in a small way is broken. A mother scaring her child is heartbreaking, even when she doesn't do it 'by purpose,' as my son would say.

People who have worked with abused children or with adults who were abused when they were growing up know that my son actually would have forgiven me. I could have left him alone all day, come home and broken both his arms, and he still would have loved me. A child's devotion to his or her parents is so deep it's almost frightening.

Your heart wasn't necessarily broken from incidents of incest or the death of a parent or even any particular time that you recall. It might have been something as normal as leaving home for kindergarten.

Most of us who are adults now didn't start leaving home when we were six months old the way kids often do today. Many of our mothers stayed at home with us, so for four or five years we were alone with Mom, and maybe some younger siblings.

I had a brother who was two years older than me, so I had Mom to myself for his first two years of school. My brother disappeared somewhere during the day, and I didn't care where he went. It was me and Mom. I loved it. Then she dropped me off in kindergarten, where there were thirty kids, including one set of twins. The twins had hair they could sit on, and the teacher liked to talk about it.

"The twins have such beautiful hair." She also said, "The twins are always dressed so beautifully," and "The twins are always so good," and "Can't you lie down and take a nap, like the twins?" Suddenly I felt like I was no longer special.

That's why kids cling to their moms or their caretakers when they get dropped off at school. Children don't want to be left there with a bunch of other kids, even though they might eventually like them. Kids want their own private grown-ups all to themselves.

The list of things that break children's hearts is endless. Kids are so involved in life, so involved in the moment, that only this moment really counts. When the unexpected happens, a child's heart breaks. When a balloon floats off into the sky, and a grown-up says, "I told you to hold onto that, now look what you've done." When a scoop of ice cream falls off your ice cream cone and splats on the sidewalk. When you do something the grown-ups told you not to, and you're punished, even though you really did forget you weren't supposed to do that and it shouldn't count when you *really* forget. Adults can't handle that the moment means so much; they get uncomfortable and try to make the kid stop expressing pain, which only serves to make the kid feel worse.

Of course our hearts get broken over more severe things as well, like not feeling welcome in a home that has few emotional resources. Hearts get broken in homes in which there is alcoholism, drug or food addiction and homes where there are already too many needy people.

Self-esteem suffers in a home where one of the other kids does it better, whatever 'it' is, where the parents favor one child over another. Children's hearts get broken when there is a grown-up in the home whose own heart is broken and who takes it out on the child.

Hearts can get broken at any age, even in the womb. From the time fetuses are about four months old, they can hear, because the amniotic fluid in the uterus is an even better sound conductor than air.

Fetuses may not understand the language, but they understand the tones and vibrations.

If you were adopted, imagine what you heard when you were in the womb. Until very recently, unmarried women were strongly discouraged from having children. They were forced to give their children away. If you were adopted, imagine what you heard from your birth mother and your birth father. Imagine what was being said by your mother's parents; your father's parents; your mother's preacher, rabbi, or priest; or other upstanding members of the community who wanted to tell her what a mistake she made. How frightening it must have been to come into a world in which you knew you'd be separated from the woman who gave birth to you.

If you experienced incest or other sexual trauma when you were a child, you know when your heart got broken. If you can't remember exactly when, at least you know that you were violated and betrayed. It's almost inconceivable how heartbreaking it is for a child to be sexually betrayed by a family member. She often feels responsible for the abuse, and her inability to trust affects every adult relationship.

If the abuse was physical rather than sexual, it can be just as terrifying. Adults are huge and extraordinarily powerful compared to children; imagine the fear that must overwhelm a child who is repeatedly hit.

Many women who have been physically or sexually abused say, "It wasn't that big of a deal." This is the coping mechanism of the child who cannot admit the magnitude of the abuse, who wants to protect that broken heart.

Some of us have more than one heartbroken child within. If you look carefully, you may be surprised by who you find. You may find that you have children of all ages inside. You may find that you have a little baby who whines when you have a bad day. You may have a toddler who doesn't have any idea what the grown-ups are saying around her. You may have a teenager who gets sarcastic at the drop of a hat.

Many of us feel we have a little boy inside; many women, whether lesbians or not, have a little boy inside that had to get lost at adolescence. Fifteen years ago, I never would have said that because I would have been arrested by the lesbian politically correct police. But now, with the coalition politics of the eighties, we can talk about our male energy, and for some, that's a relief.

You may object to this energy being called 'male,' but kids go along with what the culture sets up. So when I mention the little boy, I am talking about how children see the world. As we have matured with the advent of mainstream feminism, we have become sophisticated enough to know that no energy is exclusively female or male. However, when we are looking at the little children within us, we are looking at ourselves at an age when things were very clear-cut. Girls did girl things, boys did boy things.

How many dykes thought we were boys or wanted to be boys because the boys were having more fun? We were indoors playing with our Barbie dolls while the boys were out running around, playing baseball and basketball—being alive in the world. When I grew up, girls didn't play sports. We sat around watching the boys play sports; we were the cheerleaders.

When many of us became teenagers, we didn't know how to do this thing called 'being girls,' and we didn't want to do it. We were supposed to wear high heels and makeup and go out with boys even if we didn't like them. The worst part was when our girlfriends started going out with their boyfriends instead of us after the game on Friday or Saturday night. If we didn't know that we were lesbian teenagers, we didn't even know why we were so sad, but our hearts were broken.

How do you know if the feelings you are having in the present are related to this little kid? How do you know how old the child is, and how do you use this information to help you in your daily communication? These are questions you will be better able to answer once you start to use this process of paying attention to the little kid within.

All feelings are primal. The four biggies—happy, angry, sad and scared—are feelings we were born with. There only needs to be a stimulus to bring them to the surface. The stimulus can be internal or external. It can be large or small. Before the age of about eighteen months, a child has these feelings on a regular basis for fleeting moments at a time. She flits from one feeling to another and back again very rapidly. Once a child reaches eighteen months, she starts to separate from her primary caretaker (usually her mother) and begins to have an awareness of the rules the adults around her have made. This begins the slow descent into the mire of making feelings something other than what they are.

This little girl will learn that feelings are so scary to the people around her that she should learn to keep the feelings under wraps, because apparently they are too intense and change too quickly. Eventually, this child will learn to find reasons to back up her feelings. She will learn how to hang on to a feeling for hours, sometimes days at a time.

The adults have made up this game that goes like this: "Feelings aren't logical, thus you can't prove why you have them, and therefore they aren't really there and we should just think our way out of this." The strangest part of these rules is that the adults are feeling all the time; but because they have had more practice at this game, they can quickly make up words to make it seem as though these feelings they are having are thoughts. They act like they are thinking when they are really feeling.

For instance, when my son was two, he asked if he could take his shoes off in a restaurant. I immediately answered, "No." He asked, "Why not?" I just said, "Because people don't do that." He asked, "Why not?" again. We kept going back and forth. I came up with explanations like, "You might cut your feet," "You might step in dirt." On and on. Mind you, he was sitting down.

The real reason I said he couldn't take his shoes off in the restaurant is because my mother said I couldn't take my shoes off in a restaurant. I was afraid because my mother (long dead) had forbidden it. I made it seem like I was thinking about this and not feeling. I made up all kinds of reasons. It was hard to admit that I was actually afraid of crossing my mother.

You may think I am stark raving mad. You may think you do not protect your relationships with the people who brought you up. You may think you make all your decisions on your own. If so, check out your thoughts every once in a while. See if they are based on thought or feeling. Then trace that feeling back and find out where you got that belief. We are constantly trying to please our parents. After all, they taught us how to be, how other people are, how the world works. They taught us little things like how to hold a fork and huge things like how to speak their language. The people who brought us up had a profound influence on our lives, and our very survival depended on pleasing them.

So when we are having feelings and pushing them down, or disguising them with thoughts, we are being very little. We are being the child our parents brought us up to be. We are following their rules (sitting still at dinner, not making too much of a fuss, or using lots of big words to get our way). We are afraid to do it differently. We are also still responding to the fear we had of them. No matter whether they were abusive or not, they were big—lots bigger than we were. They were smart—lots smarter than we were. They were in control—lots more in control than we were. They made the rules. We followed them.

Even if you were a juvenile delinquent, you were reacting to them. You rebelled because you wanted their attention, or you were sad and needed something from authority figures, or you were afraid of the grown-ups and wanted to get out of their house.

Now that we are big and the grown-ups ourselves (how *did* that happen?), we still have these small beings within us who are afraid and sad and angry and happy and don't want anyone to know. So we disguise it, and then our feelings erupt in the strangest ways. We get in fights with our friends when they don't agree with us about some current event. We get scared when our lovers want to go somewhere without us. We don't tell people when we are excited because we might look like a fool. We get sad when we get left out of an event because our ex-lovers got invited instead.

Of course, all these feelings are common to adults; big people do have feelings. However, our need to hide feelings, to change them, or to get people to change to conform to our desires stems from the child within who is afraid of the pure feeling that used to bring primal relief. Our "confusion" that stops us from knowing what our feelings are is a way for the child to hide the basic feeling because it might make her parents unhappy.

When you don't know what your feelings are, when you find yourself not wanting to tell someone what you feel, when your feelings seem to last forever or your feelings seem to be out of proportion to what the situation calls for, your little child is probably running the show. There are ways to heal this little girl child within. She will not go away, but you can learn how to heal and love her. You will learn that she is valuable. She gives you so much of your humanity. She is indeed the door to that magical place within.

That little child within is perfect. That magical place within needs to be honored, but the path to that place is often covered with a lot of wild brush. The following information may be helpful in clearing a path to your magic.

See if you can come up with a visual image of who your little child is. Think back to when your heart was broken and imagine bringing that child, or those children, onto your lap. There's plenty of room.

Many of us learned as children that there wasn't enough room for us. But now there is. In your imagination—in your heart—there can be plenty of room for these children. You can bring your teenager with her stereo; you can bring your little tiny baby who was trying to decide whether to stay on the planet or not; you can bring the tomboy who had to stop playing baseball.

If you can't find an image, remember the last time you were scared. It may have been an adult sort of fear, but that's how you felt as a child too. The kid with the broken heart has that feeling all the time. That's why we're so unsure as adults whether we're doing the right thing or the wrong thing. There's a little kid in there who is scared that she's not right, that she's not good. So remembering a scary time is a good way to visualize your child.

If it's too hard for you to put your child on your lap, just let her sit next to you. If you're aware of your lover's broken-hearted little kid but not your own, do *not* put your lover's child on your lap. One of the ways we lesbians sabotage our relationships is to say to each other, "Aha! Childcare for life! You take care of my baby, I'll take care of yours, okay?" It's all unspoken, but it's a deal that we frequently make. Then, of course, we hate the way our lover takes care of our kid, and we tell her so as often as possible. "Did I tell you the 55 ways in which you pissed me off today? I didn't? Well, sit down and listen. You never listen to me. Sit down here and listen."

So please focus on caring for your own babies, toddlers, teenagers, young adults—whatever gender they are.

Take a deep breath. Try to imagine your child on your lap, or just sitting beside you. Many people think they don't know how to hold a child because nobody held them. But you don't have to do it right. You don't have to be the best. Just making room for her at all is a miracle for some people.

Now focus in on an age for one of your kids. Once you can sense how old she is, you can start to remember why you were so sad at that time, or so scared. This is only of interest to your grown-up now, however—kids don't really care about why. They just want you to hold them. They just want you to pay attention to the fact that they're here.

Imagine holding yourself as a baby, even if you have no particular memories from that time. Hold your teenager. The point of this exercise is to begin to love ourselves. We spend so much of our time hating ourselves. But as you imagine holding your little child on your lap, ask yourself, "How could this baby, this little one, be anything but perfect? How could this baby possibly deserve such pain?"

You may find yourself starting to list all the bad things you did as a child, or saying to yourself, "I must have been bad. If I weren't bad, why would they have told me I was bad and treated me like that?"

The adults taking care of you treated you like that partly because they were scared. They felt like they had to be right all the time, when actually they were very unsure of themselves. After all, no one taught them how to be parents, and it's a very tough job. So instead of letting this little kid know that they were scared of being wrong, they just pretended that they were right. In defense of this righteousness they got angry, pushy and controlling. It was all because they didn't know how to deal with being so scared. It's important to remember that this is the first era in human history that masses of people have begun to examine how they were parented and how they might in turn parent. We have the luxury of knowledge that many generations before us did not.

If you were abused, and you've recently begun to allow yourself to be angry, I'm not saying to stop being angry at those who abused you. I'm simply saying to forgive your baby, your little child.

We have to start somewhere giving this child within information that she is not "bad." She is a beautiful being who was abused or hurt in some way. Although she was mistreated by adults who didn't know any better, their behavior does not have anything to do with the worth of the child. It was not personal, even though it may feel very personal. Any child who stumbled into that place would have been treated that way.

You can argue, "Oh no, my sister never got treated like this because she was good. I was bad or they wouldn't have done that to me." It's hard to understand when you're little, but adults help to create children who get out of control and act out. Parents don't know they're doing that; they're acting instinctually. When I get into a struggle with my son about bedtime, for instance, we go round and round. Sometimes I resort to the tactics my parents used, "You are really being bad, you need to go to bed." He's not being bad. I'm not setting limits that he recognizes, and he wants to know how far he can push me. I test limits myself. How much can I get away with? That's human nature. If you were a kid who pushed everyone, it was probably because they didn't stop you, or they were ignoring you, or they didn't know what to do to help. But it was *not* because you were bad.

Keeping in mind that this child is perfect just as she is, imagine where inside your body this child stays. Most people have a favorite place to hold tension. I think that's where the children live. They're crammed into our tummies, shoulders, legs, hips, arms, face, or breasts. If you can't come up with a place, don't worry—this is not a test. This is simply a discovery. Try noticing where your muscles are tight right now. That's probably where your child lives.

Part of the reason that place is tight is because you're protecting the little kid. It's a wonderful thing to do for her. Have you seen how nurses swaddle newborns? They wrap them very tightly in warm blankets to give the baby a sense of security. That's what you're doing with your muscle tension. In our over-therapized communities, we often say, "Oh, I still carry my stress here; I'm such a bad person." No, you're not bad. This is protection for your child. It's okay. You don't need to hate the tightness.

Whatever that kid needs, give it to her. Give her attention, let her talk loudly, let her cry, give her nurturing when she needs it. Don't expect her to act a certain way to get loving care. This self-loving is the opposite of what you were raised with. You were probably raised by parents who said, "Don't spoil that baby. Don't let that baby get out of line." The Dr. Spock generation was taught, "Only pick up babies every four hours. If you pick up babies in between times, they'll manipulate you and cry to get you to pick them up all the time."

Who wouldn't? If I could get somebody to pick me up now, I would cry as much as possible. I would cry every second of every day if that would induce somebody to pick me up. We're supposed to learn how to be independent, and the truth is, each one of us would love to have somebody pick us up, whether we admit it to ourselves or not. It's okay to want that.

In fact, it's okay to give that to ourselves. You are really the best one to give this nurturing to yourself. You are the one who knows what you missed. You are the one who knows what kind of things you would have really wanted as a child. Your tiny baby may need to be rocked. You can imagine holding that baby and rocking her. You can do this with beautiful music on, you can do it while watching television. You can do it in your car at stop lights—something to do instead of taking it personally that the light turned red.

Now, if your baby or child or teenager is still in your arms or by your side, take her and put her back inside you where she lives. She's not used to being out so much. Tuck her back inside your body, imagining where she fits inside. If you cannot find a clear vision of where she lives, put your baby back into your heart. Wrap her up with warm loving care and let her know you are protecting her. She is precious cargo. She is truly a direct line to your life force.

You may want to get yourself some kids' books—books you can read to your little one when she gets scared or lonely. You can read these to her when you have a hard time sleeping—books to put her to sleep by.

You can call friends when you don't feel old enough to do something yourself. In fact, the more direct you can be, the more your friends can help. Call your friends and ask them to help you do a task or ask them to explain what would be the best way to do it. Call your friends to come and snuggle with you. Ask a friend to go to the laundromat with you because you get lonesome there. Write a list of things you would do for any child who was sad, or scared, or angry, or happy. See what things on that list you would be willing to do for your little child within.

One of the reasons it's so important to take care of these kids is because they tyrannize us if we don't. They get our attention any way they can. Our kids inside will cry for help in the most amazing ways. They will monopolize a conversation; they will get attracted to people who will not nurture us; they will stay in a job we hate because they are too afraid to leave. They will mutilate themselves, drink, use drugs, eat to the point where they can no longer feel. They are crying out for help. These behaviors get in the way of our being able to actually live life comfortably and fully. This internal acting out is not unlike kids who keep a household in turmoil. We've all been in homes in which the kids run the place. When I say, "Give the kids everything they need," I do mean that. At the same time, kids need limits.

They need to distinguish between what adults do and what kids do. I learned this in the sixties, from a mom who didn't want her daughter to get stoned. I was hanging out in a commune, and as you may recall from that era, everybody was groovy. One girl in the commune was celebrating her twelfth birthday, and we were going to give her a lid of dope. We thought this was really cool. Her mother flipped out and said, "There are things that grown-ups do and things that kids do. She is a kid, and I am a grown-up, and she can't do this yet."

It was so shocking. We said, "Oh, wow, limits, that's so uncool." But she was right. The twelve-year-old threw a fit along with the rest of us, but I am sure that her mom's decision was also a great relief to her.

The difference between what's appropriate for a child and what's appropriate for an adult becomes clearer when we begin to nurture that little child within. As we love her more and more, we begin to see what is appropriate to expect from a child and what is appropriate for a grown-up. One example of this is going to a job interview. If you send your four-year-old to a job interview, you probably aren't going to get the job. One of our biggest problems with work is that we allow our inner children to dominate our actions. This is a problem when doing nearly anything in which we feel incompetent, frustrated and freaked out, including sex or child-raising. If you find yourself feeling that way, tune in to see how old you are, who's running the show. It's probably not your adult.

If you discover this inadequacy, make sure you take your imaginary child into your arms and love her. Hold her, see what she needs. Find out what she is afraid of. Nurture her so she gets to be a kid and you get to be an adult. Both of you get your needs met.

When you feel that little child present and you need to be an adult, try visualizing childcare. Or actually call up a buddy and say, "I'm going to a job interview (or on a first date, or to telephone my parents, or to ask my boss for a raise, or to tell my lover something scary), and I have got to stay at least 25 years old, so I'm sending all my kids over. There are about 80 million of them, and I want you to take care of them for the afternoon." Then when you start to feel very small, remind yourself that your kids are in childcare. They're not with you; they are being taken care of, so you can keep being an adult.

I also suggest you get yourself a baby doll. A baby doll can serve as a constant reminder of that little kid with a broken heart. You may think I'm nuts. "Oh, sure, a baby doll. That sounds like a great idea, JoAnn." If that's your reaction, just pay attention to those voices. They probably reflect the kinds of things that were said to you as a child. You may have been laughed at, taught you weren't important, or ridiculed. You may have been told you were stupid or selfish, crazy or foolish. Or that you wasted your money and time. Those voices offer valuable information.

Some people say to me, "Won't my stuffed animals work? My little stuffed bear?" Stuffed animals—and live animals—are very lovable, but they probably won't remind you of yourself. Baby dolls look vulnerable; it's easier to look at them and remember your own vulnerability.

Many of my clients have told me stories about getting their baby dolls and telling the clerk an elaborate lie about who the doll is for.

"It's for my niece's cousin's third daughter."

We're so embarrassed about buying a baby doll for ourselves. Even the decision of which doll to buy can be instructive. Some people buy dolls that are a different race from themselves. Others buy boy dolls. Others buy dolls that are dressed the way they dressed as children.

When two partners buy dolls, the dynamics of their relationship can become clarified. One gets a doll, the other refuses. Both get dolls, but the dolls are very different. One wants to buy a doll at F.A.O. Schwarz and the other wants to buy a doll at the thrift store. Issues of class, race, size and physical abilities can become very clear when played out through the purchase of a baby doll.

Once you have a doll, set her up with her own "room" so that she has a place to be. It's important to get your doll her own bed so you can put her to bed when you want to have sex, have a serious discussion, or do other adult things. You can put the baby doll in its own room and let your adult do the talking or lovemaking or whatever. Even in a studio apartment, there's always a closet or a corner of the room, or a bathroom that can be the baby's room. There's always a corner where you can tack up a little blanket and make room for this doll.

If you were sexually abused as a child, it's especially important to give the doll her own room so she doesn't sleep in your bed with you. She's way too little to have sex. If you get scared when you're having sex, I suggest you get up, go to your doll's room, rock the doll, take care of the doll, and put the doll back in her own bed where she is safe, like you needed to be when you were a baby.

I tell clients to bring their dolls to my office, and it often takes them months to buy the doll, then even more months to bring her. Then they leave her in the car. "Oh, I forgot my doll." Then they bring her up in a brown paper bag. It's amazing how much we hate our babies, even to the point of being ashamed of a doll that represents that child within.

"I don't want anybody to see me carrying around this baby doll," they say.

"What do you think," I answer, "they're going to arrest you? My god, there's a woman here who has a baby doll! Call the cops."

Nobody's going to say anything to you. They're not even going to notice. People are thinking about their sister-in-law who's going out with their cousin's neighbor, or they're thinking about the grocery store clerk who shortchanged them this morning, or the guy who tried to mug their mother the other night. They're not thinking about you carrying a baby doll. They're not thinking about you at all.

When you find yourself wondering whether everyone is judging you, that's the time to pay attention to your little child inside. She's needing some attention, and the person she needs it from is you.

If your birthday hasn't come yet this year, or one of the High Holy Days is coming up, or Winter Solstice, or Valentine's Day, make a mental note to get yourself a baby doll by that day. This is not to suggest that when the Fourth of July comes and you haven't gotten yourself a doll, you should berate yourself. "Oh my god, it's the Fourth of July, you jerk! You haven't gotten yourself a baby doll! You could be cured by now!"

It's not a time to beat yourself up again. It's just a time to note, "Ah, look at how unwilling I am to take care of myself and love that little child inside me." If you come up with thirty other ways to take care of that kid so you don't have to get a baby doll, more power to you. That's great. It's just that the baby doll is something to hold and to rock and to buy clothes for . . . it's amazing what you can do for the baby doll that didn't get done for you as a baby.

Another way to heal the child with the broken heart is to look at old pictures. Ask your parents or whoever has the family photos to send you pictures of yourself when you were little. Pictures are so revealing. You can tell when the child stopped knowing that she was special. You can see the change from the smiling, happy, confident child to one who is sad, lonely, or afraid. Make a shrine for your child, decorating it with photos, flowers, incense, or candles. This child can be a wonderful guide on your journey of self-love.

People say to me, "So if I do these things, if I heal this baby, if I take care of this baby, does that mean she'll go away?"

Why do we want her to go away? She's so sweet. She's so good. Why do we want this little kid to get lost? She's so incredible.

Recently my son said to me, "Mommy, you know what fainting is? Fainting is like when you die, only you don't really die, you faint." Of course. Brilliant. You may have been taught that these sorts of remarks were insipid. You may have learned to keep your insights and observations to yourself. By reclaiming your child within, you can again have access to a fresh perspective on the world. Your child has much wisdom to share.

What your child needs from you may be very different from what your parents offered her. Your parents probably tried to give her what they wanted themselves—perhaps security, money, or food. You may have needed more than that.

One time my son and I were driving in the car, and he was singing. I was cheering him on. Finally he said to me, "Mommy, you don't have to clap every time I sing a song."

I thought, "Oh, I get it. *I'm* the one who travels around the country so people will clap for me. I'm the one who needs to know that people are listening and thinking I'm important. It's not his trip. He knows he's important."

When I was growing up, it never occurred to me to tell my parents what kind of attention I needed. I'm glad my son has that opportunity. Your inner child also has that opportunity. Ask her what she wants, and she'll tell you. You may be surprised how specific she will be.

I was talking to a group of lesbians in Chicago earlier this year, and I asked, "How many lesbians have their lesbian mothers here tonight?" I was kidding, so of course, I was surprised to see a woman and her mother raise their hands. It was so cool. The daughter had her head shaved. I thought, "This is what she has to do. Being a lesbian isn't enough to be different. She has to shave her head to be different from her mom." It was wonderful to see them sharing the lesbian experience, but expressing their differences in a way most of us are afraid to with our mothers.

You may wish your baby could have had a cool lesbian mom. She probably didn't. You can't change that. But you can be a cool lesbian mom for her now. You can guide her through these troubled waters. As she gets healed, she won't go away. She's a part of you. But she will become less of a burden. She'll feel less scared. She'll less frequently jump into bed with you when you're having sex. She won't need to ruin your relationships. She'll begin to believe she is important to someone—you.

Even if you don't think you're a good mom, you actually can learn to take care of this kid, or these kids. Parenting takes practice. Your idea of perfection can change, it can simply be the willingness to take care of this baby within. With your growing love for her, you will become the perfect mother and teacher.

All of that can happen if you become willing to love this kid. You have to love her as she is, including her fear, her anger, her sadness, and her happiness. See if you can love all of her, and watch how you change. Just the fact of reading this chapter is an indication that you're willing to begin this process of loving your baby. And loving your baby is, of course, simply an excellent way of loving yourself.

Lesbian
Self-Esteem

*Let me listen to me
and not to them.*

—GERTRUDE STEIN

I make my living working with lesbians, traveling around the country talking to lesbians about sex and love, self-esteem, passion, excitement and sorrow. I came out in the San Francisco Bay Area in the seventies at the height of the gay liberation movement, surrounded by a 'feminist-dykes-will-conquer-all,' 'dykes-will-inherit-the-earth,' 'separatists-forever' sort of fervor. Yet inside of me there is still a voice that says, "You mean I'm a lesbian? Aw, shit."

I think that inside every single one of us is a place in which we believe that being a lesbian is just sort of gross. No matter how much fun we have, no matter how proud we feel, no matter how in love or loved we may be, we all internalize the homophobia that surrounds us.

If we don't talk about our own homophobia, then we act like it's all external. We say to ourselves, "When the whole world gets its act together, then I will be happy." In fact, we can be a lot happier right here, right now, by taking a close look at what we're fighting inside of ourselves.

The reason that I use myself as an example is because I do have advantages that make it easier for me to be out. For one thing, both my parents are dead. That's a great advantage, because you can do whatever you want when both your parents are dead. And I wrote a book called *Lesbian Sex* with a bright pink cover. What more do you need to feel good about your sexual orientation? But even I sometimes have trouble saying that I'm a lesbian, and feeling good about it. It's very hard to do on a day-to-day basis in a world that hates women, in a world that hates lesbians, in a world in which we're trying to carve out our place.

It's hard to live in a country in which the Supreme Court decrees that you can't have oral sex, whether or not oral sex is something you actually do. The Supreme Court expressly said that the constitutional right to privacy does not extend to homosexual acts. They wrote that into the majority opinion. Then we wonder why we hate ourselves when we're having oral sex!

As lesbians, we keep thinking that we're not affected by the AIDS crisis. But every day, for years now, we have picked up the newspapers and read that homosexual sex kills. While the papers are not talking about us—once again, we're invisible—lesbians still take it in. We add it to the deep place inside that already believes there's something wrong with being gay.

Then what happens when we go back to visit our families? Our parents and siblings tell queer jokes, or, worse yet, they say nothing at all. Or they talk about AIDS. We can't talk about being queer, but suddenly they can talk about AIDS and how awful it is. They can just sneak it into the conversation. They talk about the husbands and wives and children of our siblings, but our relationships are taboo. They might go so far as to say, "How's your roommate, now what was her name, was it Jean or Joan? Or was it—no, Sally was last year, right, dear?" We just want to shoot them.

No wonder we don't feel good about ourselves. No wonder we don't come out. We have plenty of reasons. But the more we go along with the cultural mandates to be silent, the worse we feel about ourselves. Most of us don't even tell our parents who we are or anything about our lives.

Many women aren't telling their parents because they're afraid they'll get taken out of the will. But what if our parents live until we're seventy? Are we not going to be who we are until we're seventy? Or sixty? Or fifty? How many years are we going to ransom off our lives?

Women say, "Well, it's not that big of a deal to be out to my parents." But it is a big deal. Our lesbianism is a big deal.

No wonder our families think gay people are so lonesome. We never tell them about anything except our cats, our dogs, our jobs, the weather.

"It's raining out here in San Francisco. Oh, it's snowing back there in the East? Oh, uh-huh." Brilliant, thrilling conversation.

Imagine what parents say to each other. "Henry, I just got off the phone with Mary, and you know, all she talked about was that damned cat of hers, the bus, her job and that guy at work she doesn't like. Henry, I think we ought to go see that girl and find out what's the story."

So they go see her. Mary cleans out all of her lesbian books, lesbian posters, lesbian music. Her lover becomes her roommate and they "share a bedroom" for the visit and give the "roommate's bedroom" to her parents. She says, "Oh, hi, Mary's parents. It's so good to meet you. I have to go now. Mary and I hardly ever talk. Oh, don't touch that food! That's my shelf in the refrigerator. Oh, no, we don't combine food either. No food, no bodily fluids . . . ." Imagine how weird it must be to walk into an apartment where someone has taken out all the life and all the love. Imagine what that must feel like to your parents.

Yet some of us say, "I'm afraid I'll lose my family." Well, guess what? You've already lost them. They already aren't what family is for, if you can't even be honest with them.

Sometimes we convince ourselves that not coming out to our families is somehow for their benefit. I love Kate Clinton's comedy routine: "I can't tell my father. He'll have a heart attack." She says, "Wouldn't it be great if we had that much power?" Wouldn't it be great if you could just say to a rapist, "Hey, I'm a lesbian!" and he'd fall down, keel over? You could go tell anybody you wanted to, and they'd crash to the ground!

Unfortunately, we're not that powerful. The thing about our fathers is, a lot of them are going to have heart attacks anyway, and it's not because we're lesbians. They'll have heart attacks because they live in a culture that teaches men to close their hearts, and often their hearts break from the pressure.

Part of the reason why any of our hearts break is because we forget that we need to tell each other what the truth is. We forget what a toll it takes not to tell each other the truth. Consider the money secret.

"Don't ever tell anybody your salary," my dad used to say.

"What will happen, Dad?"

"I don't know. I think someone will kill you or something."

In actuality, if people started talking about money, it might become clear what a scam the capitalist system is. We mustn't have that.

When we keep those secrets, those seemingly tiny secrets, then there's a whole world of things we can't tell people about. If we don't tell them how much money we make in a year, then we can't tell them other things about ourselves. If we try to conceal a large income from friends who don't have much money, we find ourselves embarrassed to talk about new purchases. The secrecy creates distance between ourselves and other people and leads to a sense of shame. Similarly, if we don't have much money and try to hide that fact from friends who are wealthier, we find ourselves trying in vain to keep up with their spending habits.

Don't you love how everyone says, "I don't make that much money"?

"You don't? Then how come you drive a new Volvo?" I love to say things like that. I ask people how much they pay for things. It flips people out, because we all lie. We lie all the time about everything.

We lie a lot about being lesbians, because we're in the habit of lying and because we're so afraid of our own homophobia. Yet lesbians are not the only ones who have deep-seated insecurities. Most people do. We don't struggle with self-esteem only because we're lesbians.

I'm not saying it's easy to be honest. I lost my father by telling him the truth. I told him the truth not only about my lesbianism, but also about his alcoholism, and how I felt about how he had treated me, and how I see the world. After I told him my truth, he cut off all contact with me. That was a dear price to pay, but I had decided that the price of forsaking my own integrity was much higher.

The other members of my family tolerated my uniqueness until I decided to have a baby. That was the strangest thing they had ever heard of.

"You're going to have a child? I didn't know lesbians could get pregnant."

"Yes, I still have a uterus. It's amazing. They didn't take it from me at the border."

"But how will other kids at school treat your child?"

"Well, if you'd stop teaching your kids strange ideas about people who are different from you, then maybe kids like mine wouldn't have to put up with the hurt."

Once my baby was born, everyone loved him and was delighted that I'd given birth to him. But many of us get flack from our parents when we choose to have babies—inseminated babies, adopted babies, foster kids, or whatever. Sometimes this is when our parents quit talking to us. "Now you've really done it. Being queer was one thing, but now you're going to love a child? Forget it."

Consider if your parents said, "You can come home, but don't bring that baby." Who would ever do that? No one would. So why don't we insist on taking our lesbian selves and our lesbian lovers home with us? Why don't we take our lesbian selves to the office with us? Why don't we tell people the truth?

Some of us say it's because we don't like labels. "I don't want to be labeled anything; I'm one of God's children, and we are all equal, and everything is wonderful . . . ." I do understand not wanting to have labels. However, the truth is, if you eat pussy, you eat pussy.

Are there any labels you are willing to accept? Do you like being labeled a woman? Do you like being labeled working class? Jewish? Physically-challenged? Black or white, Asian or Chicana? Which labels are you willing to take? Which ones do you want to forget about? Many of us adopt only the labels that are perfectly safe.

"I'll take the label, 'I-come-from-Kansas,' okay?"

"Okay, great. That's it?"

"Yeah, that says it all."

Why do we have a hard time with the label *lesbian*? A lot of women want to be called *gay*. It's such a nice word. It's such a sweet word. Gay gay gay. Happy happy. But what's hard about the word lesbian? Who says the word lesbian is ugly? Certainly it has a negative connotation, like dyke and cunt, and has been used against us for centuries. Most of us never heard our parents say the word lesbian, unless it was in a derogatory context. But there's nothing inherently negative about the word lesbian.

If avoiding labels is not the issue, we say, "They can't accept it in my culture." I was raised Catholic in a teeny town in Ohio, so I know what it's like to think they're not going to accept it in your culture. But I have found that if you go back and just present it to your culture, there's almost nothing they can do. I recently went to my twentieth high school reunion. They asked us to write in a little catalog what we had been doing for the past twenty years. Now, I did not say that I'd been eating pussy. But I did say almost everything else. I said that I wrote *Lesbian Sex*, and that my lover—whose name I put down—and I were raising my child who was then four, and that I was a counselor. No one said anything to me except that drunk guy who says things to you even if you're straight and have four kids and your husband's with you. Everyone else was very polite. The people with whom I had been close were still close to me.

I've found that the more I show people that being a lesbian is a positive, loving thing to do, the more they are willing to believe that lesbianism can be popular, that it can be wonderful. After all, lesbianism is magical. That's why I'm a lesbian. I am not a woman of little brain. I would never pick a weirdo, terrible sexual orientation. I am just not that dumb. For me, being a lesbian is magical. It's just fabulous.

Remember the first time? Not necessarily your first sexual experience, but the first time you felt that flush of love for a woman. For me, it was for Mrs. McAndrews in second grade. I would just sit and stare for hours. She was tall, with tightly curled grey hair, and beautiful smooth skin. I was in heaven. That's lesbian magic. Remember that feeling? I remember when Mary Simmer whistled at me in fourth grade and I thought I would faint. I came out of the house dressed in white shorts and a white top with red trim, and Mary Simmer, my girlfriend from down the street, was standing in front of my house, and she whistled at me. I nearly fell over. I didn't know what the feeling was. I didn't know anything about sexuality. I didn't know who Sappho was. I was only in fourth grade. But I still remember that feeling. It's one of my favorite feelings.

That feeling is one of the reasons we go through all that we go through. We put up with a lot of homophobia in this culture, and in ourselves. We do it because we know the magic of lesbian love.

I've always found it ironic that we've been accused of converting people to lesbianism. Who would be converted to this? It's such a hard thing to do. We do it because it feels good to love another woman. For many of us, it's the way we feel whole.

Sometimes it's difficult to keep up that feeling of joy and mystical magic, and to tell others about it, when there's a gnawing place inside of us that says, "This is awful. My mom says it's awful. My dad says it's awful. My sister, my brother and my children say it's awful. Teachers and judges think it's awful. Everybody thinks it's awful."

Why is it so terrible to love women? I keep racking my brain. I really do. For starters, I don't have somebody else's last name. But for that should I be shot? Okay, so I like to put my fingers in somebody else's vagina, but is that something they should get me for? Take my kid? Take my job? Take my house? Take my family of origin? Is that why? Okay, it can't be that. So what is it? I think it's because I'm not owned by a man.

Woman-hatred has a long cultural history. Scientists have recently discovered, much to their amazement, that all of us may have one common female ancestor. They have come to this conclusion after discovering that mitochondrial DNA is virtually identical in all people. These small cell bodies each have specific genetic constitutions that are inherited from the mother, and researchers have traced the lineage of all presently living humans to one West African woman who lived 200,000 years ago. This gives new meaning to the word sisterhood. And it can help us understand how deeply ingrained the fear of woman-bonding is when the whole race has such primal connections to one woman. Men at this deep cellular level are not as integral to the human race as women.

It's also helpful to take a look at why we ourselves feel it's so terrible to love women. I call this lesbian snot. It's the feeling that there is something wrong with being a lesbian. We all have it. Why else aren't we shouting our love from the rooftops? We can tell ourselves it's because of external oppression, but we also believe their lies.

Recently I was on a plane, and the guy sitting next to me asked, "Why are you going to Chicago?"

I didn't say, "Because I'm a lesbian and I'm going to teach lesbians about sex." Instead I said, "I teach sex education." Nice and neutral.

"My wife is a nurse at a hospital and she teaches sex education," he said. "Maybe she'd like to come to your presentation. What do you specialize in?"

Why did that make me nervous? It was as if he were getting right down to it, right to the snot. I was thinking, "Uh-oh. The snot. He's going to put his foot in the snot." You know, the lights go off inside: "Snot alert, snot alert. I'm in trouble. He's going to find out I'm a lesbian."

I looked around and asked myself, "Is he an axe murderer? Is he going to pull out a switch-blade on the plane? Maybe I should reach around and put my hand on the arm of the passenger in front of me just to alert her so that if he stabs me, the blood will drip down my hand and she'll know someone is being stabbed to death."

I sat there and started saying to myself, "Tell him. Tell him. Tell him. Tell him." Like a little cheerleading squad. "Tell him about the snot. Tell him about the snot. Give me an 'L'. Come on, JoAnn, come on, you can tell him. Who is this guy to you?"

So for about an hour—seriously, an hour—I sat there. Finally I said, "I am a lesbian and I teach lesbians about lesbian sex." There was a long silence—no switch-blade, no axe, no gun, no cyanide, no nothing. He just turned to me and said, "Really? Gosh, you don't look like a lesbian."

Then, of course, my politically righteous self thought, "What do you mean, I don't 'look like a lesbian'? Fuck you, asshole! Watch me walk down this aisle. Look at this stance, man. I am a lesbian. I am a dyke!" People don't think of lesbians as normal-looking people you meet on planes. But the man never killed me or anything. He didn't reject me. We had a perfectly pleasant conversation the rest of the way to Chicago. It was, in fact, no big deal.

This conversation was not something out of the ordinary. Perhaps the subject was raised due to my work, but each of us has these conversations daily. The phone company sends a worker to our home and we explain to him that the second line is for our new roommate. The people at our child's school wonder why we are bringing another woman to the parent-teacher conference. When we say she is a roommate, the teacher doesn't understand why she is there.

These conversations last for seconds or minutes, or throughout a school year. These conversations are a continuous part of our lives. Do we come out or don't we? Our minds have great excuses in both directions. Do I tell this person or don't I? Will the phone repair person who now knows my address and both phone numbers harass us? If I don't tell a stranger that I see once in my life, who will I tell? Will the teacher treat my child badly because of my sexual orientation? If I don't tell the teacher, then my child has to do the telling in a certain way. Back and forth, back and forth, constant questioning of our own or others' actions, all surrounding this rather simple concept: we are lesbians.

Some of the ways our self-hatred is manifested are difficult to recognize as such. We may not know that drinking too much is self-hatred. We may not know that trying to be a perfect mom so our kids won't hate us for our lesbianism is self-hatred. We may not know that not wanting ourselves or our partners to look too "butch" is our self-hatred.

There's a big controversy now: is lesbianism hereditary? People are trying to find a genetic predisposition to being gay. I think part of this is positive in that researchers are trying to tell the establishment, "Don't try to cure homosexuality. They were born this way. A certain percentage of the population is going to be this way, no matter what you do."

But even if they're right, what about those for whom it's not hereditary? Many women say it's a choice. They have chosen lesbianism because of positive experiences with women. Maybe they got whistled at by a little girl down the street, creamed their jeans and have been wanting to have that feeling ever since, so they brought women into their lives. Why are we so afraid to say we chose it? It's so scary to take that chance and say, "I am choosing it. It's really what I want to do. It's not because my DNA is making me. DNA be damned, I think I'll be a lesbian."

A lesbian friend of mine was going through a period of about eight months when she wasn't having sex with anybody, and she likes to have some sex, this girl. She said, "I can't get lesbians to go out and just have sex with me. I am almost ready to stop by some straight bar on the way home from work, because I know I could get laid in about twenty minutes. And most of the twenty minutes would be getting the nerve up to get out of my car and go in the bar." So, no, we're not lesbians because we can't get a man. It's because we *want* a woman.

We spend so much energy seeking relationships, yet there's still some place inside of us that does not legitimize the relationships we do have. Some of us put down other women for trying to make their relationships into marriages. If not 'marriage,' what word should we use? Partner, lover, best friend, buddy, life partner? It's hard to live in a culture that does not even have a name for our relationships. Especially when our parents and families, even if we *are* out to them, don't legitimize those relationships either.

We also don't legitimize our parenting roles. When we're co-parenting another lesbian's biological child, and we decide we're going to leave the relationship, we often don't recognize the impact on that child, because we don't truly believe we're that child's parent. Biological moms sometimes keep the child from the co-parent, because we are more angry at the co-parent than we are respectful of that parent's right to see the child. Those of us who had kids in heterosexual relationships might hate their kids' father, but unless that father has really abused our kids, hardly anyone would say he doesn't have a right to have contact with them. Yet with our lesbian co-parents, too often either they drop out or we drop them out. It's so hard for us to take our own relationships seriously. And it's even harder for us to take our kids' relationships seriously as well. Imagine what it is like for a young child to lose his or her other mother; no matter which adult is blocking that connection, the child feels abandoned.

It's hard for us not to walk out on a relationship when it gets boring, when somebody else who is cuter, or more exciting, or more interesting comes along. It's so difficult to stay there and stay with it, so difficult for us to see our relationships as the real bonding that they are. It's also difficult to affirm our relationships to others:

"No, Mom, I won't come to your home for the holidays unless I can bring my lover."

"Yes, Dad, I am having this baby with Annie. Yes, I feel like she is the other parent."

"Well, Boss, I can't come to work next week because my mate, Gail, is having surgery and I need to be with her."

We find ourselves in the untenable position of either betraying the values of our families and the culture we were raised in, or betraying ourselves. Either choice hurts.

Everyone wants to know: how come lesbian relationships don't last long? They forget that these days, no relationships last long. We're in a fast-paced, fast moving world. Things change all the time. You can get out of anything, into anything. You can go here, go there. That wasn't happening 25 years ago. In my parents' generation, moving was a big deal. In the Midwest, it was a big deal if you knew anybody whose aunt had moved to, say, California. People said, "You're kidding! Wow! When did she move there?" It was always right after the war. "Well, right after the war, they moved to California because they couldn't get jobs around here." That's about as much as anybody moved.

Today, everybody's moving all the time. Who even knows her neighbors? Relationships of all persuasions aren't lasting for very long. Some lesbians have unreal expectations that because we're lesbians, our relationships are going to be better. They're going to be different. They're going to be stronger. They're going to last longer. All the while, somewhere inside of us, we don't believe that for an instant. We need only look at the relationships of our friends to see how flimsy that belief is.

What would happen if we allowed ourselves to stay in a relationship? I don't mean dead relationships in which you just stay to the end in order to prove that you can have a long relationship. That's been done. Several hundred generations did that. It didn't work. I think my parents, for example, should have stayed together for about a week and a half.

I'm talking about being in a vital relationship. Part of the problem with being in a lesbian relationship is that you're relating to another lesbian. Inside both of these lesbians, and somewhere in the relationship, which is a whole other entity, is the snot. The lesbo snot. It's there, and we get stuck in it.

Indeed, we *could* allow ourselves to stay in the relationship with the person we love. We could work through the fear of going against everything we were taught. We could do it even if we think that we are getting bored. We could do it even if someone comes along who is newer, more interesting. We could be honest with ourselves and admit that we would just move in with the new lover and start all this over again. We could decide to tackle it this time, no matter what the voices in our head told us. No matter what excuse we come up with to leave.

In Dodici Azpadu's novel *Saturday Night in the Prime of Life* (San Francisco: Spinsters/Aunt Lute, 1983), the two lesbian characters have had to give up their families of origin in order to be with each other for 26 years. What a crazy choice to have to make! Yet many of us are faced with that choice.

When our lover gets pregnant, do we tell our mother she's going to become a grandmother?

"Mom, you're going to become a grandmother."

"You're pregnant?"

"No, but Sally is."

"What has that got to do with me?"

Someone was telling me recently about having an independent relationship with her mother-in-law. I thought she must be straight. How many lesbians have independent relationships with their mothers-in-law? But she was a lesbian. It jogged my memory. I remembered that in straight marriages, a woman will call her mother-in-law and chat with her. It was like a distant voice from the past.

Why is it that we don't reach out to our lovers' mothers? Or fathers? Or siblings? What keeps us from creating these deep, healthy bonds in our lives? Consciously or unconsciously, we say to ourselves, "Why would she want to know me? I've got lesbian snot."

I don't think that we can even imagine the ways in which we hide our lesbianism and thereby deprive ourselves and others of our richness. I'm not laying it totally at our own door, because we do live in a culture that hides everything, and that encourages us to hide our lesbianism. We're expected to hide our lesbianism when we attend weddings, funerals, or other family occasions. We are expected to hide when we apply for apartments or jobs or credit. If we are routinely closeted, we become routinely dishonest. We always use genderless pronouns; we attend family functions alone; we may even invent boyfriends or husbands. This *must* take a toll on our self-esteem and our ability to love others.

The way I see it, we have a unique opportunity to free ourselves by living our lesbianism openly. We can, in fact, be role models for non-lesbians who will see that they, too, can live honestly. As gay men are being called upon to love each other more deeply than ever in the face of the AIDS epidemic, so, too, we are being called upon, in the face of unrelenting homophobia, to love ourselves by casting off our shame.

One way to dissipate lesbian hatred is to take time to remember the magic. What brought you to this path in the first place? When did you first start feeling the joy of loving women? Can you remember the first Mary Simmer who whistled at you, or the first Mrs. McAndrews? Or the first woman who took you to bed? The time when you just couldn't believe what was happening in your body. That time she touched your hair. That first time, when you maybe didn't even have a word for it. Or maybe you had a word for it and were scared of the word, but the sweet mystery broke through all that defense.

Remember when you found out there were more than two of you? Then when you found out that there were more than four? Remember when you discovered that you could go places and be openly lesbian? If you didn't live in a big city, you could visit a big city and walk down the streets and see women hold each other's hands. Remember that feeling? It's the feeling that reminds us of the magic of being a lesbian. It's the reminder that we are perfect, just as we are.

Let's start talking with each other about the magic of being lesbians. Not all the hard times, not all the people we know who broke up, not the awful feeling it was being a lesbian in this place or that place, but what is wonderful about being a lesbian today. We can think of lots of ways that being a lesbian inhibits us. But what about how being a lesbian enhances our lives?

Allow yourself to revel in lesbian culture. Go to women's concerts and festivals. Subscribe to women's journals, go to your local women's bookstore and read about women. Travel to cities in which the lesbian population is visible. Go to the women's buildings. See what events are happening. Make a list of all the women you have felt particularly akin to. Make a list of all the reasons why you are connected to those women. Imagine yourself standing up to all the men in the world and saying, "No thanks, I prefer women."

When I think about lesbian self-esteem, I think about both sides: the self-hatred and the self-love. We need to acknowledge both, because that's what's real. The joy and the snot. *The Snot and the Joy: A Story About Being a Lesbian.* It could be a book title, don't you think?

When Will We Love Our Bodies?

. . . a woman who wants a woman usually wants a woman.

—SIDNEY ABBOTT

We like to think that lesbians are much more accepting of our own size, shape, color and age than are straight women. But lesbians live in a culture that teaches all women to hate our bodies. As lesbians, we like to think we are immune to this indoctrination, when in fact we're not. Fat or thin, dark or pale, wrinkled or smooth, large or small breasted, all of us at least occasionally look at our own bodies and say, "Yuck." Most of us say it daily. Whatever body we have, it's not okay.

I often ask audiences, "Who absolutely loves her body?" The last time I did that, there were 400 women in the audience and thirteen of them raised their hands. That's not very many women.

See if you can remember the first time you heard there was something wrong with your body. How old were you when you first heard that you were too fat, too hairy, or too tall? When did someone tell you your hair was stringy, or your teeth crooked, or your legs knock-kneed?

You may have started hearing criticisms about your body when you were a baby. Especially in reference to girl babies, people often remark, "Oh, she's a chubby one. She sure doesn't miss any meals."

Already, before the child is even walking, her parents are worried that she will become fat. Babies are frequently put on diets. People have long debates about whether formula feeding or breast feeding is less fattening. Isn't that incredible? The truth is, babies are naturally little chubbettes. That way, they can survive for a while on their fat if they aren't fed. Yet I hear comments all the time about how fat girl babies are. Imagine what it was like to hear, at that tender, impressionable age, that you were too fat.

Bulimia and anorexia have reached epidemic proportions in the United States. In the last 25 years, the average weight of Miss America dropped twenty pounds. A recent study in California showed that 80 percent of fourth grade girls had been on diets some time in their lives. If you think lesbians are not affected, look around. Anorexia, bulimia, compulsive overeating and neurotic obsession with weight are alive and well in the lesbian community too.

Let's stop denying that lesbians have prejudices about body size. Let's stop saying, "Oh, being fat is fine in our community. Fat lesbians have no problems at all. We're so cool about body image. You can be any size you want."

I recently saw a photography exhibit of beautiful naked women at a women's coffeehouse in San Francisco. Not one of the women weighed over 110 pounds. I'm not saying it's not appealing to look at bodies that size; I just want us to consider that many of us are torturing ourselves to make our bodies be that size. When those are the only images we see, even in our own coffeehouses, we buy into the culture's myopic vision of beauty.

Years ago I went to a Mexican restaurant with a group of friends, and after eating several tacos, I said, "I'm so fat." A woman who was about my size said to me, "Don't ever say that again."

"Why?" I asked.

She said, "Because it's irresponsible for women who are not big to say they're fat. All women say they're fat. How do you think that makes fat women feel?"

Most of us don't even have an accurate image of how big we are. In my therapy practice, I ask women to draw a picture of themselves on long brown wrapping paper. They often draw unrealistic pictures. They have no concept of what their body size actually is.

The new obsession with measuring body fat as a sign of 'fitness' seems absurd to me. What if we stopped measuring our fat, stopped dieting to death and just allowed ourselves to be whatever size we naturally are? What if lots of women became very fat? What if we let our waists get huge? What if we stopped sucking our bellies in? What if we stopped thinking about our weight and started thinking about rape, or military build-up, or world hunger? A nation of big, angry women could cause a lot of trouble.

I'm convinced that the current media mania about women's thinness is related to the fact that there are now millions of women who work and millions of feminists. Women are much more threatening than they used to be. My mom, for instance, did not freak out about her weight all the time. My mom was not tiny. In fact, she was fat. I don't remember my mom and her friends ever talking about diets. But then, most of them didn't work outside the home. If they did work, they usually accepted that women didn't make as much money as men. They didn't make a lot of noise about pornography, sexual harassment, or domestic violence. As housewives, they were in a non-threatening role.

Today, women are protesting objectification, lower wages, incest and other forms of violence. Men have come up with another way to keep women in our place: if we are small, at least they can overpower us physically.

But while it has become the norm for straight women to diet, it is taboo in some lesbian communities to discuss our obsessions with body size. A friend says, "Hey, losing some weight, are you?"

You're supposed to say, "Oh, I am? I hadn't noticed. I just happen to be running a hundred miles a week."

Running, swimming, cycling, or doing aerobics compulsively is the new covert form of weight loss. Before I go on, let me confess that I hate exercise. The one time I decided I should get in shape, I got bursitis instead. I had been lifting weights for about two and a half weeks, complaining all the while, and finally I got bursitis and had to quit. I told the woman who was running the gym, and she said, "You must be really excited." I was.

My idea of exercise is a good brisk chat. You may disagree. I acknowledge that there are benefits to exercise—you can't pick up a newspaper or magazine today without reading more proof about how important exercise is. I'm not saying we shouldn't get strong. I'm not saying we shouldn't be able to run fast. One of the many positive effects of exercise is that we get in touch with our bodies. I know some incest survivors who go to the gym to remember they have a body: "Oh, here's a muscle. There's a leg. Hey, I forgot about that arm." That can be very beneficial.

Yet I believe that women, including lesbians, are hyper-exercising to lose their body fat: their hips, thighs, abdomen and breasts. If they carry it to an extreme degree, they stop menstruating. Their bodies become increasingly like the masculine ideal.

We need to ask ourselves, what's the purpose? Why swim twenty miles a week? Why ride a bike every day? Why is hyper-exercising being glorified in so many advertisements today? The exercisers I know want to have ten percent body fat. I get concerned about that. Why ten percent body fat? Who came up with that idea? I'm willing to bet that women didn't think that up.

People say to me all the time, "Being overweight is bad for the heart and joints, and the research shows . . . ." I say, what research? Men are the ones who die more frequently from heart attacks and heart disease. Constant dieting is much more stressful on the heart than being fat, and exercise can cause innumerable injuries.

Some people *do* exercise for their health, and some people eat certain diets for their health. Just be aware of the ulterior motives. So often a woman says, "I'll become a vegetarian, or a runner—it'll be good for my health." Under her breath she adds, "And I'll lose some weight."

Most of us have shame about our fat, but what we feel most ashamed of is bodily fluid. At least our fat doesn't ooze—it's just there. Bodily fluids drip.

I saw an advertisement for car oil that said, "Don't drip and drive." It reminded me how often we've been told, "Don't drip." I say it to my son all the time. "Don't drip your drink, your ice cream's dripping, your food's dripping off your fork." Dripping is a *terrible* thing.

Dripping out of some bodily orifice is especially terrible. Take snot, for instance. Isn't it awful to talk with someone who has snot dripping from her nose? I find myself wiping underneath my nose hoping she'll get the hint.

It's even worse, of course, if it's dripping from your own nose. I have allergies, so I know all about snot. I'm always conscious of the snot in my nose. I'm always asking myself, "Is there any snot in my nose?" Then I have to figure out how to remove it discreetly. Yet snot is one of the least offensive bodily fluids. Earwax, spit and other fluids that come out of our heads are also relatively minor offenses. It's a drag to wake up with our eyes glued shut and trench breath, but we get over it.

Armpit fluid is more of a downer. Don't let any sweat come out! That's the message we get from the deodorant industry. Can you imagine how much money they make by convincing us we shouldn't sweat, or, horror of horrors, smell?

When you perspire, you're supposed to keep your arms down. It's a conspiracy we all participate in: let's pretend we don't sweat, okay? Let's pretend we don't have any bodily fluids. You buy deodorant, I'll buy deodorant, we'll wash our armpits, keep our arms down, and we'll all act like it doesn't happen. We're a nation of deniers.

The worst bodily fluids are you-know-where. Down There. Shit is bad, and it's even worse if you have diarrhea. Better to be constipated, so you're miserable, but at least no bodily fluids are coming out to embarrass you.

Luis Buñuel made a great movie, *The Discreet Charm of the Bourgeoisie*. There's a scene at a big banquet table furnished with several toilets, and all the guests are shitting and peeing right there at the table. Toilet paper is being passed around on silver trays. People excuse themselves every once in a while and run into a little closet, close the door and eat. It shows how arbitrary our shame is, and how silly.

As I'm sure you've noticed, fluid also comes out of the vagina. Sometimes it's blood. Sometimes it's what I call vaginal juice. We also get wonderful infections like vaginitis because our vaginas are warm, moist and dark. If I were a bug, that's where I'd go.

Our vaginas smell. They smell different at different times in our cycle—sometimes very strong, sometimes hardly at all. Yet how many of us mention the fact that our vaginas smell? Who has conversations like this: "Hey, smell my vagina. Can you believe this? I just put my finger up my vagina. Now smell my finger. What do you think's going on?"

"I don't know. Doesn't smell like anything's wrong. Smells to me like about day ten or so in my cycle. I think you're fine."

When I go to the gynecologist, I like to go first thing in the morning because I like to have myself all clean, with no pubic hairs out of place. I like my underpants to be nice and dry, because I don't want the gynecologist to know that I have bodily fluids. It would be shocking to her, I'm sure.

This is called denial. We act as if nothing's happening in our bodies, when in fact, they're producing all kinds of bodily fluids all day long. They're little factories of pee, snot, earwax, sweat, vaginal juice.

It's so frightening for us to tell our partners how we feel about their bodies. Three weeks into the relationship, she gets her period. We don't want to tell her how we feel about our own periods, and we certainly don't want to deal with hers. We won't talk about the fact that we're freaked out about her size or her race or her tampax or her breast or her differently abled body or whatever. We won't talk about it because we're walking around inside our own, acting like we're not in them.

While we're talking about denial, did you know that one in five women shave off facial hair? One weekend when I was at Yosemite, a brave soul came into the bathroom, looked around, sucked in her breath, laid out her razor and shaving cream and went to it. You know what? I thought it was really sexy.

I mentioned it to a friend who told me she'd lived with a woman for years who shaved and she loved it. She said the shaving ritual was one of the very few things she missed about living in a house with men—those quiet times while they shaved. I suspect there's an ethnic component to our prejudice against women who have facial hair—behind those 'bearded lady' jokes—because most of the hairy women I know are either of Mediterranean or IndoEuropean background. And, of course, there's also the whole underarm/leg ritual.

We also tend to ignore our breasts. Sometimes only when breasts have to be removed do we appreciate their beauty. Many of us don't even do the simplest act of self-love, the breast self-exam. Especially if you are concerned about health, you should know that a monthly breast exam is one of the most important things every woman should do.

You may want to make a history of your breasts. When did they start to grow? When were you told you should wear a bra? How did you first get one? (I unsuspectingly opened my first bra at Christmas in front of my brother and father!) Have you ever disliked your breasts? Do they give you pleasure?

Try touching your breasts the way you do your arms, hands, face. If you don't like your breasts, begin to make friends with them. Exploring them alone is one way to find out how you would like a lover

to touch your breasts. Some women like to have their nipples stimulated during lovemaking; other women have no more sensation in
their nipples than in other parts of their skin. For some women, one
breast is more sensitive than the other. For some women, having their
breasts touched triggers memories of sexual abuse. Try to make room
for all of your thoughts and feelings about your breasts.

Few of us escape some degree of hatred of our genitals. No
wonder, since we've been told forever that women's genitals are
smelly and ugly. We hear every day about rape, pornography and other
violence directed at women through our genitals. Even if our genitals
have never been abused, we still know that we are subject to rape. Each
time we see deodorized tampons and 'sanitary' pads on drugstore
shelves, we are reminded that our genitals are offensive. Our self-
hatred can be projected onto lovers as well: we may not like oral sex
because we have internalized so many messages about how ugly
women's genitals are.

We spend much of our lives hiding and protecting our vaginas,
clitorises and assholes. We are told to keep our legs together, not to
touch ourselves and to keep ourselves clean. We are rarely told how
our genitals can be used for our pleasure. In fact, it's only been since the
publishing of *A New View of a Woman's Body* (New York: Simon and
Schuster, 1981) that we have had clear information about the true size
and function of our clitorises. This book reveals that there is much
more to the clitoris than meets the eye: attached to the outside 'head'
are two 'legs' that stretch back around the urethra, vagina and anus.

Try sitting in front of a mirror and looking at your genitals. Read
books like *I Am My Lover*, edited by Joan Blank (Burlingame, California: Down There Press, 1980), and *Labia Flowers*, by Tee Corinne
(Tallahassee: Naiad Press, 1978), that have several pictures of wom-
en's genitals. Ask a lover or friend to join you. You'll notice that
women's genitals, like women's breasts, vary greatly in size, shape and
color. Create a genital study group. Anything is possible.

For much of our lives we ignore our bodies, and when we get sick,
we act as if we've been betrayed. Even when we get a cold, we think, "I
haven't got time for a cold! I have to work. I have to go on vacation.
This is the weekend." It's never okay for our bodies to take a break.

It wasn't until several of my friends were dealing with their
hidden disabilities and their food allergies that I noticed there were
foods that I was allergic to or that gave me indigestion. I just ate them

anyway. "Onions and peanuts make me sick? Oh well. My body can just adjust." It wasn't until I met people whose bodies couldn't adjust that I thought, "I don't have to eat peanuts." It was such a novel thought. I could actually respond to the messages my body gives me every time I eat peanuts.

Permanent disability can seem like the ultimate affront to our belief that we can control our bodies. Some disabled people refer to able-bodied people as TABs, for Temporarily Able-Bodied, because we will all lose physical abilities over time. Some TABs will become permanently disabled in the future. It can be hard for TABs to walk next to their disabled sisters, or to deal with their needs, or to see them as sexual beings. We don't want to be reminded that we all have vulnerable, temporal bodies.

Differently abled women have to spend a lot of time listening to their bodies. They have to spend a lot of time educating their friends about where they can go to eat, whether bathrooms, movie theaters, or public buildings are wheelchair accessible, that they use crutches, or a cane, and need to walk slower.

Almost all images in the media are of able-bodied people. I recently saw a television show in which a judge was in a wheelchair, and the story was not about his disability; he was just another character. It reminded me that I had never seen that in the media before.

Since few therapists speak sign language and few self-improvement books are on tape or printed in Braille, people with hearing and vision impairments have restricted access to the resources that might help them improve their body image. (This book and *Lesbian Sex* are available on tape through the Women's Braille Press, Box 8475, Minneapolis, MN 55408.) Similarly, workshops and classes are often not accessible or affordable to disabled people.

People who can't wash or do their own laundry without assistance are particularly vulnerable to America's obsession with cleanliness. Women with ostomy bags, catheters, or chronic infections have to ask themselves, "What if my bag slips?" "What if the catheter leaks?" "What if I can't keep this infection clean?" These are just a few of the questions able-bodied people don't usually need to be concerned with.

When talking about body image, most people forget about racism. In fact, most white people forget about racism every chance they get. In the lesbian community, we're not supposed to be racist because we're so evolved. We've each read three books. We know people who are different colors. We're so cool.

But we actually don't mix races very well, do we? We mostly associate with people of our own race, as do heterosexuals. Latina women have friendship networks with latina women; white women have friendship networks with white women; black women have friendship networks with black women. We act like we have an integrated community, but we don't. I believe that everybody's racist; it's almost impossible not to be. Racism is difficult to admit, but the silence doesn't make it go away. Occasionally we address the racism among us and try to reach out to one another, but we're still not very good at it. The most important aspect of our community is that we do at least acknowledge racism where the majority culture totally ignores it. We must all work at trying to educate ourselves about our racism and what steps we can make to change it. We can work on our racism a little every day.

We each have internalized racism as well that's frequently expressed around our bodies. Many of us don't like the texture of our hair, the shape of our lips, eyes, buttocks. Many of us, black and white, try to change our natural skin color. Women frequently have their noses "fixed." The word "fixed" says it all: why do we need fixing? Who made up these rules? When will we have the courage to change them?

We also tend to ignore the aging process, or see it as horrifying. The truth is, our bodies change. Our skin wrinkles. Our hair turns gray. Our breasts sag. Our vaginas get drier. If your heart keeps beating, you're bound to get old.

In April, 1987, women came from all over Canada, England and the United States to attend the West Coast Old Lesbian Conference and Celebration. Somebody said to me, "Why do they say it's for 'old lesbians'?"

I said, "You have to be at least 60 to get in."

She said, "Wouldn't it be nicer to say 'older lesbians'?"

I said, "Nicer for whom?"

That's what we try to do—make things nice, so we can handle them. We're taught to say 'heavy' instead of 'fat,' 'comfortable' instead of 'rich,' 'older' instead of 'old.' If we don't tell the truth, maybe we won't have to face it. How old must someone be before we can say she's old and it won't be an insult?

Recently I gave a talk for lesbians in Ann Arbor, Michigan, and one of the women in the audience was 87. It reminded me that I rarely meet old lesbians. We live in an age-segregated culture, and the lesbian community doesn't provide much integration.

Another conference for old lesbians is held in Washington, D.C. each year. They convene a council of elders consisting of women who are all 75 or older. Too many of us have forgotten that old people have a lot to say. We want to shut them away. Their bodies remind us of our own aging process.

I also want to discuss compulsive eating in this chapter because I feel that our self-image has a great deal to do with how we use food in our daily lives. Health and nourishment are a delicate balance for women. We are not supposed to nourish ourselves in any way. The best excuse we can have is if we are doing it for someone else. Food, the primal and essential nourishment, can be easily the savior or the enemy. When we talk about body image, we must look at ways we use and distort that basic nourishment, namely food, that keeps our bodies alive.

I have had many lesbians talk with me about their compulsive behaviors with all kinds of drugs, and another chapter of this book is devoted to recovery from compulsive addictions. Many people choose food as their drug of choice. They use sugar, carbohydrates, nuts, junk food. Whether or not we are aware of them, the results of overeating are an altering of mood, feelings, and bodily function.

What exactly is 'overeating'? We live in a culture that steals food from the rest of the world. We hoard grain. We dump dairy products and other foods rather than drive down prices on food. We pay farmers not to grow crops so there is no glut of any one particular food item. Yet there are people starving in our country and in other countries around the world.

People in this country who can afford it eat enormous amounts of food. When my child was six months old and beginning to eat solid food, my pediatrician explained how little food he needed to survive. It amazed me. As my child grew, I worked hard at not imposing the 'finish-everything-on-your-plate' routine on him, which I found quite difficult. I really do think I have to eat large amounts of food to survive. Yet, when I have fallen in love, I skip meals altogether and can still do amazing things all day and all night with a seemingly unending supply of energy. Our idea of how much food we need on any given day is truly subjective. I don't think people with money really know.

The question about compulsive eating is: when does eating get in the way of feeling? When does eating get in the way of living? When does eating take on proportions that become truly unhealthy? Food addiction can stop one's inner life.

The issue here is *not* size. Women, healthy and not healthy, come in all sizes and shapes. The most compulsive food addict I knew was very tiny. She probably weighed 105 pounds, soaking wet, with a rock in each hand. She was not an exerciser; she did not vomit her food after eating it; she did not go on starvation kicks. She had some sort of metabolism that burned off every calorie she ate. She used foods like she used other drugs, to keep her from feeling. She was always occupied, either shopping for, preparing, or eating food. Her environment was totally controlled by her food.

Many of us have compulsive thoughts about food. We wonder if we should eat certain foods. We wonder what restaurant we are going to go to and what it will serve. We worry if we eat any sugar. We weigh ourselves and freak out if we are over the weight we have decided is appropriate. We berate ourselves if we eat 'too much.' Constant vigilance can be just as debilitating as overeating. The obsessive thoughts keep us from experiencing the rest of our lives.

Compulsive consumption of any substance is effective in keeping all feelings down. We weigh them down with food, caffeine, cigarette smoke, pills, or alcohol. Unlike some other substances, food is readily available and socially acceptable. Especially if you do not eat compulsively in public, you can 'do it' anywhere, anytime. There is always a way to get more of your drug of choice. You can meet someone for lunch, dinner, dessert, or coffee. We are all afraid of just meeting each other without some activity to do, and food is the easiest, most universal thing to do together. Thinking about, planning, shopping for, preparing, eating and cleaning up food can take up a whole day. You can spend your whole life planning for that donut from the cafeteria each day, rewarding yourself with a snack once a task has been completed, hiding consumption so no one knows your addictive uses of food.

As in any addiction, only the addict can decide if indeed she is addicted. No one can make that decision for her. Many big women suffer from the judgment of others who think all heavy women are overweight' food addicts. This is not true. Ask yourself: do you use food to avoid feelings or situations? Do you use food secretly? Do you use food to comfort yourself? Do you find food interferes with your relationships with others? Is food your best friend? Do you find that you eat so much that you regularly become dulled or 'stoned'? Do you plan your diet far in advance (with no real health need to do so)? Do you fear you won't get enough food? Are you preoccupied with food? Do you wish that you weren't reading this?

In my opinion, food addiction is a disease. I use 'disease' in the Chinese sense: a lack of freedom. Like any other compulsive behavior, the ritual becomes a substitute for human interaction. It is a way to stop feeling scared, angry, sad and happy. The recovery chapter discusses some of the processes of undoing addictive behaviors.

During the two years that I worked in the psychiatric wards of a county hospital, I saw only one man described on his intake chart as 'obese.' He weighed 400 pounds. On those same wards, I would estimate that one out of ten women was described as 'obese.'

This culture harasses women about their size consistently, continuously, relentlessly. There are many women who respond to this pressure with eating disorders. These women are bulimarexic.

Bulimic women stuff themselves with food and then force themselves to vomit, sometimes as often as sixty times a day. A preoccupation for bulimarexics is body size. Life is centered around weight; body measurements; exercise; clothes sizes; and food deprivation, intake and elimination. The only outward sign of this obsession is body size.

Anorexic women refuse to eat, sometimes to the point of killing themselves. Anorexics stop eating, often for weeks or months. The body goes into shock, menses stop, thinking is slowed, organs work overtime to compensate for the lack of food. Intestines can disintegrate and stop absorption. Bulimics take in great quantities of food: whole bags of cookies, a gallon of ice cream, a whole cake. Then they purge the food before it becomes digested by inducing vomiting, using diuretics and laxatives—anything to get the food out.

The behavior becomes addictive and compulsive. All thought is centered around when and if to eat. All concern is for when the 'diet' will produce results. When will the magic weight be reached? When will her body begin to disappear?

Isn't it amazing that twenty percent of young women in the U.S. are currently either starving or binging on food? Some men also have these disorders, but 95 percent of those who suffer from these disorders are women. Any inquiry into why women have eating disorders, and how they can be dealt with, has to include the political and social context of the physical and emotional oppression of women.

Of course, other factors, such as family of origin; self-esteem, power, denial of feelings and addiction contribute to eating disorders. None of these should be discounted, but I believe the oppression of women and their bodies is the greatest factor—otherwise, why isn't there an equal number of men with these problems?

Lesbians are not supposed to have these behaviors. We're supposed to be unaffected by men's concepts of female beauty. But many, many lesbians struggle with eating disorders.

As with other addictions, there is a stoned, euphoric feeling that accompanies starving. Vomiting repeatedly also produces endorphins, a natural pain killer, inducing a pleasant high. The production of endorphins is actually the body's response to stress, but this stoned feeling can also increase the addiction to vomiting. This addiction is often accompanied by addictions to drugs, alcohol, sex and people.

Recovery from eating disorders is possible, though a full discussion is beyond the scope of this book. There are many books written on this topic. There are support groups in most large cities in the U.S.— the most readily available being Overeaters Anonymous. There are also hospitals that cater to women with these self-destructive behaviors.

Perhaps the best plan is to deal with the destructive behavior, then work with our self-hatred. We can learn to love that child, learn to love our hips, our breasts. We can allow someone else to love the fact that we exist, that we have volume, size. We can define for ourselves what size women can be, reaffirming our right to exist.

Self-mutilation is another self-destructive behavior that is related to hatred of our bodies. This activity includes many actions: women mutilate themselves by cutting, burning, tearing their flesh, gouging, breaking bones, tearing their hair out, throwing themselves against objects, breaking their teeth. Women put objects up their vaginas, anuses and mouths that cut and bruise them. The action is usually not fatal, but occasionally it is. And yes, lesbians do it too.

Interestingly, more men kill themselves, and more women mutilate themselves. We are taught to endure. After all, we are the great accommodators. We have children to raise. Slow torture allows us to serve our purpose and hurt at the same time.

This torturous activity of inflicting pain is usually done in private. It's commonly a response to frustration, anger, fear and unhappiness. Many women who are remembering incest and other sexual traumas hurt themselves as they try to cope with overwhelming memories. This is variously a response to shame, guilt and self-hatred. The action feels within one's own control, in response to a feeling, thought or memory that feels out of control.

Most women who self-mutilate report that there is a great relief after the act. Part of this is emotional. "I took some action." "See, this proves how awful I am." "I've been obsessed with doing this, and now I've done it." "I can prove how sick and in pain I am by these actions." "It controls my feelings, now I won't hurt someone else."

Part of the relief is physical. Once again, the body's natural response to pain is to put out endorphins to counteract the nerve damage. The feeling is one of being just a little stoned. Seeking this relief can become habitual and compulsive.

Most women who do this do not tell people. If someone notices the cut marks on wrists and arms, they are explained away through cats, rose bushes and wild weeds. On some level, those listening know they are not being told the truth, but do not want to push. Who wants to really notice this level of pain?

Women who hurt themselves are wearing their pain on the outside. Some of them say it's to get attention; others say it's to get relief. Some say it's to remind themselves how awful they feel; others say they do it to punish themselves.

The bottom line is that these women live in a world that condones woman-hatred, a world that derives sexual pleasure from women's pain; a world that allows an enormous number of its girl children to be sexually molested before they are eighteen.

Self-mutilation is not done by crazy women. Many of us hurt our own bodies on the inside, with hurtful foods, cigarettes, caffeine, drugs and alcohol. Self-mutilation is just another little-known form of self-abuse. This physical self-destruction is frightening to all of us, mirroring the destruction the culture has wreaked against the bodies of women.

It's possible to stop self-mutilation. Women have indeed ended this painful journey. There is currently at least one hospital, Hartgrove in Chicago, Illinois, offering inpatient treatment for this specific disorder. Many institutions with programs for sexual abuse survivors and people with eating disorders treat this disorder as well. Some women find Twelve Step programs helpful in dealing with the compulsion. Others use psychiatric medication (in low doses and with a good psychiatrist) to help control the impulse to hurt. Others work on the cultural and personal hatred through therapy with a professional.

Any change takes time. Have some mercy on yourself. Try admitting your behavior honestly to yourself and then tell someone else. Changing this syndrome takes the love of your friends and the help of a professional. Bring this torture out—you don't have to hide and try to heal alone.

Whether or not we have engaged in compulsive destructive behaviors, we have an opportunity to change our vision of ourselves and to accept the bodies we've been given. We can work to form support groups, to stop judging other women, and to encourage each other in loving ourselves back to health.

It's difficult to feel sexy, self-loving and uninhibited in these bodies the dominant culture has taught us are too big, or don't work right, or are the wrong color, or sag too much. It's difficult to live in bodies that all the commercials, movies and billboards tell us are not attractive. It's difficult to lie down next to another woman, which books, churches, and our laws tell us is disgusting, and then make love together.

In the beginning of a relationship, we're not embarrassed at all—we're so overcome with passion we'll have sex anywhere, any time. But after a while we start fearing she'll see our moles—or, worse, our cellulite. We turn off the lights or blow out the candles, sneak out of our clothes quickly and zip under the covers. Eventually we may become so afraid our lover will dislike our bodies as much as we do that we avoid sex altogether. Sexual inhibition due to poor body image is not unusual.

I recently saw a blue jean advertisement directed at teenagers that said, "Maybe it's not your body you need to change. Maybe it's your blue jeans." I thought, "Thank heaven!" Let's recognize that teenage girls are killing themselves in order to lose weight. Let's recognize that lesbian-feminist women are preoccupied with their weight. Let's recognize that lesbians are cutting off other women in the community because of their size, their color, their disabilities or their age.

The next time you want to say something derogatory about your body, stop yourself. Don't say, "I'm too fat." Try *not* saying, "I'm too fat" for a year. See what happens. What if every time you thought or said a negative statement about your body you replaced it with a positive one? What if all women stopped saying, "I'm too fat," "I'm too old," "I'm too" anything?

What if every time you had a negative thought about your body, you stopped yourself and said instead, "I love this body." No matter what you've been taught about your body. No matter what you feel about your body. Even if your body doesn't feel good physically, or doesn't work the way you'd like it to. Even if your body isn't the age you want it to be. Or you've been oppressed forever because of your race. Or your size. Every time you have a negative thought, try saying, "I love this body. I'm so grateful for this body." Find one place in your body that you really like, and start with that, saying to yourself, "I love my fill-in-the-blank." See what would happen if you practiced that daily.

Try not commenting on weight loss. Even if the thought comes to your head, don't tell another woman she looks 'better' when she is thinner. She may want this sort of opinion, but how will she then feel when she regains the weight? Do you then tell her she looks worse? If you know a compulsive eater who has lost weight due to her abstinence, offer her support for not eating compulsively, but don't tell her she's more attractive because she's thinner. The struggle against compulsivity of any kind is a struggle against self-hatred, not weight.

If you suspect a friend of yours might be hurting herself through starvation, binging, or self-mutilation, let her know you've noticed. Offer assistance and guide her toward counseling without criticizing her.

If you familiarize yourself with images of women's beauty from other eras and other cultures, you'll notice that the ideal size and shape changes frequently. Go to women's music festivals, where you can see thousands of women of all body types and colors. Hang pictures in your home of real women, not just women who conform to male standards. Don't make jokes about fat or disabled people—even in private.

When you find someone either attractive or unattractive, examine this feeling to see if it can be traced to the dominant culture's prejudice. See if you can be willing to find many different kinds of bodies attractive. Talk to disabled people about bodies and about sex. Ask how you might make their lives easier. Don't ignore them.

Look at your body naked, and write down all of the feelings you have, positive and negative. See if you are willing to throw away or burn the negative list. Read the positive list to a friend. Then read it to yourself every day. Add new positive feelings about your body to the list each week.

Imagine if we rejected the male ideal of female beauty. What if we created our own definitions? I'd like us to begin honoring the beauty in all women's bodies. Love those hips, love those breasts, love those legs that don't walk, love that little girl who thinks she is ugly.

Even if your body looks ugly to you, or doesn't function how you want it to, say to yourself each day, "I love this body, I'm grateful for this body." Thoughts are very powerful. See what happens.

Celibacy: Having a Love Affair With Yourself

If you want some-thing done right, do it yourself.

—UNKNOWN

Women have used celibacy for centuries, perhaps since time began, to keep themselves from men and to protect themselves from the violence that men have perpetrated. In the United States, where women were not allowed to vote until 1920 and not allowed to own property without the permission of their fathers or husbands until the late 1800s, being an 'old maid' has sometimes been a woman's only way to retain a sense of selfhood. No wonder celibate women have a bad reputation. They challenge a basic tenet of patriarchy: that women are obligated to have sex with men. They deny men access to their bodies, and thereby deny men the right to control them.

Celibate lesbians have different motivations. Sometimes we choose celibacy in order to give ourselves a reprieve from the difficulty of relationships; sometimes we feel forced into celibacy when a lover leaves; sometimes we become celibate in response to illness or disability.

But what is celibacy? Having debated for years the relative merits of such things as monogamy and nonmonogamy, makeup and no makeup, we lesbians could spend months trying to arrive at a collective decision on what celibacy is. Can it include masturbation? How long must one be celibate before she earns the label? Does two weeks count? Does celibacy include sexuality?

As is true with so much of our lives as lesbians, there are no rules to go by. No one taught us how and why celibacy might be valuable, or what exactly it entails. For the purposes of this discussion, let's define celibacy as an extended period of time in which a person is not sexually active with others.

Note that with this definition, one can be celibate and still feel sexual. People often think celibacy implies a total lack of sexual feeling as well as expression. But even though we may not be having sex with other people, we're still sexual beings. It is possible—and indeed likely—that when we're celibate, we also feel sexual.

Before exploring what celibacy is and can be, let's think about sex. How is it that we identify ourselves as sexual beings? What is our sexual energy? We have been taught by our society and families that women are only supposed to be sexual with men. As lesbians and as feminists, we have turned that around and said, "Women can be sexual with other women." We also have claimed the right to masturbate. But I think we have to stretch more and acknowledge that we can be sexual even if we're not having genital contact with ourselves or another being.

By 'sexual,' I mean our unique physical feelings: the special warmth, the genital throbbing, the 'butterflies' in the stomach. The sensations and responses vary from person to person and time to time. We may crave masturbation or partner sex, hugging or orgasms. We may just enjoy the sexual feelings and feel no need to act on them.

The Chinese say sexual energy is our 'life force' which is energized by our kidneys and adrenal glands. I'd add that the brain is also instrumental in the creation of sexual energy. All of these organs are inside us—we don't need other people around in order to feel sexual. And our sexual energy doesn't necessarily involve orgasms or even genitals. Even nuns are sexual.

When *Lesbian Nuns: Breaking Silence* (Curb, Rosemary, ed. Tallahassee: Naiad Press, 1985) was published, everyone flipped out over the fact that nuns actually see themselves as sexual beings. Not only are they sexual, some of them even have a sexual orientation, and a taboo one at that. As I was reading the book, I was thinking, "Well, of course, nuns have sex with each other in the convent. They are human beings—sex together makes perfect sense." Then I got to the chapter by a nun who has been with another nun for twenty years. They've lived together, they've never had genital contact with one another, they've never masturbated, yet they identify as lesbian and see themselves as sexual.

I said to myself, "Wait a minute! Best buddies are one thing, but lovers are a whole other category." It was interesting to watch myself come up against my prejudice about what exactly is sexual.

Women have come to my workshops and lectures and said, "I've been celibate for ten years." Or, "I've been celibate for most of my adult life." Or, "I've never been sexual with another woman." Yet they still identify as sexual beings, and as lesbians.

The reality is that we're sexual from the time we're born until the time we die. Even children have sexual feelings, just as they have emotional feelings. It's part of who they are, whether or not they're given words for those feelings. It's part of who all of us are.

Lesbians are often surprised to learn that celibacy is common. We've been defined by our sexuality, and some of us have come to think of ourselves as very sexual people, but in fact most of us go through celibate periods in our lives. In my survey, 79 percent of the women had been celibate for some period of their lives. Thirty-five percent were celibate for one to five years; another eight percent were celibate for six or more years. What is actually surprising is that twenty percent of lesbians have never been celibate at all.

How does one become celibate? Sometimes it's not by choice. Seventeen percent of the women in my survey said they were celibate against their will, either because a lover had died, or left them, or for other reasons. Disabled women are from time to time forced to be celibate because of physical problems or chronic pain. Post-operative women, women who have environmental and food allergies, or women going through the process of gradually becoming disabled may find themselves being celibate while they adjust to physical circumstances that change their sexual needs or abilities.

Then there are the women who choose celibacy. In my survey, 35 percent of the women who had been celibate said that celibacy had been a choice, and 49 percent said it had "sort of" been a choice. You may know this feeling: "I have had my last insane relationship. No joke. Really. I've had every kind of insane relationship there is to have, and now, before I get together with a mass murderer or something, I think I will try being celibate for a while and see how it goes. Who knows? It could be wonderful." Often it does turn into something wonderful. Relationships can be very time-consuming and very other-oriented. Celibacy is a good way to get back in touch with one's self.

Incest survivors often go through a period of being celibate, particularly when they are first having memories of the incest, or are beginning to look carefully at its effects on their lives.

Women who embark on spiritual paths often spend time being celibate to keep the distraction of sex away. When you sit in meditation, it's difficult enough not to be concerned about your checkbook, much less the lust you feel for that woman you met a couple of weeks ago. Not that celibacy makes the lust go away, but it may help you focus on yourself and your own spiritual process.

Sexual addicts also often choose a period of celibacy. These are people who tried to get their self-worth from sex. To choose not to have sex, and to search for other sources of self-esteem, can be very empowering. It is also usually very scary, just as it is when giving up drugs, food, or other addictions.

Some women are celibate when they are teenagers or young adults because they have difficulty finding lesbian partners. Other young lesbian women are out there, but they are hard to locate. In addition, some young women choose celibacy because they are afraid of sex or really don't want to engage in it just yet.

Some people choose celibacy because they simply prefer to be alone. I have a great-aunt who is 86. She still walks five or six miles a day and has an amazing memory. It occurred to me recently that she is probably an "old maid" because she enjoys her own company.

In *Journal of a Solitude* (New York: W. W. Norton and Co., 1977), May Sarton describes the life of a celibate woman. Of course, Sarton was in her sixties when she wrote that book. Old people are expected not to be sexual. Isn't that strange? We each seem to have in our minds an imaginary cut-off age after which people stop being sexual. Often the ages are different for women and men. Why do we think that when a person crosses some magic birthday, all of a sudden her sexual needs disappear? Throughout our lives we experience changes in our sexual needs, most of which have little to do with age.

In my survey, lesbians over 60 masturbated two to five times a month, in greater numbers than any other age group. More lesbians over 60 also have partner sex two to five times a month (the average frequency for all lesbians) than lesbians in any other age group. Women over 60 also made up the largest group that hadn't had partner sex in a typical month. What all this makes clear is that none of the common generalizations about age and sex or celibacy are very accurate.

I once chose celibacy for two years. I had decided that I needed time alone to think about who I was and what I wanted in relationships. My parents had not done a very good job of teaching me how to love myself or how to choose sexual partners who would be good for me. I was also planning a pregnancy during this time. They were two different processes, but they served each other well.

During the pregnancy and the first few months afterward, I was able to focus my attention on my own body and my growing baby without having to concern myself with a relationship. It was a very special time for me and my son.

In the early part of those two years, my friends kept trying to fix me up, even though I told them I wasn't interested. Then I discovered that once you become obviously pregnant, people don't try to fix you up anymore. They stop thinking of you—and sometimes you stop thinking of yourself—as someone who's sexual. Or maybe they assume that no one would want to start a relationship with a pregnant woman. It was interesting to spend that time being deliberately single, not talking about dating and relationships. I learned so much about myself: what I was willing to do by myself, what kind of protection I had relied on from a partner, how my free time after work and on weekends was almost frightening. I learned a great deal about how hard it was to structure my time without someone by my side recommending activities. I also found out how hard it was to go to parties, restaurants, movies and clothing stores alone. I learned to rely on myself and my instincts. I began to learn what my own tastes were. I had no one else to worry about, so I ate at odd hours, stayed up late or got up early depending on my mood. It was frightening and empowering at the same time. I recommend it, with or without pregnancy.

I also recommend acting as if you've chosen celibacy even if you're in fact celibate against your will. If your lover leaves you, or you're post-partum, or you become sick or disabled in such a way that you're not able to be sexual, it's a good idea to approach celibacy from a place of strength rather than of victimization. Try looking at it as a wonderful opportunity instead of saying, "Ain't it awful?" You might discover that it's actually not such a bad choice.

Women who choose celibacy, who really come from a place of wanting to explore it, often have a kind of extra lift behind them. The act of choosing feels powerful and becomes a very positive thing, a gift to the self.

This is a time you can have a love affair with yourself. You like to do the same things as yourself. You like the way you make love to yourself. You enjoy the same movies, friends, food and vacations. So how about taking yourself as your lover? This could include sex if you like. However, you may not want to have sex in this relationship. Whatever you want, there will be no complaints.

You may want to actually take yourself out on dates. Give yourself a bubble bath by candlelight. Treat yourself to a lobster dinner. Read whatever trash you want to—you have the freedom to please yourself.

Write letters to yourself about what you would like to do. Write love letters to yourself. Rhapsodize about how wonderful you are. Imagine writing down all the things your parents told you never to say about yourself, all those things we were taught were vain. Now you can write them down and not show anyone but your lover—the woman inside you. See what it is like to read them to yourself in a mirror. Send yourself flowers with a love poem written on the card.

If you do want to be sexual with yourself, light the candles, take out the sex toys, turn on your favorite music, get out your massage oil. Read literature that turns you on, watch a video that makes you excited. Tell yourself what a wonderful lover you are. Take a long time to make love to the body that you are most familiar with, your own. There are many things to do that will allow you to carry on a mad, passionate affair with yourself.

Often, a woman who has been celibate is actually much better equipped to be fully present, to be loving, warm and caring about others, because she has already tapped into a source of self-love. I've met many women who have been celibate for years and years, and their centeredness is often uncanny. They have gone through all kinds of things by themselves, and they have redefined their sexuality. They have amazing things to share with those of us who are so addicted to other people's energy that we can't imagine spending that much intimate time with ourselves.

However, celibacy presents difficulties. When you're sexually active with a partner, at least you're complying with the cultural mandate that in order to be worthwhile, you have to have sex. You may be having sex with the 'wrong' gender, but at least you're having sex.

Sex is supposed to be where it's at. But a celibate woman rejects that notion—or at least seems to. Celibate women are called old maids, dried up, cold, frigid, uptight; they're presumed undesirable. Imagine how undesirable the celibate lesbian appears—even lesbians don't want her!

Especially for women, there is strong pressure to be coupled. Capitalism is fueled by selling two of everything. Women aren't supposed to be alone—we're told it's not safe. Women are supposed to offer their love and nurturance to another person, not to themselves.

Celibate lesbians may find themselves questioning their lesbianism. "If I'm not eating pussy and rubbing clitorises, if I don't have somebody sitting on my face, does that mean that I'm not a lesbian?"

If your partner dies, the thought of being sexual with another may feel like betrayal. The grieving process can take a long time and being sexual with another may be the farthest thing from your mind. If you are in this position, you may eventually ask yourself, would you want her to stop being sexual if you had been the one who died? That's a hard question, but one that often needs to be asked. Don't forget that she loved you and supported your happiness.

When a woman in an ongoing relationship decides not to have sex with her partner, it often creates great distress in the relationship. This celibacy usually appears gradually with little acknowledgement between the two women. There is often, in fact, a tacit agreement that if nothing is said, the problem may go away. Perhaps the person who wants to stop sex will change her mind and everything will return to normal.

Often the woman who does not want to be sexual with her partner keeps this decision at a subconscious level. When asked, she may not even feel she has entered a celibate stage, but merely that she is not having sexual desire. Her partner may feel very insecure and not want to mention the subject. What if she asks her partner what is going on and finds out she is no longer loved? Maybe, she'll tell herself, if we just ignore the fact that we aren't having sex, it won't matter. Who needs sex anyway?

The couple may stay closely bonded through other interests. However, if nothing is said, an opportunity is being missed. The two women will learn a great deal about each other if they each are willing to share their feelings. It may be surprising for the partner to find that indeed she is loved, just not sexually desired at this time. She may be relieved to learn that the celibate period has little or nothing to do with her. The woman who is not wanting to be sexual may find that the word 'celibate' validates her feelings. "Oh yes!" she may say to herself. "I'm not an awful person, I'm just being celibate. This is a time of introversion, or healing, or re-evaluation. I am a whole person, I just don't want to have sex with anyone else right now."

The difficulty with taking that kind of stance within a partnership is that women often feel terrible about withdrawing from a relationship in any conscious way. We were taught that would be selfish. We are supposed to be available. We often believe sexual intimacy is supposed to be consistent throughout a relationship. In fact, in my survey, four percent of the women who were celibate were currently in a relationship—this does not include the women who were in relationships and did not have partner sex, but who did not identify as celibate.

I don't believe celibacy within a relationship is particularly unusual. What is unusual is talking about what we are doing and why we are doing it. What is unusual is taking care of ourselves even if the person we love the most is threatened. We are more accustomed to slipping unconsciously into behavior that feels safe.

Friends often react to our celibacy by trying to change it. This is particularly true if we are single. People put so much emphasis on relationships that if we say, "I don't need a relationship in order to be happy," it can threaten people. They may start to question their own sexual choices, which can be scary. So despite what we may say about choosing to be alone, friends may keep trying to 'fix us up.' As if we need fixing.

Though we don't need fixing, we may be lonely. When the day is over, and we've talked with our friends on the phone all evening, there we are, stuck with ourselves. We eat with ourselves, watch television with ourselves, and go to bed with ourselves. No one is arguing about what to do, but also there is no one with whom to share the tearjerking movie on television. No one to tell about what happened at school or work. No one to ask in the middle of the night if they heard that noise. No one to help with the kids. The hardest part is listening to the chattering of our own brains. Often we start another relationship as soon as possible so we don't have to face this aloneness, and the loneliness that can accompany it. Part of why celibacy has such a bad rep is because it's so frightening to just be with ourselves.

Contrary to the popular assumption that celibacy is a dormant phase or a waiting phase, celibacy can in fact be a time of tremendous change and growth. As with all aspects of sexuality, there is a great deal of variation among women. For some, sexual drive decreases. This can come as a welcome reprieve if sexual feelings have led to obsessive or addictive behaviors. For others, sexual energy increases or stays constant. During the periods of my life in which I have not been sexual with another person and have not masturbated, I've had even more sexual feelings.

There's a certain freedom in not being sexual with other people, because you can go around feeling sexual all the time. It's not being saved for any particular outlet or place or time of day. You can just be sexual.

When you're single and celibate, you don't have to perform. No one is expecting you to be a good lover, or a consistent lover, or any kind of lover at all. Your sexual feelings become a private matter; no one will argue or be offended or demand anything of you. You don't have to worry that your lover will freak out because you're masturbating. You can be sexual exactly when and how you want.

How do you like to have your clitoris stimulated? Celibacy is a good time to find out—not so you can show your future lover, just for your own enjoyment. Often we use masturbation in a goal-oriented way: hurry up and have an orgasm so we can release tension, or relax, or take the edge off a sexual urge. We act as if it's something we have to get over with quickly. Try doing it slowly, luxuriously, throughout an evening, or with the tenderness and passion you usually reserve for lovemaking with another.

Another wonderful thing about celibacy is fantasy. You can, through fantasy, have perfect sex. Ask yourself: exactly how would you like to express your sexuality and with whom and when? Then imagine doing it. Make your real or fantasy lover perfect.

Instead of finding somebody to fall in love with so that they will love you, try using celibacy as a path toward self-love. Then, once you love yourself, you'll be much less vulnerable to the vicissitudes of relationships. The love will already be there, inside you. What could be more worthwhile than embarking on a journey in which you are doing nothing but loving yourself?

I'd like celibate women to start talking about their sexuality. We have a difficult time talking about sexual feelings no matter what they are. The closest we come is, "She's hot. We're hot. The sex is very hot." But we don't talk about sex. Imagine what it would be like if you, as a single celibate woman, started talking to your friends about your sexual energy.

"I didn't know you were dating anybody!" your friend says.

"I'm not dating anybody. I'm just feeling really sexual," you say.

"Well, let me fix you up with somebody."

"No, I don't want to be fixed up with anybody, I'm just feeling really sexual."

"What do you mean? Are you celibate or are you sexual or what?"

This could be an interesting conversation: the celibate woman turns her friends on to her own sexuality, educates them in a new way of defining sex, sexual energy and the expression of that energy.

You could add more detail: "I was just sitting there, reading *Golden Apples*, and I got turned on."

"What did you do?"

"I put the book down, put one hand on my nipple and the other on my clitoris, my body had this very tingly feeling for a few minutes, then I picked up the book, and started reading again."

"You what?!?!?!"

I'd also like to see more women celebrating celibacy as a way to love themselves. Imagine what it would be like to assume that you're sexual, assume that you're a lesbian, and assume that you have sexual energy inside you that can make you feel good, without having to have someone on your arm or between your legs.

Imagine spending each day knowing that you're not going home to snuggle up next to somebody. Imagine how it might feel to sleep alone night after night. There are advantages: you wouldn't have to give up the friends you have. You wouldn't have to argue over what program to watch on television. You wouldn't have to be home at any particular time. You could spend your time with yourself, uninterrupted. You could have quiet in your home when you want it. Some of us know that experience well. It doesn't have to be a bleak, terrible time. In fact, it can be a healing, loving time. You can get to know yourself intimately and learn to take care of your own needs.

When you're newly celibate, and you feel like you have been forced to be celibate, it's hard to imagine a love affair with yourself—especially when you're feeling homicidal, still wanting to murder your ex-lover. But that passes. Eventually a love affair with yourself may come to sound appealing. It can be very empowering.

Nobody laughs at you when you say you want to have a relationship and you'd like it to last longer than six months, but how many times have you a heard a single celibate woman say she wants to have a long-term relationship with herself? It is possible. It might even be easier or more rewarding than coupling. When you begin a loving, sexual relationship with yourself, you can choose to make it lifelong. The decision is entirely yours—no one can break up with you. That loving relationship is with you for the rest of your life, in every part of your life.

Can you imagine what would happen if we learned how to love ourselves? We might find a powerful centeredness. Having gone through both difficult and joyous times alone, we could become stronger and more compassionate. What if we started thinking we were absolutely perfect without being sexual with anybody? What if we were not only independent of men, but independent of women too? Celibacy is about learning to love ourselves. I can't think of a better way.

Passionate Friendships

Women are women's best friends, women are men's best friends; if it weren't for women, there would be no friends.

—UNKNOWN

My friends are the people I always talk to when I have a fight with a lover. They are the people I call when I meet someone new who's attractive. They're the ones I ask for advice and whose remarks I treasure. I want to be with them whenever I want; I resent their lovers sometimes, as they resent mine. When I'm single, I make sure my friends and their lovers will take me in when there are things I don't want to do alone or when I don't have a date. I've adopted the parents of my two dearest friends as my surrogate parents. I have friends who connect on all different levels with me. I have friends who enjoy different kinds of activities, so I always know exactly who to call when I want to go out. I show my friends my deepest love, and I know they show me theirs.

Our lesbian friendships are so integral to our lives; we believe in each other, we trust each other, and often our connections change our lives. For years, my best friend has been my former sister-in-law. We were once married to brothers. When I started graduate school, I began taking courses in sexuality, one of which explored all aspects of a person's sexual orientation. One night the class was taught by a lesbian, and I flipped out. I said to myself, "This is it, I only wish someone had told me something about this earlier." I went right home and called my best friend.

"Judy?"

"Yeah?"

"This is JoAnn."

"I know who this is. What's up?"

"I know what's wrong."

"What?"

"We're lesbians."

(Very long pause.)

"Really?"

"Yeah."

This began my coming-out process, and hers too. I jumped in with both feet, which is my nature. She began a slow, measured investigation, which is her nature. She eventually left her husband, moving out on April Fool's Day two years later. We're still best friends, family and more—sisters in more ways than ever.

Probably the most intense passion in the lesbian community is between friends. Lovers, jobs and roommates come and go, but friends can last a lifetime. Our friends often become our chosen families—the people we trust and cherish above everyone else. Friendships are sometimes the most important part of our lives.

When our friends are lesbians, we often feel additionally bound to them out of a sense of being 'other.' We each know what it is like being lesbian in a hostile culture. We shelter each other from the storms created by families of origin, and we nurture each other through bouts of external and internal homophobia. We are mother, daughter, crone, healer, mentor, enemy and angel for each other. We go through breakups, illness, childbirth, death and political upheaval together. Often we are bound by a pact, silent or spoken, to stay together through everything. Our friendships are similar to what we expected from our families of origin but usually did not receive.

This passion for friendships seems universal for lesbians. I have met lesbians from all over the country, and friends always play a central role in our lives. Of course, heterosexuals also form serious, abiding and important friendships, but lesbian friendships have a different quality. Lesbian oppression looms large; when we find friends we can trust, they become not only playmates but deeply trusted confidantes. Even though families and straight friends may be supportive, they don't know what it's like not to have any validation for our relationships. They don't know what it's like to have the Supreme Court decide what we can and cannot do in our bedrooms. Lesbian friends play the ancient role that clans once provided. They provide safety, understanding and preservation of 'the lesbian community.' Though the members of our 'clans' may change, the role friends play in our lives remains the same.

Though friendships and romantic relationships often overlap, friends are very different from lovers. With a friend, we feel committed through thick and thin. We stay connected with friends for long periods of time, and even across long distances. We aren't as ego-invested as we are with lovers. Our friends can wear what they want, eat what they want, hold the political or spiritual beliefs they want; if our friends disagree, we do not feel threatened or try to change them. Since our friends' behavior does not directly reflect on us, as our lovers' behavior seems to, we allow our friends room to be themselves in a way that few lovers do.

Friendships seem freer than lover relationships because in this culture friendships between women are acceptable. We can be openly friends without announcing our lesbianism. Friendship is indeed a lesbian act—since it is an act of loving between women--but since women friends are not discriminated against as such, they can more openly express their love. I've even caught myself walking down the street arm-in-arm with a dear friend, sure that it was safe because everyone would know we were 'just friends.' For some women, friendships are the only way they express their lesbian feelings and let their love for women shine through.

Our friendships tend to last longer and be more stable than lover relationships for similar reasons. Lesbian partnerships are at least as fragile as heterosexual marriages, and have the added pressures of not having medical or job benefits for our lovers, not having our lovers regarded as true parents to our children, and not receiving approval from our families. By contrast, lesbian friendships suffer from none of these pressures, though the individuals themselves do.

Perhaps the greatest difference between our lover and friend connections is the kind of passion that imbues the relationships. With lovers, the major reason we pair is sexual passion. We find the other person irresistible, then create ways to form a union. We give up old lovers, change the way we dress, move to new cities, and take on projects we never thought we would—all to satisfy sexual passion and to receive from our lover a healing of our emotional pain. Yet our lover never does that fully, and we once again depend on our friends.

Our passion for friends is different. We bond primarily because we enjoy each other's company. Even if our friends were once our lovers, their roles have now changed. We give them room to express their individuality, without seeing them as reflections of ourselves. We do not expect our friends to make us Number One. We may be hurt when they don't, but we don't insist that they do. Our passion for friends is more elastic, less rigid. In friendship, we share hope, love, anger, grief, joy and other emotions, but we do not see our friends as the cause of these emotions, as we often do with lovers. With a friend we are not trying to merge, but to support and appreciate each other. There's more room to allow each other just to be, rather than to be something in particular. This makes the relationship more dependable and less primal.

Wonderful though they are, lesbian friendships also have their problems. My straight cousin Sandie once said to me, "My lovers are men and my friends are women. Out of all those women, how do you choose who will be your lover and who your friend?"

It certainly can be confusing. Friends become lovers; former lovers become friends; friends become lovers with our lovers; our lovers become lovers with our friends' lovers, and on it goes. The boundaries can become very fuzzy. These fuzzy boundaries are the source of some of the most painful problems lesbians face.

When two lesbians are very fond of each other, especially if they are both single, the question of whether or not to become lovers inevitably arises. Sometimes friends make the best lovers. With them, we have developed trust and mutual respect that goes beyond sexual passion. But we must ask ourselves how becoming lovers will change the relationship. "If we become lovers and then break up, can we retain the friendship without being bitter? Will my friend want to be more involved than I do? If I hurt her feelings, will friends of hers be angry with me?" Many friendships have been destroyed and entire friendship networks have been lost when two friends became lovers. Because friendship is so paramount to lesbians, we try very hard to stay friends no matter what, but it is not easy.

That sexual passion gives friendship a special energy for a while. If it dissipates, the friendship can either disappear or become stronger. If it lingers, the energy is very confusing.

Another complication occurs when a woman who is committed to a monogamous partnership meets someone she is very attracted to. The debate starts. "Is it worth it jeopardizing what I have with my current lover to be sexual with this woman? Do I want to violate my principles by flirting with this woman and perhaps forcing a break with her lover? Can I be satisfied being friends with her, or will I always want to have sex with her?" It's easy to fantasize that she may be a life mate; she might be the greatest lover ever or more willing to be intimate.

For a compulsive thinker, this liaison is great material. One can obsess about it for years. Sometimes the only cure is abstinence; not seeing the woman, talking to her, or manipulating to run into her at parties helps cure these obsessive thoughts. We usually have to just choose not to do anything about being lovers, so we can let the friendship grow. Sometimes just setting rules takes the pressure off.

Making friends a priority while being in a lover relationship is also difficult. We have few role models. We have been raised in a culture that says our family of origin is *it*, and there should never be any interference with that union.

When we take a lover, she becomes our significant other. This woman becomes our mate, and most of the rules our family applied to 'mate' get translated to this relationship. We may try to change some aspects of how we relate, but way down deep, we abide by the rules our parents used.

The strain between family and friends becomes intensified for lesbians, because our friends are so integral to our emotional survival. Prioritizing friends often becomes a major issue between lovers. Since many of our friends include ex-lovers, the issues become even more loaded.

Many lesbians (like most humans) take their friends somewhat for granted. We like to assume that our friends will always be there for us. We like to believe that they will be present even if we have abandoned them for a lover relationship. But many friendships will disappear if they are not nurtured. Many of us have received (or made) calls like this one:

"Hello, Edna?"

"Well, haven't heard from you in a while."

"Yeah, blast from the past."

"My feelings have been really hurt. You were supposed to call me right after you got back from your trip."

"I know, but you know how things go."

"I know how new affairs go. That's what I know. We've been through this before, Patty. You never change. Do you think I'm always going to be willing to go through this with you?"

"Well, to be truthful, I guess I think you'll always be there. You know."

"I don't know, not really. I mean, what do you think, I'll just drop everything and be friends again? What do you think I've been doing for support all this time?"

"The phone works both ways."

"It's always me calling you."

"So? I love to talk to you. Can I come over?"

To nurture friendships, we need to make our friendships important in our daily lives, and to let our friends know what we need from them. We must remember that our families were never all we needed. Too often, when we take a lover, we make her our best friend. We make her our reason for being happy. We make her the only one we can go anywhere with. Friends often are pushed aside. We expect lovers to fill us up in a way friends cannot. The odd part is that no one can fill up that empty space inside of all of us except ourselves.

This intense expectation of a lover usually creates a situation in which the lover is eventually sucked dry. The relationship has no vitality because we stop bringing in fresh input from friends and activities outside our lover relationship.

This is when we turn back to our friends, whom we expect to be waiting patiently in the wings. And usually they are, because we are just as important to their well-being as they are to ours. The problem is that these absences often create little chinks in the foundation of the friendship; if too many occur, the friendship cannot survive.

I believe that even if our lovers don't like our friends, we need to keep them actively in our lives. Our friends represent a certain part of us that is important. They may be part of our history; they may be supportive of an aspect of us that our lovers cannot stand. We must make sure we don't lose touch; friends are truly part of our foundation.

Lesbian friendships are so deep and so complex that we also have the power to hurt each other deeply. We deal with these pains in ways similar to what heterosexuals do with their mates. Our friendships are so intimate that they cross over an invisible boundary that mainstream culture uses to separate friends from mates and family. Our friends actually become our family. At times, this level of intimacy may feel overwhelming and we may react with anger, fear and sadness, feelings that sometimes have to be worked out in therapy, meditation, or informal community healing.

The events in my own life surrounding my pregnancy, giving birth and the months that followed formed profound bonds with four of my friends, and allowed some of those deep conflicts to surface.

When I was inseminating, I was single. The women who were around me at that time were close friends and have remained close. They gave me all the encouragement that I could need. They were excited when I got pregnant; they celebrated with me when I could feel the baby move.

The baby was born two weeks late, on my ex-lover/friend's birthday, no less. They all came to the hospital with me and stayed throughout the birth. One friend stayed at my home a few more days and my sister/friend came to visit every day. My ex-lover/friend stayed the whole next week. My surrogate mother (my sister/friend's mother) took care of me and the baby for another week.

We were all excited, exhausted and thoroughly entwined in each other's lives. Then something began to break down. We all have different versions of it, but probably the intensity of the situation became a little too much. We really got on each other's nerves. We started arguing, being angry and having unreal expectations of each other.

The question was, would we continue snapping at each other, blaming each other, talking behind each other's backs, or would we do something about it? Being therapy junkies, we decided to do something about it. We found a perfect facilitator. The session was painful, and no one enjoyed herself, but I feel it transformed the fear which had brought us to the office in the first place.

We all worked very hard at maintaining our relationships. We spent time away from each other, receiving nourishment elsewhere. All five of the main characters took new lovers within a five-month period after the birth. (Two of the main players became lovers with each other.) We needed so much from other sources—our system had become depleted.

We may each never be fully forgiven by the others, or be able to fully forgive. Sometimes intimacy causes permanent tiny sorrows. The friendships that survived, however, are strengthened by the intensity of the connection we all had during such a miraculous time.

This is one illustration of how friendships become intensely integrated into lesbian lives. Each woman reading this has a story of her own that is equally powerful and profound. Friendships are the safety net we all need to survive in this homophobic world. Our attachments to our friends must be honored and encouraged even, and especially, through the difficult times.

Deciding who to become friends with and how to maintain friendships can be problematic for many of us. Your current friends become critical parts of those decisions. Can you befriend a friend's ex-lover if the friend is still in pain about the breakup? Can you befriend someone who has very different values or life experiences? Can you be friends with people of different ages or class or race backgrounds? Can you be friends with someone your lesbian community may deem politically incorrect? Such pressures from the lesbian community influence us to form and break apart friendships.

There is a phenomenon in lesbian culture that has profound influence on lesbian friendships. We 'vote' on the correct positions to take on all sorts of issues. We all know there's a correct position on skirts, Republicanism, men, money, S/M, children, bisexuality, AIDS testing, monogamy, lipstick, rock music, therapy, pornography, whether our favorite lesbian musician can use men in her band and so on. From the crushing issues of our time, like racism, classism and apartheid, to the issues that are really none of our business, lesbians are supposed to vote.

If we don't pass our friends' 'Lesbians For Correct (never Right) Voting' vote, we remain in limbo, like Catholic babies used to if they died before they were baptized. The Catholic Church has done away with limbo (I always wonder what happened to those babies I personally prayed for), but lesbians still cling to the idea that someone has to have pledged her allegiance to particular things or she isn't in the Club. Lest my vote be misconstrued, please do not assume that I consider the Catholic Church more evolved than the lesbian community. I know the right (I mean correct) vote when I see it.

Anyway, this politically correct stamp of approval has an enormous effect on us as lesbians. Friendship networks form and break apart over current issues; we each have given up parts of our belief systems to fit into the latest politically-correct stance.

The history of being 'politically correct' is based on the Marxist philosophy of dialectical materialism, which asserts that all materialistic concerns (from where you buy something to your position on class analysis) affect how the world runs and the conditions of those living in it. This is easy to understand.

The process breaks down when we deal with those who have a view that differs from our own. Among lesbians, as in other oppressed communities, we tend to have a difficult time tolerating difference. Any one faction of the community has stringent rules, and judges those who do not agree with them. Because we are so dependent on one another for solace and safety, that emotional acceptance is often essential. Being politically correct becomes not just a method of perceiving the world, but a way of judging your own—or someone else's—self-worth.

When we judge and condemn each other, we do the work of the forces trying their best to divide us. We keep our energy tied up. We stop creativity and drive each other into inactivity. Of course, we need to keep challenging, questioning and educating ourselves—and each other—but not at the expense of each woman's heart and true nature.

Another way that lesbian friendships function like families is that we apparently are much more likely to stay friends with former lovers than are straight people. The inclusion of ex-lovers in tightly-knit friendship circles cements the connections even further.

In her forthcoming book, *Unbroken Ties: Lesbian Ex-Lovers* (Boston: Alyson Publications, 1988), Carol Becker writes about the effects of including ex-lovers in lesbian friendship circles. The women she interviewed discussed both negative and positive experiences in having ex-lovers as close friends. One common problem they cited was triangulation between a woman, her lover and her ex-lover. Sometimes not only one but both women in the current partnership remain emotionally involved with ex-lovers. There can be three, four, or even more significant players in a relationship that appears to be between two women.

This triangulation is often comforting. The woman who remains friends with a former lover can keep the positive parts of a former relationship. It is also comforting to know that even if relationships don't remain sexual, those women aren't lost to us forever. A former lover can be a source of great solace. She knows all our secrets and still loves us. Different from a friend, she has gone to that deep sexual place with us and is still willing to give us great abiding love. She may be the one we turn to in some of our deepest struggles.

This inclusion of former and present lovers in our family structure can create jealousy and hurt feelings all around. The current lover may feel like the newest kid at school, who is left out of the game. The old lover may feel like she has to take a back seat to an interloper who has just moved to town and taken the starring role in the play. "After all I've been to her, along comes someone who sweet-talks her hormones and it's curtains for me!"

Conversely, this phenomenon can also help to create security in the relationship. The two women currently relating as lovers do not have to be everything for each other. Their former lovers may provide love, continuity, support for children, or a family atmosphere that enhances the primary sexual relationship, much as extended families can for a heterosexual union. Everyone can gain from the overlapping unions. As the button says, "An army of ex-lovers cannot fail."

Many women entering a relationship are quite threatened by their partner's former lover. The pet names, code words and in-jokes can create distance between partners when the ex-lover is present. The ex-lover may actively maintain such intimacies since they establish her place firmly in the old lover's life. As the 'ex,' she has great power. The new lover hasn't been through numerous ups and downs, family rejections, job changes, years of a child's upbringing.

The new lover, on the other hand, has other ways in. After all, her power rests in her position between the legs of her lover. Of course, we are all very polite and would never talk about it in this way. Her fear is that she will lose that sexual position or may even end up sharing it with the 'all-finished-honest-really-I'm-not-kidding-this-time' ex-lover.

Her fear is not unfounded. Many women find, when they become involved with someone new, that indeed they are not emotionally or sexually finished with a former lover. Frequently when a woman renews a bond with her old partner, they also begin having sex again. Sometimes all three women have sex. Lesbians are endlessly creative, and the foggy boundaries between friends and lovers lead to all sorts of experiments (and disasters). Almost all of us have at one time or another blurred the boundaries between friends and lovers.

What is particularly devastating about instability in friendships is that our self-esteem is often closely tied to the group, clan, or community with which we identify. When friends withdraw, when a lover alienates our friends, or when our lover does not fit with our clan, it can be devastating. We may incessantly try to change the situation, explaining to our friends how nice our lover is, or pleading with our lover, "Oh come on, honey. Come out with us just one more time. I know you'll like my friends."

Often, both sides merely tolerate each other. We may find ourselves trying to explain a friend or lover to the other, trying desperately to get them to accept each other. We sometimes have to listen to our lovers complain about our friends when they aren't around; friends may do the same thing when our lovers aren't there. When a breakup occurs, our friends often tell us all the things they didn't like about our lovers. This only serves to make our self-love take a nosedive.

In our need to be close to a new lover, we often ignore our friends. It's as if we believe friendship can take that kind of separation, while lovers cannot. Many women isolate themselves from their friends for the duration of a relationship; when it is over, they go back to their friends and are often accepted into the group as if all that time had not elapsed. Even during this period of separation, the idea of a clan or friendship tribe remains important, but drops into the background.

How can we make time for friends while we are in a lover relationship? How can we stay friends with former lovers after the intense disappointment of separation? How can we keep from choosing sides when two friends break up with each other? All of these questions are vigorously and constantly discussed in lesbian circles. There are no easy answers; we need to proceed with all the sensitivity, honesty and courage we can muster.

We often explain to others that we are 'just friends,' which is probably meant to clarify who our lovers are. A lesbian friend, however, is hardly ever *just* a friend. Our friendships may be the strongest and most enduring bonds in our lives. In the mainstream culture, such bonding is reserved for families, and friends are relegated to 'just friends.' Perhaps lesbians can invent new phrases—the way Eskimos have hundreds of words for snow—for the myriad bonds of friendship we know.

The best advice I have for keeping friends is to love them, as unconditionally as possible. That is what you are asking of them. We all want that, and friends often give that kind of love to one another with greater ease than do lovers.

Despite the problems that arise, we love our friends passionately, sometimes more than we love anyone else. Friends sustain us through the troubled waters of partnerships, and become family, mirror, sounding board, stamp of approval, shelter, and an endless source of love and support. We accept and tolerate more from friends than from almost anybody in our immediate circle. Our friends are our life source. We see reflected in our friends parts of ourselves that we find valuable. Our friends make us feel good about who we are as individuals, as women, and as lesbians. The passion we have for our friends is compelling and powerful. They deserve our best efforts, our most rigorous honesty, our relentless loyalty. The rewards of friendship are great. Let's continue honoring our friends as much as we do our lovers.

The Lesbian Date

*All I love
is always being born
what I love is
beginning.*

—OLGA BROUMAS

*T*here are two possible outcomes of a lesbian date: either the two women never date again, or they get married. At least, that's how it usually goes. Now, lesbians *could* date without immediately getting married. This is a possibility.

If we don't know how to date, the reasons are obvious. Our parents never said, "Now come on, honey, don't be nervous. I'll sit here while you call Mary." Our parents didn't take us aside and tell us about lesbian lovemaking, the way some of our brothers were taught about heterosexual sex. We didn't get to practice dating girls in high school, inviting them to Valentine's Day dances or proms.

In my generation, we didn't even get to ask boys out. We were taught to wait. So there are a lot of lesbians now whose concept of initiating a date is sitting close to the phone and praying.

Feminism has evolved to the extent that girls can now ask boys out, but can girls ask girls out? How indeed does one go about asking a girl—or a woman—for a date?

Because we don't know, we coach each other. Mareet gathers fifteen of her closest friends and asks, "Do you think I should ask Sally out? Do you think she'd go out with me?" That way she can get a consensus, so she'll reduce her chances of looking like a jerk. We all go to great pains not to look like jerks. Once Mareet decides to ask Sally out, she has to be quick about it, because if someone else asks Sally out first, Mareet may lose her chance, since usually the first date is the last.

After Mareet summons her nerve, she calls Sally on the phone, and they both try to act nonchalant.

"Hi, this is Mareet."

Sally has to say, "Oh, really?" She can't say, "Mareet! I'm so excited that you called me. Six hundred and seventy people told me you were going to call, and I am so happy!" She has to act really cool, on the outside chance that Mareet only called to ask her what happened on *Cagney and Lacey* last week. So she says, "I was just watching *The Cosby Show*," acting mildly irritated that she has to stop watching television to talk to Mareet, of *all* people. In fact, the lesbian grapevine has already informed her that Mareet thinks she's cute, and like most of us, Sally will go out with anybody who thinks she's cute. She'll follow her anywhere.

Mareet, sensing Sally's deliberate casualness, acts as if she dialed Sally's number by mistake. "Oh, who's this? Sally? Oh, hi." They're off to a bad start. Of course, there's a lot of pressure: if they don't act cool, the minute they hang up the phone, 670 lesbians will know they blew it. That's one big problem. Every lesbian community is a small community, regardless of the size of the city, and everyone knows everything about each other.

Still trying to be as cool as humanly possible, Mareet says, "You know, Sally, like, you know, like, uh, I don't know, ever thought about going to a movie?"

"Yeah, I've thought about it, Mareet. I've gone to a few."

Okay, Mareet says to herself, pick up the pace a bit. "Well, um, ever thought about like, I don't know, like, maybe, I don't know, going to, I don't know, a movie with me?"

At this point Sally is whispering to her roommate, "It's Mareet on the phone! It's Mareet on the phone! It's Mareet on the phone!"

Her roommate is saying, "You're kidding! Get off the phone so I can call everyone and tell them Mareet called."

Then Sally says to Mareet, "Oh, well, go to a movie, I don't know, like, with you, Mareet? Yeah, well, sure." Not wanting to seem overly aggressive, Sally adds, "Like, when?"

Mareet, afraid to insult Sally by assuming she has no plans for the upcoming weekend yet also afraid to wait much longer, says, "Well, uh, like, uh, well, um, I don't know, do you, like, I don't know, have plans, like, I don't know, like, for the weekend?"

"The whole weekend, Mareet?"

"No, I mean, could you go to a movie one night?"

But what Mareet really means is the whole weekend. She's trying to figure out whether to ask for Friday or Saturday, because some people are tired from work on Friday, but if they make the date for Friday, they could spend the whole weekend in bed. She pretends she's not thinking this. They make the date for Friday.

The real test comes at the movie theatre. They know it's a real date if neither one brings along any friends or roommates. Neither of them see the movie, because they're both sitting there thinking, "I wonder if she's going to want to have sex with me?" The 670 friends have already made their predictions, based on their information about the two women's past relationships, which is vast. After the movie, Mareet has to figure out how to get Sally to her house. One of the tricks is to have Sally meet her at Mareet's house before the movie, so Sally leaves her car there.

Mareet finally gets Sally to come over to her house, and they try to talk about the movie, which is difficult because neither one noticed it. They drink tea until the wee hours of the morning. That can be especially painful for Sally if she doesn't drink tea. But they keep drinking pot after pot, thinking, "I wonder if we're going to go to bed. I wonder if she'll make a move." At that point they can't exactly slip away and call their friends to see if or when they should make a move. The friends would laugh.

What is Mareet so nervous about? Why doesn't she just say, "Let's fuck!"? What if she gets rejected? So what? She could just go ask someone else.

Mareet is nervous because, like the rest of us, she has a little girl with a broken heart inside who is petrified that somebody's not going to like her. She says to herself, "I'm not so great in bed anyway. I'm a dud. If I ask her to have sex with me, and then it's really a drag, I'll be embarrassed. But if I can just sort of sneak up on her, getting her excited as we go along, then maybe she'll want to have sex with me, and won't expect me to be a superstar."

Let's not forget that we live in a very homophobic culture, a culture that has an inordinate fear of women who love women, so initiating a date is more stressful than it is for straight people. If you ask a lesbian for a date, you're admitting you're a lesbian and not just falling into bed with someone as if by mistake. There is a very large population—western civilization, eastern civilization, civilization since written history—that is not helpful when we're trying to dial the phone or ask for sex. Somewhere in our unconscious minds we're hearing, "I'm not supposed to do this." That's why we call dozens of friends—so we don't feel so isolated and afraid. Where are we going to get ideas about who might be a good person for us to date? Or how to ask somebody out on a date? We certainly can't read about it in magazines.

I laugh about how we ask all our buddies their opinions, but it's so hard for us, making up our whole own world. Every time a lesbian asks another lesbian out on a date, she's making it all up all over again.

No wonder we're so afraid to date more than one person. It's hard enough to make up the whole world at one time, much less having to make it up several times in a month. Or even several times in a year. I think that when relationships come to an end, the hardest part is thinking, "I have to make this whole world up again. I had my little world all set up."

Back to our story. By now, it's four in the morning, and Mareet says to Sally, "Oh, well, like, you could just like, sleep here. It's awfully late."

"Where, I mean, where could I sleep?" says Sally.

Now Mareet feels like saying, "Let's cut the crap, Sally, just fucking get in my bed and let me eat you out!" But no. She was raised to be sweet and polite and nice, so she says, "Well, here. I'll give you one of my t-shirts. You can sleep with me. I sleep much better when I sleep with people. I usually sleep with my housemate." Now she's babbling some sort of bull because, after all, it's four in the morning, and she's getting tired.

They get into bed and lie there in their long t-shirts and underpants, as if they always sleep with their underpants on, and they lie stiffly, like two-by-fours, not touching each other. Nobody can sleep, of course.

Then Mareet rolls over, sort of pretending she's asleep, and flings her arm around, hoping it will land in a fortuitous place. "Did I touch you?" she says. "Did I wake you up?"

"Oh, no. But I like where your hand is."

Finally, they get to have sex.

Dawn comes, and they're still having sex. Noon comes, and Mareet sneaks out to the kitchen like a little mouse to grab something to eat. After all that tea, Sally has to go to the bathroom, and she sneaks out like a little mouse too, because she doesn't want to run into Mareet's roommate, who is Sally's ex-lover's best friend.

By the time Sally goes home to change clothes—Monday morning, perhaps—everyone knows she slept with Mareet. I think that's part of the reason we don't date more—we're afraid other women in the community will find out we actually may have had sex with more than one woman in a month. Oh, my god!

In these days of safe sex, a lesbian date looks a little different. Mareet calls up Sally, they go to the movies, they get to Mareet's house, they drink tea for hours. But when they're on their way to the bedroom, Mareet says, "Excuse me, exactly who have you had sex with since 1978, and who have each of your lovers had sex with since that time? If you are at risk for having exposure to HIV that causes AIDS, I need to get out my rubber dams, my finger cots, my nonoxynal-9 and my sex toys with condoms."

It would make Mareet's job easier if someone would make up a lesbian sex tree as a community service. Every woman would be listed, and branching off from her name would be all her former lovers, and all their former lovers. Of course, it would get very complicated, because unlike family trees, most people's names would be listed more than once.

Anyway, in this age of AIDS, these first dates become even more difficult. There lie Mareet and Sally, stiff as boards in their long t-shirts and underpants, and at least one of them, probably Mareet, is thinking, "I need to ask her about safe sex. I know she's in a Twelve Step program; I wonder if she's ever shot drugs. Okay. Just get it out of your mouth. Come on. Just say it. Just open your mouth and say it. You're in the dark. She'll never know. She'll never know it was you."

Deciding to use street terms, she finally blurts out, "Ever shot any horse?"

"I've never shot a horse!" says Sally. "I never shot anything in my life."

Mareet ascertains that Sally is not, in fact, an IV drug-user, but then she has to ask her about men. How can she ask the lesbian lying next to her if she's had sex with men? This is a very delicate question.

"I just thought I'd ask," begins Mareet, "a very funny question—a thought just came through my head, a silly thought, but, uh, how long have you been out?" That's a good place to start: how long have you been a lesbian?

Sally says, "I've been out for fifteen years." That sounds pretty safe. But some lesbians have sex with men. So Mareet coughs it out: "Okay, I was just wondering—oh, I don't know, since 1978 or somewhere like that, have you ever had sex with a man?"

"Sex with a man?!" says Sally. She's offended. But she's reacting so strongly, thinks Mareet, could she be trying to cover up? Would Sally admit this sort of thing on a first date if it were true? Sally doesn't even know Mareet—maybe Mareet works for the lesbian police. "Okay, lady, you've had sex with a man. I'm going to have to take you in. How many times? Just the facts, lady, just the facts."

If Sally is a recovering alcoholic, she might not even remember who she has had sex with. Sometimes drug addicts and alcoholics will say, "There's a shaky period there of about five years. I don't quite remember what their names were or where we were or what we did." Sex addicts don't necessarily remember everyone they had sex with either. All of this can make the first date even more difficult.

When Mareet and Sally finally get out of bed on Monday, they are no longer dating. Now they are in a relationship. Now they make their first therapy appointment. Already Sally doesn't like the way Mareet talks to her friends on the phone, and they have to work this out. Mareet thinks it's a class issue. After all, Mareet's parents were teachers and taught her to be polite, so she didn't tell her friends she was busy in bed when they called. Sally, on the other hand, was practically raised in the streets, and she thinks the only way to talk to friends is be honest; when you're in bed, tell them to call back.

Mareet and Sally have to get married because, as women, they were raised to believe that if they're going to have sex, they have to be in love. Mareet has to ignore the fact that maybe she made a mistake going out with this white girl. Sally has to ignore the feeling that she wanted to date for longer than once before she settled down. The lesbians who aren't in love and just go around diddling with the girls can get terrible reputations. One woman says to another, "Let me tell you what I heard about Frances. I heard that she had sex with three different women, just last month. Can you imagine?

"You're kidding me!" says Mandy. "What a male-identified lesbian!"

"And I know all three of the women."

"What a creep. Objectifying those three friends of yours. I hope you told each of them that she had sex with the other two."

"Oh, absolutely. It is my professed duty to make sure that the moral values of the community are kept to a high level."

With attitudes like that in the lesbian community, it's hard for each of us to find our own way. We vote on everything, including how many different people we can have sex with.

The CIA doesn't need to infiltrate because we keep ourselves in line. We don't challenge the rules that we've made up; we're too afraid of alienating our peers. We didn't create these rules because we're uptight weirdos. We made these rules because we live in a culture that hates women, especially lesbians. No wonder we're so afraid to date several people at a time. If our community rejects us for not living up to their standards, then where will we turn?

I work with lesbians all the time in private counseling, trying to help them understand that going out on a date doesn't have to mean you're marrying the person. A date is just a date. You don't have to commit to her for the rest of your life. You don't have to bear her children. You can just have a date.

I love our euphemisms. We say, "I'm really attracted to you." That's a nice, polite, middle-class word: attracted. Anything with more than one or two syllables we're allowed to say. We can't say, "I want to have sex with you." *Sex* is a one-syllable word. *Fuck* is another one-syllable word. It's much safer to say, "I'm attracted to you."

If you ask somebody over the telephone, it's a great way to save face, because she can't even see you. If she says no, you can just quietly hang up the phone. "Oh, you don't want to? Thanks a lot." SLAM.

If she says she doesn't want to date, but she'd like to be friends, you can say, "No thanks. I don't want to be friends. I have six good friends. I've got a list here of women I want to be sexual with, and I'm going to call the next person on my list. Thanks for helping me narrow it down."

Most of us are far too busy being polite to be so direct. But if we would just be up front about it, we'd avoid a lot of embarrassing situations. Have you ever tried to kiss someone and it feels like you've kissed a stone? That's her little hint. She glues her arms to her sides, bends at the waist so there's no body contact whatsoever, and gives you a little pebble kiss.

If you had known that she was going to do that, you wouldn't have even tried to kiss her. As is, you have to act like you meant to be giving a pebble kiss, too. You suddenly change your lips from soft and puffy and sweet to tight like hers, so she doesn't think you had anything in mind.

I'd like to see single women premeditate sex and cop to the fact that they've planned it and they want it. It would eliminate a lot of misunderstandings between women who do and don't like to fuck on the first date. That's the real question, and it's not addressed in the proposal, "Would you like to go on a date?" If we just asked, "Would you like to fuck?" things would become a lot clearer. This would be helpful both for the women who do want sex on the first date, and those who would rather explore someone's brain before exploring her vagina. Both kinds of women think about sex before going on dates, and it would be great to be up-front about it.

Once when I was giving a lecture in another city, someone showed me a matchbook that someone had given her at a bar. It said, "I fuck on the first date." Inside, the woman had written her name and phone number. I thought that was the coolest thing! I said, "We should get cases of those, and pass them around."

If you do want sex, you're probably afraid she'll think you're too aggressive, too forward, too male-identified. (Anything a lesbian does that isn't passive and wimpy can be called male-identified. But no, we're not sexist, oh no.) If you don't want sex, you're worried that she will and you'll have to say no.

I'd like to see one woman say to another one, "I think you're really attractive and I have ulterior motives. I already have plenty of friends. More friendship I do not need." (You may not in fact have any friends at all, but she doesn't need to know this.) "Are you willing to have safe sex?"

If you don't want to get married, make *that* clear. Say, "I'm looking for someone to jump in the sack with occasionally." Find out if that grosses her out. See if she says, "Hey, wait a minute. I want you to want me for my heart and brain and political sensibilities."

You can do it gently. You can say, "I just think you're so sweet, and I would like to take off your blouse." That way, you don't have to spend all evening wondering if she'll take her blouse off or not. How many dates have been wrecked because you're sitting around worrying?

You may find someone who has no interest in casual sex. She may really want to have sex only with a woman with whom she can have an ongoing relationship. "You know, I find you very attractive, but your proposition of fun sex with no strings attached just doesn't appeal to me. I get attached very easily and recreational sex makes me too nervous and feels too empty."

"I really respect that, and I appreciate your telling me instead of our getting sexually involved and then your being angry because I don't want to get married. You sure I can't talk you into it while you're waiting for the woman of your dreams?"

Instead of having direct communication like this, you get signals about how far you can go. It's a lot like it was when you were a teenager. First you kiss. Then you sort of rub against the side of her breast. If she doesn't object, nipples are the next step. If you can get to a nipple, it's a pretty clear sign that you can go down further, but the waist is a critical cut-off point. All the time you're thinking, "I wonder if this is freaking her out. It's freaking me out. I hope she doesn't expect me to be this assertive in bed or anything . . . ." (As they say, butch in the streets, femme in the sheets.)

This is how we tell each other whether it's okay to have sex. I'm not discounting this as a method. Nonverbal communication is very exciting. I'm just suggesting that we admit—even to ourselves—that we're actually planning sex.

We didn't learn to date as teenagers, so we have to learn now. We don't have to pretend we're cool. You could say, "You know what, Star? I feel like I'm thirteen. I've asked twenty-five people if I should ask you out on a date. So here I am on the phone, feeling like a total fool."

Star could say, "I feel like a complete fool, too. I'd love to go out on a date with you."

You could also make a promise to yourself, "I'm going to go out on fifteen dates with fifteen different people." Then afterward, you could decide to get to know a few of them better and, if you want, eventually get "married."

You could say, "Listen, I read a book called *Lesbian Passion,* and JoAnn Loulan says to ask fifteen people out on dates, and you're number five."

She'll probably say, "Well, fuck you. If I'm not number one, then I'm not going out." Click.

That's our problem. If we're not first, we're not interested. This is the United States of America, and we're going to be number one or nothing.

Lesbians act like we're different. "The military-industrial complex is one thing, but I'm a lesbian. I am cool." Yet we can't go out on a date with somebody if she's dating somebody else.

"Do you like me best? Do you have the most fun with me? Do we have better sex? If I'm going to put my tongue on your clitoris, I need to know that we only do this with each other, and that this relationship will last until we're eighty."

Well, honey, unless you're seventy-nine and a half, don't count on it.

One reason we want our relationships to last is because we don't want to show somebody else our body. If we had a choice, most of us wouldn't show our bodies to more than one woman in a decade. Being vulerable and exposing our bodies is another reason the lesbian date is so difficult. It's not just about going to the movies, because if you just want to go to the movies, you would go to the movies with your buddies. Part of the reason to go on a date with somebody is because the potential for sex is exciting; it's different than going out with your buddies. And we have to love ourselves to be able to do that.

As with anything else, there is always another side of the coin. There are women who have had problems with compulsive sex, women who have been preoccupied all their adolescent and adult lives with being sexual with another woman. These women have a difficult time with the notion of premeditated casual sex. It's just an invitation to exercise compulsive sex thinking. You may have found that you have used sex with women to fill up that empty space within. In fact, you can find other ways to feel full. You don't have to use women and the attention they focus on you to feel whole.

Dating may not be something you can do when you are first recovering from being compulsive; it may be something for the future. The discomfort you feel may not be the same as what I have been describing here. Unlike Mareet, you may have an easy time asking women out on dates. The difficulty is being alone with yourself.

When you become aware of compulsive sex, it's scary to then start imagining dating, having sex, and not having it be compulsive. This is hard to do unless you have gone through a period of abstinence and have begun to learn what you have been using sex for. You can begin asking a woman to go out with *you*, not your self-hatred. You can ask her to go out because you would like to get to know her and have her get to know you, not because you're great in the sack. Undergoing a process of recovery from this compulsive behavior is much like drug and alcohol recovery; it takes time, humility, honesty and action.

When we are dating, having sex is really not the whole of it. We can acknowledge our feelings to a new person. We can experience a bit of self-love—what else would get us to do something simply for fun?

We have an opportunity to be honest about who we are. I heard someone say recently that she was a recovering liar. I think in this culture we have been taught to lie and have lies glorified. How else could someone like Oliver North become a folk hero for sending millions of dollars to the Contras in Nicaragua? He lied and he did it with such aplomb that lots of people in this country fell for him. He lied for protection. Our culture promotes this, and we do it daily to protect ourselves.

Telling someone how you really feel in the moment will begin the process of learning to love the magical self that you are. The truth can be as simple as, "I'd like to go to the movies with you." Or as scary as, "I'm really attracted to you, I mean, you know, sexually." How wonderful to be able to love yourself enough to tell another human being who you are.

Beginnings are traumatic. All of us are beginners at being single and creating a new way to make dating fun and fulfilling. Calling somebody up for a date, not dating compulsively, trying to get her to your house, trying to get her into bed with you, starting to be sexual—all those beginnings are scary. For most women, being in the midst of sex is not scary; they're swept away by it. But it's the beginning that's so hard, so scary, so traumatic. It's the beginning of everything.

I think we make the situation worse when we pretend to be at ease, pretend not to want sex, pretend not to care so much. Think of it this way: wouldn't you rather get to know someone first before committing yourself to spending the next six holidays with her? Wouldn't you rather have someone tell you honestly what she wants, rather than making you guess? Wouldn't you rather come clean with your compulsive tendencies than have her find out later? If you start being honest about who you are and what you want, and if you open to the possibility that the first date does not necessarily have to be the engagement party, you may find that you and your partners will have a much better time on all your lesbian dates.

Sex Toys and
Other Hot Ideas

*It doesn't matter
what you do in the
bedroom as long as
you don't do it in the
street and frighten
the horses.*

—MRS. PATRICK CAMPBELL

*H*ave you ever used sex toys? If not, try to read this chapter with an open mind. Sex toys can add a lot of spice to your sex life. After reading my last book, *Lesbian Sex,* some people said to me, "There wasn't enough juice in it. Don't just tell us that lesbians have oral sex and kiss a lot—we know all that stuff. Tell us something new that can spice up our sex lives."

So I'm telling you about sex toys. I call them 'toys' to remind us that, ultimately, the purpose of sex is to have fun. I know that sex can be deeply spiritual, or deeply emotional, or so deeply traumatic that you end up in therapy over it. But I think it's important to keep in mind that sex can be fun. It can be a hoot. This chapter is about ways to make sex a hoot.

Let's start with vibrators. Vibrators come in all different shapes and forms. Some vibrators run on electricity; others run on batteries. They can go in your vagina, in your anus, in your mouth. You can rub one all over your body—anywhere that you like to be touched.

One vibrator is great for stimulating the head of the clitoris. Its soft, spongy head is about the size of a tennis ball, so you can lie on it and move around, or put it between you and your lover and both be stimulated at once. Hitachi is the most common brand.

Another vibrator has a long part with the shape of a woman's head on the end. That part goes inside the vagina. Another part in the shape of a baby bear rotates around on your clitoris. This vibrator runs on batteries; you can take it anywhere.

Most vibrators have a few speeds so you can receive the level of intensity you want. Vibrators produce wonderful sensations because, after all, sex is mainly a matter of stimulating nerve cells. I know that's terribly unromantic, but it's true. Vibrators are great at stimulating nerve cells. In fact, vibrators are so good at stimulating nerve cells, they'll often help a woman have an orgasm when all other methods have failed. Many women find that masturbation is boring unless they have the kind of stimulation that vibrators can give.

Vibrators can also make partners jealous. Often women say to me, "My partner wants me to be orgasmic, but she won't let me bring a vibrator to bed, and the only way I'm orgasmic is when I use a vibrator." I try to explain that it doesn't have to feel like a ménage à trois. A vibrator can just be an additional object that makes sex exciting, the way some women are excited by teddies or other lacy lingerie.

You can buy vibrators at special sex paraphernalia stores (see the list at the end of the chapter) or at regular department stores, in the small appliance section. (But you won't find the special rotating bear one there.) The instructions on the vibrators you find in department stores say they are good for easing tension in the shoulders. I suppose you can use them for that too.

Some vibrators come with attachments. One is called the 'G-spot Stimulator.' The G-spot is a popularized word for the paraurethral sponge within which is the paraurethral gland. Since the area is, after all, a part of our anatomy, and not Graffenberg's—the male doctor the 'G' refers to—I prefer to call it the 'Our-spot.' Many of us knew about it long before he did. Anyway, it's an area about an inch to an inch and a half in diameter, located behind the vaginal wall and wrapped around the urethra. When stimulated, this gland swells and produces a fluid that comes out through tiny ducts into the urethra. It feels wonderful. Many women think they are urinating when this fluid comes out, but what is emitted is not urine. When you are having sex and feel like you have to pee, try to keep going with it—you won't pee, and you might experience intense pleasure. Some women don't have a sensation of needing to urinate; they just suddenly realize that the bed is wet, they don't know how it got wet, and they don't want to ask anybody. Other women don't experience sensitivity in their Our-spot at all.

Back to sex toys. There is a little tool that fits over the head of those vibrators with the tennis ball-sized heads, and it has a curved, carrot-shaped projection, which you can insert into the vagina to stimulate the Our-spot. It's curved in such a way that you can put it into your vagina and have the vibrator's big head stimulate your clitoris at the same time. It's really very lovely.

There's serious controversy in our communities over any act that might be considered sado-masochism. I'm not going to touch that with a ten-foot pole. But I will discuss some fun things that might be considered mild S/M. If you want to know about braces, whips and things like that, you'll have to get a catalog.

Soft restraints, for instance, can be fun. Soft restraints are essentially handcuffs, made of silk, leather, or other soft fabrics. They have velcro strips that close them, and long straps that can be tied to bedposts or something else sturdy.

You might be thinking, "If you think I'm going to let someone tie me down, you're nuts." If you have been out of control in a violent sexual situation in which you were not participating as a peer, soft restraints might be too freaky. So don't use them. But if you're just afraid of feeling silly, go ahead and try it. Or at least, don't knock it until you've tried it.

Some soft restraints come in a box with a little blindfold. It's black satin and has an elastic strap on the back. When you put it over your eyes, you have the opportunity to relinquish responsibility for initiating or sustaining sex. You might be able to feel physical sensations more acutely, since you can't see anything, can't go anywhere, and don't have to be worrying about pleasing your partner. We try to control so much of our lives, it can be a real relief to stop trying to manage every second of every day. Some women enjoy giving up control to somebody they trust and love.

When you play with soft restraints, you have to make agreements with each other before you begin so you can stop if you feel uncomfortable. Some women like to say "stop" when they mean "keep going," so they choose some other word to mean "stop." This is something you should agree on before having any kind of sex that feels scary or out of control.

Another popular lesbian sex toy is the dildo. Isn't that a beautiful word? Dildo. Yuck. Can't we find another word? How about Agnes of Goddess? Fortunately, we now have at our disposal dildoes that no longer look like penises. Inventive women that we are, we have now made things that fit into all kinds of orifices—mouths, vaginas, anuses—and come in all sorts of colors and shapes. 'Orifice,' incidentally, is a fancy word for 'hole.' I learned it in college so I wouldn't have to say things like, "I'm going to put this in my hole." Instead I say, "I'm going to put this in my orifice." It's much more polite.

Some dildoes are hollow so you can put things in them and make them as soft or hard as you want. Some are made of silicon. Silicon can flop around like a fourteen-day-old carrot. Some are thin, some are thick, some long, some short. Some are very long and two-headed, so you can stick them in your own and someone else's orifice at the same time. Then you can roll around together with this double dildo connecting the two of you. It's fun. But in doing any sort of penetration, it's important to go slowly and be respectful of what your partner likes.

Some lesbians think penetration is a heterosexual activity. Of course, it's our right not to participate in any sexual practice that makes us uncomfortable, but let's not rain on anyone's parade. Personally, I enjoy having people explore my vagina. There's nothing heterosexual about that. I'm a lesbian, and it is my right to have the kind of sex I want to have. It's my vagina; I'll play with it how I want. Heterosexuals don't have a corner on exploring vaginas.

Then there is the much maligned asshole. I mean, we even use the word to put someone down. We often associate our anuses with yuckiness. But they are filled with the most wonderful nerve endings, thousands of them. With just the slightest touch, the tiniest finger stimulating those nerve endings, the pleasure can be intense.

Some women like to use toys in their assholes. Appropriately enough, they're called butt plugs. You put them in your butt. This stimulates nerve endings in the rectum and anal sphincter. Butt plugs come in all sizes and shapes: sometimes they resemble thin Christmas trees; sometimes they are a string of marble-sized balls; sometimes just a thin finger-like projection. Some butt plugs are electric and will rotate and vibrate. They all have something large on the end, such as a ring, so you don't have to worry about them slipping up your ass and disappearing.

Some people like small butt plugs; some people like big butt plugs; some people don't like them at all. If you don't like them at all, don't use them. It's a free country. (Well, it's free if you're white, upper middle class, male, able-bodied, and heterosexual . . . but that's beyond the scope of this book.)

If you're afraid of poop, you might be interested to know that the poop usually isn't right down there near the anus, it's up several inches. So, often you don't get any poop on your fingers or sex toys if you stick something in your anus. If you do, wash it off. No big deal, really, especially if you've raised a baby. I changed my son's diapers for three years. After a while, poop just becomes poop. (That's part of why we have such a strong bond with our mothers: they're the only people who didn't mind our poop.)

Enough on poop. On to the next sex toy. Some women used to cut holes in their underpants to hold dildoes in place, but now there are harnesses that even come in lavender, the lesbian color. A harness is something you can strap around yourself, sort of like a sanitary napkin belt, or a G-string. It wraps around your waist or hips and has little holes to hold dildoes or butt plugs or whatever you fancy.

Some people say, "Now, that's really male-identified." I say, why not? Why should men be the only ones who get to put something in a woman's vagina and still keep two hands free? I think it's wonderful because it gives you more opportunities to feel her up.

What else is wonderful about you and your partner both having vaginas is that you can take turns wearing the harness. Androgyny at its best. You can put a dildo through one of the holes in the harness and position the end of the dildo over your clitoris, so as you're pushing the dildo into your partner, it's also rubbing against your clit. You can also put one dildo on the outside, pointing toward your partner, and one facing inward, into your vagina. Some women like to put on a harness, equipped with a dildo or two, and go out on the town. This is called 'packing.' They dance with the girls, and rub up against them and confuse them. It could be fun.

To facilitate some of this sex toy action, you may need lubricants. Lubricants are the gooshy substances that help you have smoother movement in and out of your orifices. Some women don't have enough fluid in their vagina or anus to facilitate things moving in and out of it. Old women and women who are postpartum, for example, often don't produce enough vaginal fluid for easy penetration. Stress can also cause the vagina to secrete less fluid, and it can be drier during certain phases of the menstrual cycle. This may differ from woman to woman, but dryness usually occurs between bleeding and ovulating.

The important thing to remember about lubrication is that it should not have a petroleum base. Vaseline, for instance, is not good because it is not water-soluble, clogs the pores and can cause infections. KY jelly is good and available in most drugstores. Sex toy stores also sell squishy, good-tasting lubricants, including lubricants that warm when you blow on them.

Keep in mind that sex toys can spread disease. Don't put one in a vagina after it's been in an anus. Clean it or put a condom over it if there is any chance that either one of you is infected with AIDS. You can get up and wash it in one part bleach, ten parts water, but do you really want to do this in the middle of having sex? Condoms are cheap and can be used easily.

It can be scary to introduce the idea of sex toys to your lover. I recommend the direct approach: "I like to use sex toys. Do you like to use them? I have a catalog; which ones would you like to use?" Or, "Here are my sex toys. Have you ever used any of these before?"

When a lover first showed me her sex toys, I had never seen any before, and I thought, "Is she kidding?" She wasn't kidding. Now I'm the one saying to new lovers, "Have you ever tried sex toys?"

If your lover hasn't and she doesn't want to, she may have negative reactions. What is important to remember is that her reaction is not personal. It does not mean you are bad or that she is bad. It simply means she has different tastes. She may be afraid; most of us are afraid of new things. Or she may have some history with sex toys that is not pleasant. Remember to ask her what is going on; don't just hide behind your own fear of rejection.

This reaction to our sexual enthusiasms is not easy to accept. It is probably a big reason why we do not experiment in new ways with sex. The old ways worked and new ways may get us rejected. We have this idea that we aren't allowed to think of new, exciting, different things, that we're 'supposed' to have sex this certain way. And yet, if anyone said that we should only have heterosexual sex or that we should only have sex in the missionary position, we'd all flip out. Remember that experimenting is just another opportunity for you to love that magical self within. Coming up with new ideas about sex, using new toys, and experimenting is often another road to self-love.

RESOURCES

Good Vibrations, 3492 22nd Street, San Francisco, CA 94110 (415) 550-7399. Catalog available, all items mailed in parcels marked "plain brown wrapper."

Harmony, PO Box DDD, Albuquerque, NM 87196. Catalog available. This is the only lesbian-owned and operated sex toy store I know of.

Eve's Garden, 119 West 57th Street, New York, NY 10019 (212) 757-8651. Catalog available.

Fanning the Flames: How Couples Can Keep Their Sex Lives Exciting

Joy was a flame in me
Too steady to destroy.

—SARA TEASDALE

*H*oney, are you awake? Are you there?"

"I'm here. What do you want?"

"Oh, nothing. Are you tired?"

"Yeah, I am. I'm almost asleep. 'Night."

" 'Night, honey."

Do you know that routine? You lie awake for another two hours listening to her snore. "What am I doing here?" you ask yourself. "She's supposed to be my lover. How come we never make love? I love her but . . . I don't know if I can go on like this."

My research shows that frequency of sex among lesbian couples drops off dramatically after the first year, then keeps sinking, sort of like Beethoven's Fifth: Dah Dah Dah . . . Dum. It fades away until it becomes a peck on the cheek.

If this is what you're going through, you probably thought your present relationship was going to be different. During those first six weeks, it probably seemed like this was going to be the relationship when you got to have sex however and whenever you wanted. You thought you'd be jumping through fields of daisies, the wind in your hair.

Now that it's been a year, or two years, or ten years, or maybe just six months, you can't remember the last time you had sex. You almost don't remember what it feels like. You and your lover are having battles about it:

"We haven't had sex for a month."

"No, we had it last week. Don't you remember? Let's see. Wasn't it after *Cagney and Lacey?*"

"*Cagney and Lacey?* You fell asleep in the middle of that show!"

"I *know* we had sex last week."

"Well, when?"

Then she starts marking it on her calendar, so she can point to it and prove she's right: "See? It hasn't been that long!"

Sex is what differentiates friends from lovers. It's magical; it can give us intense pleasure and a feeling of closeness unlike anything else. Sex can also help partners stay bonded during difficult times. It's a form of nonverbal communication that can sometimes heal more deeply than words.

In a long-term relationship, I think it's crucial to make a conscious effort to take each other to that magic place. Too often, sex fizzles out in a relationship, then one partner finds someone else who will have sex with her and leaves the relationship.

Fortunately, decline in sexual expression is not terminal. It is possible to reignite sexual passion between longtime lovers. But first let's consider how this decidedly dispassionate state of relating came about.

Freud had some weirdo things to say, but he also said some things that were true, and one of these was that sex is the first thing to go. Sex is an expendable activity; you can live without it. When energy gets diverted to other concerns, such as work, children, illness, or school, sex can take a nose dive. It can also slack off if there is disharmony in the relationship.

Often sex slows or even stops when two women move in together. This can be attributed to many things. The move may create fears of intimacy or uncertainty about making a deeper commitment.

The women may begin to take one another for granted, devoting less of their attention to courting and more to homemaking. Living together may also trigger painful memories for survivors of incest.

There is an extra strain in lesbian unions because we aren't legitimized by the majority culture. One of our ways of compensating for this homophobia is to bond through activities, opinions and clothes. Lesbian partners often combine incomes, wear the same clothes, read the same books, ditch those friends the other doesn't like, and watch TV or not depending on the other's preference. This creates a needed sense of belonging for people who may feel like outsiders in the general culture, but it doesn't do much for the sexual connection between them. When we emphasize how similar we are and deny our differences, we become bored. There is no more newness to intrigue us.

Many of us are embarrassed about the fact that sex has become routine. Why shouldn't it? Other things become routine: we know how late at night we can call; we know how early in the morning she's coherent. We know how many cigarettes she's still smoking a day; we know when she pays her bills. It's no different with sex.

Often, boredom leads to insecurity. We'll have discussions *ad nauseum* into the night: "Are you attracted to me? Aren't you attracted to me? You know, since we've gotten together, I've gained about 35 pounds. In between relationships I lose a lot of weight, and that's when people are attracted to me. I know now that you're not."

Or she now knows that you get pimples on your butt during certain parts of your cycle, which she didn't know before you started being sexual. She's been through vaginal infections with you. She's been through your period more than once, probably. You pull out your tampax and drop it in the toilet right in front of her now. It's very unromantic. She's been in the bathroom while you shit and pee, and your genitals have become unglamorous. She knows you get constipated, and you know she has diarrhea, so you can't idealize each other anymore.

Couples often polarize into two camps: one wants sex and the other doesn't. Rather than viewing the lack of sex as a mutual problem, we each tend to blame the other. It doesn't matter whether she wants to have sex and you don't, or you want to have sex and she doesn't. It's always her fault. "She wants to have sex too fast." "She wants to have sex too slow." "She doesn't have orgasms." "She has orgasms so fast it intimidates me." Or this one: "I found out that fifteen years ago she faked an orgasm, so I don't want to have sex with her because I can't trust her." Isn't that a convenient reason not to have sex with her anymore?

Often I hear from clients, "I'm very sexual, and she never wants sex, and it drives me crazy."

I say, "Then why did you choose her?"

I think our subconscious self makes choices without regard for intelligent concerns. We all have our radar. "Yes" people choose "no" people. People who have orgasms as soon as you look at them find people who have never had an orgasm. Call it karma, call it romance, call it fate, call it recklessness. In any case, we often find ourselves with lovers who have dissimilar needs and desires.

I don't know what kind of built-in radar there is, but if you are a therapy junkie, you can find the one person who's never even been to a therapy session. I'm an adult child of an alcoholic and I can pick an alcoholic out of a crowd of millions.

Believe it or not, we choose our partners for the very reason that drives us crazy. Yet we refuse to learn the lesson, because we want to make it her fault. It's as if we say, "How did you get in my movie?" In fact, we very carefully picked her out and said, "You come with me."

Another reason I think "yes" people choose "no" people is so that someone else will say no. That way the "yes" person can continue to be cool. It's why women who love being in therapy choose to be involved with people who don't want to be in therapy. Then they can go around feeling superior: "If you went to therapy . . . ." We love those people so we can feel superior to them. That may not seem nice, but it's true.

Why "no" people choose "yes" people is obvious. Why would a "no" person choose another "no" person? They'd never get to have sex. They'd break up within an hour and a half. "You're kidding! You're going to say no, too?" Each "no" person would either immediately go find a "yes" person to have an affair with or turn into a "yes" person herself.

We're taught in this culture that you can have fun in this place, at this time, for this amount of time, but then you can't have any fun after that. We all have to work, and we all have to be very serious. I mean, what if *both* people in the relationship made an agreement to keep on having a good time?

We trap ourselves with 'shoulds.' Sex should be sacred. Sex should be a spiritual union between two people. I don't know about you, but I have done some things during sex that are not at all sacred, and I wouldn't particularly say my spirit was unified with that of the other woman. I got off. Sometimes sex is indeed a deep spiritual experience; sometimes it's just fun.

Our families taught us, verbally or nonverbally, most of the rules we live by. "Sex isn't supposed to be fun." "Sex is shameful." "You shouldn't have sex more than a certain number of times per week." "You *should* have sex more than a certain number of times per week."

We did break one rule by becoming lesbians. None of us were told, "Oh, honey, when you grow up I want you to find another woman to be with. I think it would be heaven." But beyond our lesbianism, we've hardly changed the rules at all. We feel ashamed of our bodies unless the light is out. We refuse to be innovative. We feel afraid of venturing beyond the lesbian missionary position: your face between her legs, then her face between your legs (or if you don't like oral sex, lying on top of each other fondling and rubbing each other).

You may be surprised how many sex rules you actually follow. Sometimes a new lover can bring this to light: her sex activities may be very different from yours, and you may find yourselves struggling to have familiar sex. This can be very scary. One woman's rule book says she should say no to sex during menstruation, no to anal sex, and no to affairs while in a long-term relationship. Imagine her horror to find that her lover's rule book doesn't include any of these. Both women may find themselves arguing about who is right.

We find it disturbing to explain or justify something that seems so obvious and true. When we confront this kind of difference, we tend to put the other person down. "Sex during her period?" you may say. "She's nuts! That makes me sick. We'd get blood all over the sheets."

What if the blood washes off the sheets? Would that make sex during menstruation okay? Does the resistance come from a religious upbringing? Is the taste or smell of blood disgusting? Are you afraid your partner might be turned off by the smell of your blood? Is it even clear why certain practices are taboo?

When sex in a long-term relationship starts to become boring or infrequent, I think the first place to look is inward, at your inner child. If you've read the first few chapters of this book, you've heard several variations on this theme, but I do think it's crucial that you turn to that little girl with the broken heart and find out what is happening with her.

When our little kids are not taken care of, they start acting out in ways that we don't even notice. They may throw fits like real children do; they may couch their frustration in sarcastic statements to lovers or friends. We walk around looking like grown-ups—going to jobs, going to welfare appointments, cooking and cleaning and being responsible. We don't want those little kids with broken hearts to be here, so we pretend they're not. But whether we acknowledge it or not, the kids influence what goes on, especially in relationships.

The way people act in relationships to get their little kids taken care of reminds me of the Chicago Grain Mart. At the Chicago Grain Mart, they have little tiered stands, like a mini-stadium. One side of the floor has oats, the middle of the floor has wheat, and the other side of the floor has corn. Someone rings a bell, men run down to their place in the pits, and then everyone starts screaming at each other. They all scream constantly and make hand gestures. It's the most insane thing I've ever seen. Then the bell rings again, and everyone has to shut up immediately and go back to their places. (I want that job, actually. I'd love to get paid to run someplace to scream and gesticulate at somebody else. It would be a great job.)

That's what we're doing all the time in our relationships with our lovers—making deals. "If I sell you ten bushels of corn, you give me two bushels of oats. Okay? Now wait a minute. Why did I say I'd give you ten bushels for just two bushels? If I'm going to give you ten bushels, you're going to have to give me ten bushels back!"

We say to our lovers, "If I'm going to take care of my little kid, you're going to have to take care of your little kid. But if you don't do it the way I want you to—for instance, a minimum of one therapy session a week—it's illegal. All right, I'm going to call the lesbo police."

Can you imagine not having that deal? What if you simply said, "I will take care of my child with the broken heart as my offering of devotion to this relationship." As women, it's so hard for us to understand what devotion and surrender are about. Devotion and surrender don't have a very good reputation among feminists. By devoted I mean devoted to your own little kid. By surrender I mean surrender to the reality that she is the only little kid that you can care for.

The little one who dwells within especially affects our sex lives. If you're a survivor of childhood sexual abuse, for example, and you're in a sexual relationship with another person, your kid may be feeling safer and more familiar, and thus is being exposed in ways you're not used to. This could lead to you feeling 'little,' young and scared. You may or may not be aware of this. You may want to be held in a nonsexual way for hours. You may find yourself crying at the slightest things. You may not want to do much that entails thought or planning. You may not want to be sexual. This may be because your little girl inside is open and vulnerable, and kids don't want to be sexual with adults.

So if you're not wanting much sex, take a look at your youngest self inside. Go to the baby, or go to the very young girl with the broken heart. This little one needs your care, support and understanding. Unless we're taking care of our little kids, our teenagers—who are filled with sexual energy—don't get to come out and play. If unattended, the kid can drain all of one's energy.

Early in our relationships, we let our teenage energy out. We call our friends several times a day to share stories about our new lover. We let go of responsibilities while spending long weekends in bed. We become more obsessed with our appearance or we disregard it entirely, preferring wrinkled, dirty clothes to spending time doing laundry. We stop going to the grocery store. We only want to be with our new love; we think of her all the time; we fantasize about living together happily ever after. But after those first six weeks or six months of a new relationship, we stifle this teenage energy. We start paying bills again and acting mature and going to couples counseling.

How can we get that teenaged energy back into our sex lives once we're old, boring married couples? Start by admitting that it's boring. "You want to know why I don't have sex with you? I'm sort of bored. I know everything that's going to happen. It's like going to the same movie fifty times, you know? And it's not like the *Rocky Horror Picture Show*, I'm sorry to say. It's not that much fun. No squirt guns, no umbrellas, no toilet paper, no dress-ups."

All of which are great ideas about how to get your teenager out. Dress-ups, squirt guns, toilet paper, umbrellas . . . you could do all kinds of things with your sex life if you were willing.

Who balks at this? The little girl with the broken heart. Sometimes it's because she's actually suffered sexual abuse, so she's afraid of what's going to happen. It may also be that she's tried new things before and felt like a dope, so she's embarrassed. It may be that she's never taken sexual risks before, so she thinks she's a wimpy, inadequate lover.

It is helpful to challenge those thoughts. When your mind is saying, "Don't do that, stop, you'll get in trouble," try responding with the opposite: "Go ahead, there's nothing to fear." You probably won't get in trouble. No one will know you had anal sex, or used squirt guns, or had sex in the bathtub. No one will know you used a vibrator or dildo, dressed up as someone else, or teased your girlfriend with your tongue for an hour, always stopping short of her having an orgasm.

If you were a teenager, you would be willing to try new things, as long as your buddies were doing it with you. You would hitchhike all over the country, or climb into dryers at the laundromat. When I was a teenager, we'd make our bodies into an X, hold onto the sides of a huge dryer at the laundromat and spin around. What grown-up would do that?

I'm not suggesting that you go out and do dangerous things. In fact, if you go spin around in a dryer, I'll deny I ever wrote this. But you could allow your teenager to come out and have fun. Perhaps you could trade off with your partner, each one coming up with a new idea every other month. A big part of the problem is, we simply get bored.

To begin to get beyond boredom, write down all the sex rules you live by. If your partner is willing to make a list too, you can compare. You may be surprised to learn what rules she has. This may shed some light on problem areas in your sex life. For instance, you may not have known that her rule book says no sex toys, but that would explain why she never has used that vibrator you gave her for her birthday. One of your rules may be that women aren't supposed to have fun with sex; this may help explain why you have been saying no. If it can't be fun, why do it?

We hold onto our beliefs about how it should be. "Yes" people say, "I want to be turned on. I want to be excited. But I want her to do it this way, and I want her to do it this often." "No" people complain, "She pushes me all the time; she wants to have sex all the time." Unfortunately, we can't program other people. The "yes" person can't make the "no" person want to be sexual. The "no" person can't make the "yes" person not want to have sex.

Our first task is to accept who this other person is. Often we don't even accept the way she brushes her teeth. How are we supposed to accept when and how she wants her clitoris stimulated?

The next task is to surrender. We've been taught to acquiesce, be passive and surrender all of our lives, but that's not the kind of surrender I'm talking about. I'm suggesting you try giving up your position for just a minute or two.

It's scary to surrender our positions, whatever they are. The duality between two women isn't always about frequency; it can be dildo/no dildo, vibrator/no vibrator, oral sex/no oral sex, things in vaginas/nothing in vaginas. It doesn't matter how you set up the polarization. What matters is how you work with it.

Just for an hour, one day a week, let go of your side of the dichotomy. If you normally say no, see what would happen if you said yes for one hour. You can still have your list of things you absolutely will not do, but beyond that, be willing. It's okay if you're thinking, "I'm not going to have fun, but she can go ahead and do what she wants."

Rules can be broken, but not all of them have to be. Note the rules on your list that you would like to break. Tell your lover which of her rules you'd like her to break, and ask her to tell you. Talk about which ones each of you might be willing to break. This may not be easy. Everyone in your family may follow certain rules. You may be the first person in generations to challenge them. Go for it.

If you normally say yes, try letting go of the stipulations about how your lover has to behave. What if you were willing to give up your need to have her come on to you like a dog on a bone? What if you had sex even if she's not turned on, even if she doesn't want to but is willing to accommodate your need? What if you were willing to masturbate while your partner simply held you?

If you're a "no" person, you might have to have a conversation with your parents—the ones inside your head who say, "If you're going to be a lesbian, at least don't have sex. At least don't have fun." You might say to these parents: "I'm sorry I'm in a lesbian relationship. I know it's against your religion. I know you don't like it. I know she's not my race, my size, my class, or whatever, and I'm really sorry. I can't even use the excuse that I got pregnant. I am just having fun, and I'm really sorry." Apologizing to your parents might help you let go of some of their rules. It might sound crazy, but many of us are actually very worried about going against our parents' wishes.

I have a friend who apologizes to her parents for things that her lover does. She has these long conversations in her head with her parents, saying, "I'm really sorry that she does not have the respect that I have for you. I know how important it is to pay your bills on time, and I am so sorry that she doesn't have enough respect for you to pay her bills on time." Instead of harping on her lover, she has these discussions with her parents because, after all, that's where the problem lies. It doesn't really lie with your lover, because you chose her for a very particular reason.

What if you made a list of all the fantasies you could each think of, then shared them with your partner? What if you got the telephone company to do a conference call, and several of your friends had group sex over the telephone? If you and your girlfriend are attracted to the women in another couple, you could have phone sex together instead of ruining both relationships by having actual sex. It could be really fun. There are all kinds of things you can do to make sex interesting if you let your teenager out.

Write down interesting things you've heard of people doing. Or write on little pieces of paper all kinds of things that both of you are willing to do, put the pieces of paper in a hat, and choose your evening's activities that way.

You might make a list of things you will not do. Maybe you don't like her to touch your asshole. Maybe you refuse to have sex outdoors. But as you try new things each month, you may be surprised to find that you're erasing things from your 'I'll never do that' list.

What if you decide ahead of time that nobody is going to have orgasms? That way, if somebody has a lot of orgasms and somebody doesn't have orgasms at all, you take away that problem.

This may seem really crazy, and in fact impossible, if you believe orgasm is the true form of sexual expression. But orgasm is only one aspect of our sexual response. However, most of us gauge our sexual activity by who has had an orgasm and who has not; it helps us know when we are done.

"Did you come yet?"

"No."

"Then I guess sex isn't over."

It's sort of odd that a muscle spasm is how we decide when sex is over. We even use orgasm to decide whether we have had a good time or not.

Women who easily orgasm usually are not concerned with whether this muscle spasm is sex or not. Women who do not have orgasms, or whose partners do not have orgasms, are often preoccupied with orgasm. However, fourteen percent of the women in my survey do not have orgasms. Nineteen percent of respondents don't have orgasms with their partner. This is a significant number. It is important that we don't define sex in such a narrow way. It's also important not to take our own or our partners' orgasm personally.

Orgasm is a function of the nerve and muscle structure. Of course, there are psychological issues as well, but these are complicated by a culture that says orgasm is essential.

If orgasm is difficult and also a focus for you and your lover, this may be a major reason why the flames of sex are dying. There is no reason why either one of you has to have an orgasm to have sex or have fun with sex. There are lots of other things you can do with your bodies. There are lots of ways to stimulate, be stimulated and get excited. When orgasm is not the goal, there is pleasure to be had.

Another way to be creative with sex is to draw straws; the person who draws the short straw can initiate or be responsible for coming up with a new position, sex toy, or idea.

What if you had sex in the bathtub? Sex on the kitchen floor, sex on a countertop, sex in the living room, sex in the hallway, sex down a flight of stairs? Let your teenager out.

Say to your girlfriend, "Let's go out on a date and get turned on." Try to figure out ways you can 'lesbianate' in public. Can you get your finger down her pants at the movie theater? Oversized clothes are great, because you can easily get your hand underneath her clothes and into her pants. If she wears skirts, you can sneak your finger under her skirt at the movie theater or at a restaurant with a tablecloth. It's a good reason to pay another ten bucks for your meal, because you can put your hand underneath the tablecloth and get it up into her vagina. I also know two women who have done this on an airplane with the plane blanket over their laps.

Let yourself dress up as a character in the teen movies that are so prevalent today. Or dress up as the girl in your math class who you wanted to go down on in eighth grade, before you had any idea what sex, much less lesbian sex, was about.

It might be difficult for you if your partner wants you to pretend you're somebody different. You might be scared of her fantasies about other people. You might feel judgmental: "If she wants me to dress up as someone else, she must be wanting to avoid reality." But what's wrong with pretending?

If you'll pretend that you're her eighth-grade girlfriend one night, then the next night she can pretend she's your eighth-grade girlfriend. You could do this. You could make it be fun. You don't have to be competing for this nameless woman she hasn't seen in 30 years. You could just let it be part of the sexual fantasy and energy that is inside each of us—if you're willing.

You could tell your partner before you leave for work, "I'm going to be somebody different when I come home today." Then go to a thrift shop and try a few clothes on. Come walking in as somebody else. It's so scary because we want her to love us just the way we are. We don't want to change anything, and we don't want to have to jump through any hoops. But this can be part of who we are: willing to try on new roles. This is what happens in a new affair. We don't really know who is going to be coming to our door when we are first falling in love with someone. We love this unknown and exciting energy then. Why not bring some into the relationship now?

What if you made a sex date? Not a movie date, not a dinner date with friends, not a date to go shopping. Don't say, "Let's watch television, then afterwards, if we feel like it, we'll make love." Plan to have sex. We can make dates to do other things without fearing it will destroy our sense of spontaneity; try planning sex as well.

Premeditated sex doesn't have to be boring. In fact, planning sex can be fun. We plan to go to the movies, or to an amusement park, or on a long bike ride, and we look forward to it. We call each other up at work and say, "I've got time between 6:00 and 8:00. You want to go out to dinner?"

Why can't we call up and say, "Listen, I have from 8:30 to 10:00 free Thursday night, and I would like to get in your pants. Is that okay with you?" Why do we giggle at the thought?

When we call up and ask our girlfriend out to dinner, she doesn't say, "Don't ask me that. Let's just see if it happens. If we both happen to be in the same restaurant at 6:00, and neither one of us has eaten, and we both have money, and it's open, and we don't have something else to do, then we'll have dinner. But let's not plan it."

So why is it so funny to say, "When shall we have sex? Where? What kind of sex? For how long?"

One of the reasons we have a lot of sex at the beginning of relationships is because we're having a lot of sex. It's true. Because it feels good, we keep doing it and doing it. When people set up sex dates, they often start having more spontaneous sex as well. They remember that sex is fun, and they start making it more interesting. Don't wait for things to get exciting again, because sometimes they won't get exciting again for a long time—like until the next relationship.

I'd like women to start saying to each other, "I would like you to touch my vagina. I would like to suck your nipples. I would like to blow on your ear. I'm sick of watching the people on Dallas do it. I want us to do it ourselves."

Because we're so scared to set up premeditated sex, we wait until it's been three weeks and we're resentful. Then it's hard to ask for sex in a loving way. "You coming to bed, dear?"

"No."

"It's been three weeks and one day, and you haven't come to bed when I've asked you if you're going to come to bed."

"Why are you saying that?"

"No reason. Just happened to notice."

The next night, you walk into the television room with a submachine gun. "Okay, are you going to bed with me tonight or not?"

Why didn't we say in the first week, "You know what, honey? I need a little nooky. There are lots of ways to do it. I have lots of ideas, and if you don't want me to eat you out, that's fine, baby, but I want you to be sucking on my pussy in about half an hour."

We're so afraid of being demanding. We'd rather wait until we're at the machine gun stage. Then we can walk into therapy and say, "Okay, it's been three weeks and two days!"

Try making dates for premeditated sex that you both agree to. That's what your therapist is going to tell you if you ask her, so you'll save yourself a lot of money if you do it on your own. Make a pact with each other that you'll have sex on some particular schedule. Say to each other, "Each month, I need to have sex three times"—or 30 times, or whatever it is for you. Maybe you need to be physically close and connected but not necessarily having orgasms a certain number of times per week or month. Maybe you just need the kind of touching that lets you know you're not buddies or sisters or roommates.

It's okay to start thinking about sex. It's okay to use our brains to create the physical and even spiritual connection that sometimes comes with sex. It's okay to set it up ahead of time. It's scary, because we just haven't been taught to do it.

Premeditated sex is a great way to get out of that couples syndrome of one person always wanting sex and the other always saying no. People say to me, "Well, that doesn't count. Saying it ahead of time, setting up a date doesn't count, because it's not romantic and it doesn't mean that she really desires me. She's supposed to be turned on first."

Who made up those rules? Now, I'm no dope. Of course it's wonderful to have spontaneous sex. It's what our dreams are made of. But that doesn't mean we can't have other kinds of sex, and it doesn't mean spontaneity won't come back. Often after having premeditated sex, the person who had been reluctant to have sex says, "I don't know why I've been saying no. It's so much fun when we do it. It's just that after it's done, the next day, I don't even think about it again, and then I forget how much fun it was."

There are some tricks to remembering. Write a note to yourself, and put it on the refrigerator or on your desk at work. It could be in code at work: 'Remember.' Short and to the point. At home you could be more specific and have it in plain view for you and your lover: 'Remember how great we felt after Saturday night. The wet, the hot, the fun. Let's do it again.'

Put notes all over the house that all say a different word that reminds you about how good you felt. 'Remember.' 'Smell.' 'Fun.' 'Loving.' 'Wet.' 'Sex.'

You could also write in your calendar when you had sex, and rate the encounter. Rating helps us remember that we have different experiences—it's not all hard. Put up gold, silver, purple, red, green, blue stars. Or use one of those wonderful stickers that are available with all kinds of pictures. Make sure each of your sexual encounters with your lover gets acknowledged visually. We have so few reminders in this culture that lesbian sex can really be wonderful, so we have to create those images, those visual helpers.

You may be someone who is visually impaired, or someone who learns better with verbal messages. You may want to make a tape of your lover and you making love. You may want to make a tape of the two of you talking about how you like sex. Make it right after you have made love. With that warm, sweet, exciting energy, communicate why you like to do this. Then you can play this tape occasionally to remind yourself why you like sex and how much feeling is generated by the encounters you have with your lover.

Premeditating sex can also be very helpful for women who are physically challenged. If you're receiving acupuncture, homeopathy, chemotherapy, or other treatments that make you feel ill for a few days, plan to have sex before the treatments. If you have premenstrual syndrome and have a hard time just being on the planet in the days preceding your period, plan to have sex during or after your period. All of us—particularly disabled people—know which times during the day we're most fatigued. Plan sex for a time in which you know that you're going to be at your best. Usually that's not late at night, after the kids are in bed, the chores are done, and you're exhausted.

Sex is supposed to be romantic. She's supposed to want you. But after a while, she doesn't want you. She wants you to pay the rent on time. That's what she's passionate about. Keeping love alive is perhaps our greatest task. Not companionship and camaraderie. Not roommate energy or best friend connection. The love that is difficult—but important—to keep alive is that kind of passion we have for our lovers.

After a while, it's so much easier to become passionate about the things we don't like about each other. But who would want to have sex with someone who is critical? What if we started to tell our partners only the things we love? Try telling your partner the ways she turns you on. Tell her the ways she has touched your body that got you excited. It may have been a long time since she touched you in a way that turned you on. That's okay. Instead of bemoaning the amount of time it has been, just tell her how much you liked it. Tell her something complimentary every day. When you call her up at work to tell her what else to get at the grocery store, say, "Oh, by the way, you know what? Remember that time you slipped your two fingers in my vagina while we were watching TV and we just rocked back and forth? I loved that." Let her in on what you love about her. Remind her that you just love it when she comes up with an analysis of the political situation in the Persian Gulf. Let her know how much you respect her for telling her boss she won't fix his coffee. Tell her how valuable you find her ability to be honest. Too often we forget to say out loud in varied ways how we love our partner.

Often we are afraid of looking like fools. Maybe your partner is not very good at receiving love, and so you've stopped giving her specific examples of how you love her. Maybe you can't receive love very well, so you work at hiding love between the two of you. Keeping love present is a scary proposition.

These ideas are just the beginning. Make a pact with yourself, and then later make a pact with your partner if you want to, that you're going to let go of a sex rule each week. See what it's like to bring something new into sex, to plan sex, to make sure sex happens. Bring your teenager back. And remember to love your child, so that your teenager and grown-up have more of your energy available for sex.

What Do Lesbians Need to Know About AIDS?

You don't get to choose how you're going to die. Or when. You can only decide how you're going to live. Now.

—JOAN BAEZ

What is the story here? Why is JoAnn bumming us out at this point? Why do *we* need to know about AIDS? I thought that was something only gay men and drug addicts get. I think I'll just skip this chapter."

Please read on. We need information to keep ourselves safe. Think what could have happened if only gay men had known what we know now. Because lesbians have the lowest percentage of the population contracting AIDS, we have a unique opportunity to act wisely now, and to keep the incidence of AIDS in our community very low.

Read this chapter with a loving light around you. Make sure you keep breathing, and call a friend if you are scared. Call one of the resources listed at the end of this chapter if you need more information. It is so painful to learn about a disease that has unleashed so many emotions, so much fear and sorrow. We need to engage our minds, however, as well as our hearts.

Many lesbians feel that they are immune to AIDS. We go into denial, saying, "Luckily, this has nothing to do with us." The reality is, AIDS is caused by a tiny virus, and viruses are unaware of sexual preference. They can infect anyone.

Research on AIDS—Acquired Immune Deficiency Syndrome—is proceeding so rapidly that by the time this book is published, some of this material may be outdated. Nevertheless, much is now known about AIDS, and lesbians need this information. My suggestions may sound extreme, but as a sex educator, it's my responsibility to be conservative about this often fatal disease.

What exactly is AIDS? AIDS is a disease caused by a virus called the Human Immunodeficiency Virus (HIV). When the virus enters the bloodstream, it attacks certain white blood cells, called T-lymphocytes. The virus damages the body's immune system and allows otherwise controllable infections—'opportunistic infections'—to invade the body. While the opportunistic infections may be treatable, there is no cure for the underlying immune deficiency that causes them. Most people with AIDS die within two years of diagnosis.

The AIDS virus is transmitted by blood, semen and vaginal secretions. HIV is also found in urine, feces and breast milk, and may be transmitted through these. HIV has been found in very low concentrations in tears and saliva. To date, the virus has not been transmitted through either tears or saliva, and researchers believe the virus probably cannot be transmitted this way.

Originally it was believed that the virus had to enter the bloodstream directly to cause infection, but in recent laboratory studies conducted in test tubes, the HIV virus has permeated mucous membrane cells of the colon and rectum. This research suggests blood contact may not be necessary.

The incubation period for HIV—the period of time between exposure to the virus and manifestation of symptoms—is anywhere between several weeks and seven or eight years. AIDS has only been studied since 1981, and researchers expect the incubation period to be longer as time goes on.

An available blood test can determine fairly accurately whether an individual has been infected with HIV. This test, called the AIDS antibody test, measures the presence or absence of HIV antibodies in the blood. If antibodies are present, the test results are positive and the individual is presumed to be infected (and infectious—that is, capable of passing the virus on to others through the usual routes of transmission). If antibodies are absent, the test results are negative. At that point there are two possibilities: the person has not been infected with the virus, or they have not 'sero-converted' but do have the virus. Sero-conversion is a fancy way of saying that antibodies have not been produced yet.

Some lesbians want to find out if they have been exposed to HIV but there are many concerns women have about this test. Some of the most common will be discussed. Before having the AIDS antibody test, you need to consider: how accurate the results are; how confidential the results are; and what the results actually mean.

Accuracy: As medical tests go, the AIDS antibody test is one of the most accurate ever developed. Nevertheless, there are times when the results might be inaccurate. For example, some period must pass between the time a person is exposed to the virus and the point at which antibodies can be measured in the blood. For most people this period is six to eight weeks. For a few it may be as long as six months. If the antibody test is taken during this 'window' period between the time of exposure and the development of antibodies, the test results may be negative even if a person is infected with the virus. For very few people, antibodies may never develop.

Occasionally test results will be 'false positive,' meaning that the result registers the presence of antibodies, when in fact there are none. This may occur because the test is reacting to the presence of some medication, an illness, or some other oddity of an individual's chemistry. This is *extremely rare*, since all labs will do two and sometimes three different kinds of antibody tests on anyone who tests positive. The results are well over 99 percent accurate if even two different tests have been used.

At the time of this writing, tests for the virus itself (as opposed to the antibody) are complicated, expensive and not entirely reliable, but it is possible that a simple and accurate test for the virus will be developed in the near future. This might allow testing to be even more accurate.

Confidentiality: People with AIDS and those with HIV infection who are not yet ill have experienced tremendous discrimination in employment, access to insurance and housing, use of public services, medical care and many other areas. In addition to the discrimination already documented, some policy makers in state and federal government advocate restrictions on people who carry the AIDS virus. They would like to institute quarantines, prevent these people from holding jobs, or make it illegal for them to have sex, even though there are ways to be sexual and be safe.

For these reasons, most people who have an antibody test do not want their results to be recorded. This is especially true if the test results are positive. But even a negative test result in a medical record might lead an insurance company to refuse coverage, because insurers may worry that such a person might be at risk for contracting AIDS in the future.

In most cases, it's a good idea to be tested anonymously. With anonymous testing, no one records your name, address or phone number. When you take the test you are given a code, and you use that code to receive your results. But even with anonymous testing, the testing agency will usually not give positive results over the phone. If you test positive, workers at some sites may put pressure on you to reveal the names of your current and past sex partners. This usually does not happen in large cities. Understandably, health officials want to inform partners who may be at risk, but this is something you should consider when deciding where to be tested.

In some states, there is no anonymous testing available. While confidentiality is usually guaranteed, confidentiality is not always failsafe. There was a burglary recently in a government office, and one of the items stolen was a list of 500 people with positive antibody tests. As with other sexually transmitted diseases, positive results are always reported to the Centers for Disease Control, but this information does not include the person's name. In Colorado and some other states, positive antibody tests including the person's name must be reported to the state health department. These policies can be dangerous for those who test positive.

Find out before you are tested who will have access to test results. If possible, take the test at a clinic which offers anonymous testing, rather than through a personal physician who might write the results on your chart. You can also give a false name if you cannot get anonymous testing in your area.

What the results mean: A negative test result means one of the following is true: you have not been infected with HIV, or you have been infected with HIV, but have not yet developed antibodies to the virus. Negative results do not mean that you are immune to the disease, so always consider safe sex with partners.

Barring error, a positive test means that you have been infected with HIV and have produced antibodies. You are probably infectious, so you should not share needles, exchange blood (including menstrual blood), vaginal secretions, breast milk, urine, or feces with anyone else.

What is not yet clear is how many people with HIV infection go on to get AIDS or an AIDS-Related Condition (ARC). The statistics, unfortunately, are not very hopeful. By conservative estimates, it appears that at least 50 percent of those infected will develop AIDS or other HIV-related illnesses within five to ten years from the time they were first infected.

Even with all these considerations, some lesbians have decided to take the test. Some feel anxious and want to have information to quell their fears. Others who plan to get pregnant want to know the risk to their yet-to-be-conceived child. Some are already pregnant and are fearful for the unborn child. Still others want to be socially responsible and use safe sex practices if there is a need. You may have other reasons. The results can be helpful for those who test negative. But before taking this test, consider how you might feel if you test positive, even if the chances of this are slight.

Positive test results can be devastating. Many see it as a death sentence, or feel as though a time bomb lives inside their body. Others who test positive for the antibody have experienced great discrimination even if they are symptom-free. They have lost lovers, jobs, housing, friends and families as a result. Many women are uncertain who to tell, and where they can get support. This is especially true for lesbians who may fear being ostracized by their community if they have had sex with a man in the high risk group, or have shared needles. The emotional and economic consequences can be overwhelming.

There are many symptoms of AIDS. If you think you may have the disease, go to a physician who can diagnose the disease. Many of the symptoms of AIDS are also symptoms of other diseases, but in the case of AIDS they are persistent (lasting many weeks or months) and severe. They include fatigue, fever, chills, drenching night-sweats, unexplained weight loss greater than ten pounds, swollen lymph glands, pink or purple blotches or bumps under or on the skin, persistent white spots or unusual blemishes on the face or in the mouth, persistent diarrhea and persistent dry cough.

In 1981, when AIDS was first described, researchers did not know it was caused by a virus. They defined the disease not by the presence of the virus but by the presence of certain opportunistic infections. They decided that, in order to be diagnosed with AIDS, one had to have either Kaposi's sarcoma, pneumocystis carinii pneumonia, or one of several other opportunistic infections. This definition has changed some over the years and is now more expansive.

However, many people who are ill as a result of being HIV positive do not meet the diagnostic criteria for AIDS. These people are said to have AIDS-Related Conditions (ARC). People with ARC generally are not eligible for the same federal, state and local benefits as those with AIDS. Though individuals with ARC may be quite ill, even terminally ill in some cases, they are offered less support than those with AIDS. This arbitrary distinction was necessary when we did not know much about the disease, but today it leads to much suffering. Furthermore, it makes the epidemic look less serious. In June 1987, there were reports of 35,000 cases of AIDS in the U.S. Yet there were an estimated 150,000 additional cases of ARC, which we rarely hear about.

What is known about women and AIDS? As of June 1987, seven percent of people with AIDS in the United States are women. That's about 2500 women (based on June 1987 statistics from the Centers for Disease Control). Half of the women who have AIDS are or were intravenous drug users. Another 29 percent of the women had had sex with men in a high risk group. Eleven percent had had blood transfusions. Some of the remaining ten percent have no known risk factor, which could mean that they died before they were interviewed, they did not want to say what their risk was, or they did not know what it could have been.

It is also important to note that 80 percent of the women with AIDS are women of color. There are a variety of factors that contribute to this statistic, the most influential of which is racism. Women of color have traditionally had limited access to health care services. Because AIDS was initially publicized as a gay, white, male disease, women of color have not sought out AIDS information, and information about AIDS prevention has not been made readily available to them.

It is not known how many women with AIDS are lesbians. Some are probably lesbians, though they most likely have contracted AIDS from some way other than through lesbian sexual transmission.

To date, there are not many cases of suspected lesbian sexual transmission of AIDS. In fact, at this writing (June 1987) only two such cases have appeared in the medical literature. (Sabatini, Patel, and Hirschman. "Kaposi's Sarcoma and T-cell Lymphoma in an Immunodeficient Woman: A Case Report." *AIDS Research* 1: 1984. Marmor, Weiss, Lyden, et al. "Possible Female-To-Female Transmission of Human Immunodeficiency Virus." *Annals of Internal Medicine* 105, no. 6: 1986.)

However, lesbians may be at risk for AIDS. The absence of data on lesbian transmission may reflect an actual low risk; but it might be in part due to neglect of lesbian health concerns, as is typical of the medical establishment.

Historically, lesbians have had a lower incidence of sexually transmitted disease (syphilis, gonorrhea, etc.) than any other group: bisexual people, heterosexuals, and gay men. But we are not immune. Many of us have herpes. Many of us have had syphilis, gonorrhea, trichimonas, gardnerella, or yeast infections. We've passed all kinds of diseases back and forth between our vaginas, our clitorises, our tongues. So it stands to reason that indeed we could pass AIDS back and forth since it is found in blood, vaginal secretions, breast milk, urine and feces.

Which lesbians are at risk? Before I cite the risk factors, I'd like to reiterate that I'm very conservative on this issue. You could certainly be in a high risk group and never contract AIDS. Also, I would like you to breathe; we can only take things in if we are also using oxygen liberally. Keep reading and breathing.

You may be at risk of having AIDS if, since 1978, you have:
- shared needles while using IV drugs;
- had sexual contact with men who were bisexual or gay, were IV drug users, were hemophiliacs, or were known to be infected with HIV;
- had sexual contact with a woman who either uses or has used IV drugs or has had sex with men in the high risk group;
- had a blood transfusion in the United States between 1978 and 1985. By mid-1985, blood banks began screening all donations for the AIDS antibody. (Blood in some other countries might not be screened. In developing countries in partic-

ular, resources for widespread testing of blood donations do not exist); or

- had donor insemination by a donor whose sexual or drug-using history is unknown to you, or is in one of the high risk groups: IV drug users, hemophiliacs, gay or bisexual men.

Most lesbians do not belong in the above list. However, there are a good number of us who do. In 1981, I was donor-inseminated by a man in a high risk group, a gay man in San Francisco, so I am in the high risk group. If you have an unknown partner or a new partner, and you don't know her sex history from 1978, then you should be using safe sex. You might also be at risk if any of your lovers had sex with someone in the high risk group, or even if your lover's lover, or your lover's lover's lover had sex with someone in the high risk group. Your chances of having AIDS under these circumstances is small, since the virus does not seem to be easily transmissable between lesbians. But if you have an unknown partner or a new partner, and you don't know her sex history and the sex history of her partners since 1978, then you should be using safe sex.

I hope everyone will be able to look back in five years and say, "JoAnn, what was your trip?" I do feel strongly about safe sex. I believe it's hard to be *completely* safe unless you have not used IV drugs, have not received blood, and have been monogamous since 1978 with someone not at risk for AIDS. However, testing is very accurate, and many lesbians ask me, "If we get tested and we are negative, then are we at risk for AIDS? Do we have to use safe sex?" If you and your partner have both had negative test results and neither has engaged in any high risk behaviors since taking the test, then you can consider yourself safe.

You must be able to trust your partner, and know what her sex activity was three months prior to and since having the test. If you are secure that she had safe sex, or sex with no one in the high risk group, and her test is negative, then it seems at this writing that you are safe.

The greatest risk for lesbians is probably through intravenous drug use. In some areas of the U.S., about 80 percent of IV drug users have been exposed to the HIV virus. If you use IV drugs, the most effective way to make sure that you don't get AIDS is to stop using IV drugs.

The second best strategy is never to share needles. If you continue to use IV drugs, and share needles, clean them and the syringes with a solution of one part bleach to ten parts water after every use. Flush the needle and syringe twice in the bleach solution, then rinse by flushing twice in water.

You'll probably want to be tested for HIV antibodies if you intend to get pregnant and you have reason to believe you are at risk. A woman who has AIDS or is infected with HIV has a 50 percent chance of passing the disease to her fetus in utero or at birth. This is done through the blood exchanged between the mother and infant, in the uterus or in the vaginal canal. There are also two documented cases of mothers passing AIDS to newborns through breast milk. Therefore, women at risk for AIDS are advised not to breast-feed their babies.

Babies born infected with HIV generally show symptoms of the illness by the age of six to eighteen months. Infants transfused with infected blood in their first year may be clinically well from one to four years before symptoms appear. Pediatric AIDS usually has different symptoms than adult/adolescent AIDS. Children with AIDS often have developmental delays, severe and recurrent bacterial infections that respond poorly to treatment, and a general failure to thrive. These are very sick children. Usual bouts with ear infections or other child-hood diseases do not suggest the presence of AIDS. See a physician if you are concerned. Over the years, innumerable lesbian mothers-to-be have received semen from gay male friends or acquaintances, but the days when we could use gay men's sperm without caution are over. If you're planning donor insemination, you might need to begin by mourning the loss of gay men as relatively hassle-free donors. Many lesbians have said to me, "I'm afraid to use a straight man for the same reasons we didn't want to use straight men years ago: we were worried that they might try to take our kids."

In fact, not all gay men have been exposed to the HIV virus. If you do want to use a gay man as a donor, get all the information you can about his health and his sexual activities since 1978. It's hard to ask someone how they have sex, how often, and with whom. We get a little puritanical. We don't even talk about what we do with each other! But this is important information to have.

Receptive anal intercourse is known to be the riskiest of gay men's sexual practices. Active anal intercourse, receptive oral sex and receptive anal fisting are also very risky. If your potential donor has engaged in these activities, it's important to find out how many partners he has had. Has he had one partner in a mutually monoga-mous relationship for years? Has he had just a few partners? If your potential donor has to use complicated mathematical equations to figure out how many partners he has had, he probably would not make a good donor.

Any potential donor should be asked to take an AIDS antibody test. If he can't get an anonymous test in his town or city, hopefully he can get one nearby. Of course a gay man has all the considerations, if not more, that lesbians do when deciding whether to take the test. The Women's AIDS Network in San Francisco suggests that your donor have two tests, six months apart, before you inseminate. Between his first test and the time you inseminate, he should use safe sex practices. If he has two tests and both are negative, you have the best assurance possible that he does not have the virus. There is still a slim chance that he could have the virus and infect you or the baby—there are no guarantees.

I suggest that you have any donor, gay or straight, follow those guidelines. If you're going through a private physician or a sperm bank, make sure that they have the same guidelines you do for choosing a donor. Talk with them in specific terms about how they choose donors, ask for any and all information they have on your donor, and let them know any additional questions you want answered. Make sure you get the agreement in writing to ensure they are going to back up what they say.

At the time of this writing, there are no documented cases of lesbians infected with HIV through insemination. However, there have been four cases of HIV transmission reported in heterosexual women in Australia after being inseminated with semen from the same asymptomatic virus carrier (a donor who was HIV positive but had no known symptoms of AIDS or ARC).

If you are in the risk group, or are having sex with someone in the risk group, or are unwilling to ask someone her sex history, I suggest you practice safe sex. Lesbians have the opportunity to be ahead of the game; if we practice safe sex now, we won't be saying five years from now, "Yikes! I was at risk after all! I wish I'd been having safe sex too!"

What is safe sex for lesbians? The following information is from the Women's AIDS Network pamphlet on "Lesbians and AIDS."

Safe sex includes massage, hugging, body-to-body rubbing, social kissing (dry kissing), voyeurism, exhibitionism, fantasy and masturbation. French kissing is considered 'possibly safe.' Also considered possibly safe is oral sex with a barrier such as a rubber dam. A rubber dam is what some dentists use to isolate a tooth they're working on. It's a thin, stretchable sheet of latex, sort of like a flat, square condom. To have safe sex, you can put it between your tongue and somebody else's vagina, anus, or clitoris, and lick. The hard part about using the rubber dam is that it is somewhat awkward; it moves. It's small and you have to mark it or somehow remember which side was on your tongue and which side was on her vagina, so you don't inadvertently turn it over and lick her vaginal juices off it. You may want to have several available so if you forget which side is which, you can just reach for another.

Hand-to-genital or finger-to-genital contact is considered possibly safe. To be safe, one should wear latex gloves, or a finger cot, which is a glove for just one finger.

Definitely unsafe for lesbians at risk is blood contact of any kind, including blood from menstruation; IV drug use; or traumatic sex. Traumatic sex is sex which creates cuts or abrasions. This could include fist fucking, rectal or vaginal penetration with something which causes breaks in the skin, and sado-masochistic bondage or discipline which draws blood.

Also unsafe are rimming (which is putting your tongue directly on somebody's anus) and sharing sex toys that have had contact with somebody else's bodily fluids.

Rubber dams are available in dentists' offices. I got my first dams from a lesbian dentist, and she thought safe sex was a fine idea. Dams also come in roll-out sheets that you can cut into whatever size you want. Wrap one around yourself or your lover or both—it could be exciting. They come unflavored and in vanilla, chocolate and mint. Now if somebody could just invent a vagina flavor . . . .

If you're concerned about embarrassing yourself in front of your dentist, don't worry. Your dentist will never know why you are asking her or him for rubber dams, I promise you. You can also order them from a dental supply company. Many of them have toll-free numbers. Ask them to deliver you a box or two. That's what I do. They come right to my office, and the delivery person never says, "Hey, you're not a dentist. What are you getting these for? I'm going to call the CIA!"

A substance called nonoxynol-9, used in some spermicides, has been found to kill the HIV virus in the laboratory. Spermicides are available in drugstores in a cream or jelly form. Straight women use them with their diaphragms. You use this cream smeared in your vagina or on a condom. Try some on your wrist before you use it on your genitals; if you are allergic, it will itch and burn. Another draw-back is that it tastes terrible. Check the level of nonoxynol-9 in any spermicide you're using for AIDS prevention—you want at-least five percent nonoxynol-9. Keep in mind that this offers additional risk reduction, but is not an effective prevention technique on its own.

You might also join the condom bandwagon. Put a condom on your sex toy—vibrator, dildo, or butt plug—and take it off and put a new one on before you use it on your partner. You can also put a condom over your fingers before putting them in your lover's anus or vagina. If you have sex with men, please use condoms all the time. Some condoms are covered with nonoxynol-9 to provide chemical as well as barrier protection.

Latex gloves and finger cots are also available at drug stores and at dental supply stores. Gloves and cots are especially important if you have cuts, scratches, chapped skin, or even hangnails on your fingers. Viruses are tiny.

Luckily, the HIV virus is very fragile once outside the body. It can be killed by almost any good disinfectant, such as soap and water, hydrogen peroxide, rubbing alcohol, or household bleach (one part bleach to ten parts water). Remember to wash all sex toys (unless you're covering them with a condom) and rubber dams. Better yet, don't share sex toys at all.

No one wants to have to worry about getting AIDS, and no one wants to have to start using rubber dams and condoms or thinking about which sex practices are safe and which aren't. Lesbians have already been through enough trauma just figuring out that it's okay to have sex with other women. We shouldn't have to worry about AIDS. But we do, and we need to inform ourselves.

I want to acknowledge that the prospect of no longer exchanging bodily fluids may be devastating. Sex can be exciting without the exchange of bodily fluids, but there's something almost primordial about exchanging fluid. Bodily fluids are an intimate part of ourselves that we only share with selected people, and the sharing of them can create deep bonds. Bodily fluids create life—even if that happens in a Petri dish. Fluids are what we are fed at birth to keep us alive. No longer sharing fluids with another person can be very disturbing.

We must be honest with ourselves about our feelings about this deadly epidemic. We're being called upon to open our hearts even wider to the suffering of other human beings on this planet. We're being called upon to inform ourselves and take appropriate precautions. If we are careful now not to contract the disease, we'll be very grateful in the years to come.

RESOURCES

Organizations

All of the following organizations will give you information confidentially:

Women's AIDS Network: 333 Valencia Street, San Francisco, CA 94103 (415) 864-4376.

Association for Women's AIDS Research and Education (AWARE): (415) 476-4091.

National AIDS Hotline: (800) 342-AIDS.

Books and pamphlets

(Please call or write the sources listed for prices and ordering information):

Mobilizing Against AIDS: The Unfinished Story of a Virus. Institute of Medicine, National Academy of Sciences. Cambridge: Harvard University Press, 1986. Order from Harvard University Press, 79 Garden Street, Cambridge, MA 02138.

This is a thorough review of AIDS in nontechnical language.

Teaching AIDS: A Resource Guide on Acquired Immune Deficiency Syndrome. Marcia Quackenbush and Pamela Sargent. Santa Cruz, California: Network Publications, 1986. (408) 429-9822.

This is a curriculum guide designed for educators working with teenagers. It has clear general information sections and is a good resource for any health educator, teen educator, or other people interested in knowing more.

Women and AIDS Clinical Resource Guide. San Francisco AIDS Foundation, 333 Valencia Street, San Francisco, CA 94103 (415) 864-4376.

This is a collection of technical papers and articles, most from medical journals, relating to women and AIDS.

Lesbians and AIDS. Pamphlet by the Women's AIDS Network in conjunction with the San Francisco AIDS Foundation, 333 Valencia Street, San Francisco, CA 94103. To order, call (415) 861-3397.

This is a simple, excellent brochure which can be ordered in large quantities for distribution. It lists which lesbians are at risk, safe sex practices and answers to questions most commonly asked.

Confronting AIDS: Directions for Public Health, Health Care, and Research. Institute of Medicine, National Academy of Sciences. National Academy Press, 2101 Constitution Avenue NW, Washington DC 20418.

This is a very comprehensive review of technical knowledge about AIDS and recommendations for public policy.

AIDS Safe Sex Kit and Book

The Institute for the Advanced Study of Human Sexuality offers a safe sex kit that includes rubber dams, condoms, adult toy cleaner and two lubricants. It comes in a box with lavendar wrapping. The cost is $19.95, plus $2.50 handling charge. They also offer a book, *The Complete Guide to Safe Sex* (San Francisco: Specific Press). The cost is $6.95, plus $2.00 handling. Checks should be made to The Exodus Trust. Write or call the Institute at 1523 Franklin Street, San Francisco, CA 94109 (415) 928-1133.

Marcia Quackenbush and Cheri Pies read this chapter, adding a great deal of specific information about AIDS. Both of these women helped me sort out my concerns about how to word certain passages, and how to present information about safe sex.

anything. What the compulsive behavior or obsession gets transferred to is not the issue; the issue is how much this behavior alienates us from our emotions.

I sometimes even feel addicted to paper clips. For some reason, I never buy them; but when I get one, I feel very attached. I debate with myself, "Now where should I put this one? Should I put it in my purse? Will it get lost? How about my wallet? No, I'll forget it's there and never use it. I'll put it on my desk, so I know I have it." Then I save that one paper clip, not using it, in case I never get another.

Once we begin to see how much our daily lives are dominated by addictive behaviors, we have the option of becoming willing to let them go. This can be frightening, because our addictions are comforting in their familiarity. What would we do with our time if we weren't acting compulsively? How would we fill our emptiness if not with food and drugs?

The good news is that serenity can replace that frantic need to fill ourselves with a substance or occupy our time with some activity. Serenity comes from allowing a quietness to develop within. Stopping the addictive behaviors does not in itself lead to serenity; we must love and work with the part of ourselves that is filled with fear. Usually, it is a slow process.

In my recent survey, 30 percent of the lesbians considered themselves to be in recovery from drug or alcohol addiction. This figure does not include lesbians who are recovering from food addiction, people addiction, sex addiction, or other addictions.

A recent Los Angeles survey found that 30 percent of lesbians are *currently* addicted to alcohol or drugs. (Rofes, Eric. *I Thought People Like That Killed Themselves.* San Francisco: Grey Fox Press, 1983.) When we add women who now have or have had addictions to food, sex and other substances, it becomes clear that there are many, many lesbians who are in recovery or who are still practicing addicts.

I believe addiction is an epidemic in our culture in general. There is so much pain here that we are willing to use anything to take our pain away. This becomes even more exaggerated in the lesbian community, since we are oppressed by the mainstream culture for our lifestyle. In addition, in most cities, lesbian activities still center around the bars (although this is changing in large cities because so many lesbians are getting sober and are creating other ways of socializing).

The result is that lesbians are profoundly affected by substance abuse; not just the women who are addicted themselves, but also their friends, lovers, family members and children are profoundly affected.

Sometimes it seems as though everyone in the lesbian community is touched by the ravages of substance abuse in some way or another.

Co-dependents are those of us who are engaged in all kinds of ongoing relationships with addicts and recovering addicts. The co-dependent is the woman who has spent her life pleasing others. She believes, consciously or subconsciously, that if she isn't in a relationship, she doesn't have a right to exist. In order to feel good, she must be making someone else feel good. 'I help, therefore I am' is her motto. The popularity of Robin Norwood's book *Women Who Love Too Much* (New York: Pocket Books, 1985) is a testament to the pervasiveness of co-dependence among women. We were raised to put others' needs before our own. I have been in recovery from co-dependence, or people addiction, for eight years. Still, every time I pass a hitchhiker, I feel like I should pick him up. "After all," I tell myself, "I have a car and he doesn't. I should help." I don't do it, but I am tempted to allow a strange and potentially threatening man into my car just because he is there and apparently in need. When the co-dependent goes into recovery, she often feels a great emptiness inside. If she's not helping others, what can she do with her time? Sometimes she even becomes suicidal.

I have known women who feel that their only purpose in life is to help others. In fact, the co-dependent is usually dependent on others for her self-esteem. So when she begins to recover from co-dependence, the conversation goes like this:

"Honey, are you getting up for work today?" Translated: "If you don't get up for work, my friends are going to think I got involved with another alcoholic who doesn't pull her weight."

"Aren't you supposed to stop telling me what to do?" Translated: "Actually, I don't want to go to work at all, but I'd better not tell you, you'll just nag me more."

"Well, sweetie, I know, but it's getting late, and I just thought you might like to know what time it is." Translated: "Stupid idiot, I'm trying to stop telling you what to do, but if you don't do anything right, how am I supposed to keep my mouth shut? Really, I'm afraid my friends will be right."

This dialogue demonstrates the co-dependent's inability to let the alcoholic act like a grown-up. Her fear is that she will look like a fool being involved with someone who can't take care of herself.

To me, getting sober is about becoming serene, becoming peaceful. For instance, I can let my paper clip trip happen for just so long.

Then I tell myself, "Okay, honey, just let the paper clip go. Okay? You've put it wherever you've put it, and it's over. Let's not even think about it again. Next time you get a spare 39 cents, you can go buy a box of paper clips. It will really be okay."

I have to talk to myself like that about many things because I grew up in an addicted home and nobody gave me that kind of everyday, simple, clear information. They were too busy worrying about drinking or keeping someone from drinking.

It is difficult for anyone to give up addiction. Most of us learned our addictive behaviors in childhood. Fifty-seven percent of the women in my survey who were recovering from drug and alcohol addiction were raised in alcoholic homes. These women have been in chronic trauma for years; they don't have any concept of what it's like not to live in a chaotic state. Even if there was no physical abuse in their homes, there was probably tension and stress most of the time during their childhoods. It's so hard for those of us who grew up in those crazy homes to just accept reality for what it is.

People don't get sober because it sounds fun. They do it because they've finally figured out that if they keep using drugs or behaving compulsively, they're going to kill themselves or have a life that's not worth living. It's either sobriety or the morgue. So people usually come to recovery desperate. They are often emotionally drained, physically worn out and spiritually bankrupt.

Women who are in their first year or two of recovery from alcohol, drugs, or other substances and activities are often exhausted. Just getting out of bed, going to work and making dinner may be all they can handle. It's purely physical—the adrenal glands are worn out from having been pumped up by drugs or drama. When the addiction stops, the adrenals, being depleted, take a rest, and the result is fatigue.

Some people in recovery from drug and alcohol abuse lose interest in sex; others trade drug or alcohol addiction for sexual addiction, trying to fill themselves up or repress unpleasant emotions by having lots and lots of sex. Their shy friends will sometimes say, "I wish I could do that too." But it's not as fun as it looks, because sex doesn't fill the empty places inside any better than alcohol, people, food, or cigarettes do. Other women choose other types of compulsions to trade for the addiction they are giving up.

The first thing to expect when you're getting sober is that things are going to be different than they were when you were loaded. The actual activity will not have changed, but your relationship to it will have changed drastically. You will no longer have that fog that separated you from the rest of your daily activity. You will no longer be anesthetized. Work, cleaning your apartment, talking to people, going to parties, taking a bath and sex will all be different. These things get easier the longer you are sober, but they are never the same as when you were under the influence of drugs, alcohol, food, people, etc.

When people talk about being newly in recovery, they often say that the feelings are so overwhelming that they feel like they're in the middle of a cyclone. Feelings that the drug of choice had been holding down for however many years will start to flood into your consciousness. This is why it is so important to get the support of others who are also going through recovery. This can be done in various private or public meetings: therapy support groups; Women For Recovery (meetings of this nationwide group may be in your city); Alcoholics Anonymous; Al-Anon (a group for the family and friends of substance abusers); Overeaters Anonymous; Sex and Love Addicts Anonymous; Women Who Love Too Much support groups; Narcotics Anonymous; Coke Enders—the names are numerous. Choose what works for you. Go even if you don't want to or don't think you need to. Getting off the drug is only the beginning. Then comes the real part, learning how to live.

All kinds of feelings begin to surface:

"I can't believe I started crying right in my boss's office, just because she told me that I needed to speed up a little on the job. She wasn't even mad, she was just telling me what she needed from me."

"Sometimes when I'm driving, I feel like the cars better get off the road. I get so angry over nothing."

"I am terrified that my lover will leave me. She's given me no indication, but I'm afraid she won't be able to tolerate my mood swings."

"I love being sober. I'm sober and clean, and I haven't used any chemicals in five years. I have such a hard time with the happiness I feel. My family is still drinking and miserable. What right do I have to be this happy?"

The changes during recovery are numerous. The rewards are never ending. The first three years of recovery are just a beginning. It takes a while for the physical, emotional and spiritual healing to take hold. After these first three years, there is a long process that entails much work. The recovery process is really a process of learning how to live. It took many years to get where you were when you were loaded; it will take time to change all that programming.

Women who have been in recovery for years are often discouraged. They have worked diligently to stay off their compulsion of choice, and they feel like their support groups are failing them because they still have depression, mood swings, or occasional bouts with wanting to do the behavior or use the drug of choice again. All of this seems unfair after years of being sober. This is common, and can be dealt with by using the tools you have learned in support groups over the years.

Alcoholics Anonymous, Al-Anon and other anonymous programs use the slogan, "One day at a time." This is not just for newcomers, but also for people who have been around for years. Our compulsive behaviors and compulsive use of drugs are insidious. You never know when the sneaky feelings will re-enter your thinking and you will want to use, just to feel that sense of abandon again. The problem is, it's not the caboose that kills you, it's the engine. The first drink, joint, needle, piece of chocolate cake, cigarette, cut on the arm, or inappropriate affair is what starts the destructive cycle. If you can *not* do it just for today, you have a chance to live.

The recovery process is similar for alcoholics, drug addicts, food addicts, self-mutilators, anorexics, bulimics, compulsive gamblers, sex addicts, compulsive spenders, co-dependents and many others you can name. The questions seem to be the same no matter what the compulsive behavior: How can I go to parties? What will I do when I feel frustrated or overwhelmed? How can I get by being conscious all the time? When lesbians I work with get into recovery, the issues that surface are myriad.

Communication in intimate relationships seems to be the hardest change. What do I do when my lover and I get in a fight? What do I do if she wants sex and I don't? What do I do when her parents take us out to dinner? What do I do when I feel like hurting myself? How do I tell her when I'm angry, sad, or scared? How can I tell her I want to drink again when we are both trying to recover?

This process of changing communication patterns is very tedious. Instead of withdrawing when a feeling surfaces, women in recovery start to learn how to express those emotions. If the feelings remain buried, frustration and resentment will eventually build to the point where there is no way to keep them down. This often results in mood swings from depression to anxiety. With compulsive behavior or drug use gone, the feelings seem explosive.

Feelings of excitement and joy often come with recovery. These feelings were often too scary in the past, and so a drug was used to stop the feeling. In recovery, the passion returns: passion for loving, for work, for recovery meetings, for healing oneself.

"I never let myself get this excited about anyone or anything before sobriety. I was always terrified of my energy. It seemed to push through my body, beyond my control. When I took drugs, the fear disappeared."

"You and me both. I stopped starving myself, and I had no idea what feelings were underneath my compulsion to stay thin. I can't even look at a regular old tree without crying sometimes."

Body image often changes drastically in recovery as well. Many women with compulsions have a distorted image of their body. This is true for women who are addicted to food as well as those addicted to self-mutilation, drugs and other things. Compulsiveness takes us away from our sense of self. When we enter into recovery, the body comes into focus once again.

Women who stop food addiction often lose weight. This can be frightening. Self-mutilators often have a bizarre sense of their bodies since it is the vehicle through which the compulsive behavior is expressed. They may find in recovery that their body is not the enemy they thought it was. They may find themselves ashamed of their previous abuse of their bodies. Women on drugs often have an unrealistic sense of themselves that extends to their bodies.

I have a friend who is a recovering alcoholic/addict. Once, when she was still using, she bought herself a pair of flip flops. She wore them around for a while and then gave them to me. Her foot was at least four sizes larger than mine, and they fit me perfectly. She was completely out of touch with how big her body was. We all hooted at the time, but later in recovery, she was horrified to recall how little she had known about her body.

In sobriety, our homophobia frequently comes to the surface. The substance abuse that used to cover that particular self-hatred is no longer available, so it becomes painfully apparent. Once the fog clears, we may begin to admit for the first time that we are in fact lesbians, or that we have been trying to drown our own homophobia with alcohol or other drugs.

Recovering addicts also experience a strong fear of change. I recently made plans to buy food at a grocery store and make dinner with a friend who's a recovering alcoholic. When we arrived at the store, I realized there was a good restaurant right down the block.

"I'd rather go to the restaurant," I said.

She was freaked out. "Oh, my god. Go to a restaurant now? I thought we were going to go home and cook. What do you mean?"

"I mean I want to change our plans and go to the restaurant."

"But we'd agreed to cook!" Addicts usually have the picture all set out. We're already at the end of the evening, or at noon the next day. And then the plans change suddenly. "What do you mean? The evening was already over. And you're changing it now? It's over. You can't change it because I'm already at tomorrow morning."

Of course if *she* had wanted to change plans, I might have been equally unnerved. My people addiction was no less debilitating, and my recovery is equally slow. People in recovery feel very brittle, as if they're on a narrow ledge. For once, they can walk a straight line, and they feel afraid that one more change will threaten their balance.

It's during recovery—even two or three years after the substance abuse has stopped—that memories of sexual abuse sometimes start to surface. Of the women in my survey who were raised in alcoholic homes, 50 percent were sexually abused as children. Fifty percent! That's a staggering statistic. In other words, of the women in my survey who were raised in alcoholic homes, one in two were sexually abused. Women who were raised in alcoholic homes frequently become alcoholics themselves; so quite often, women in recovery are also dealing with first-time memories of sexual abuse.

Our addictions often serve to cover up things that were too painful for us to fully face as children. In an odd way, it's lucky that we have this ability to keep things down until we're able to deal with them. For those of you who are in early recovery and who have just started to have these memories and feelings, it's very important that you simply keep believing yourself. The hardest thing for those kids was that people didn't believe them. Start by showing yourself a little mercy now.

Alcoholic families have other dysfunctions that put the offspring at a disadvantage when they grow up. Blurred boundaries abound. Probably the biggest question is: who are the children and who are the adults in the family? Too often, the children have been caretakers of their parents. There are many more compulsions that keep the alcoholic family engaged in drama: workaholism, over-eating, money, over-achieving, compulsive cleaning, sex addiction, gambling and others. You name it, an alcoholic family has tried it, and tried it, and tried it.

In my family, we had plenty of money, but bill-paying was still a major drama. Were they going to pay the heating bill? Were they going to pay the telephone bill? Not a month went by when those simple tasks didn't become elevated to the status of major quarrels. Whether someone spilled the dog food or my mother had to go to the hospital, the events were given equal weight.

I was an adult before I realized that in other houses, when someone spills the dog food, people just say, "Woops, the dog food spilled," and they clean it up.

In my house, my mom would yell, "You spilled the dog food! I can't believe you spilled the dog food! Do you know how much dog food costs?" Then my dad would enter into it. "My god! JoAnn spilled the dog food? Where'd she spill it? Didn't she spill the dog food last week too?" They could go on for hours.

I hadn't spilled it down a well, of course, just on the floor. I could pick it up—even put it back in the bag. But that didn't matter. It was still a crisis. It kept us all occupied so we didn't have to talk, or feel our feelings. Or be bored.

If you were raised in an alcoholic home, you'll need to learn that life is simple. Watch reruns of *Leave It To Beaver* to find out what normal life is like. It's boring. Beaver says, "Hi Mom, hi Dad." They mow the lawn. They go to work. They make peanut butter sandwiches for lunch. That is how life is for most people. It's not really a big deal.

I am not saying we should emulate the Cleavers. I'm just suggesting that life can be a simple process. People get bored with each other, and they don't call a lawyer. Now if June Cleaver were an alcoholic, she'd be saying, "I'm bored to death! Get me out of this relationship! I can't stand it. Where do I sign?"

If her lawyer were also an addict, he'd say, "You're bored? Oh, my god! I'm coming right over to divorce you immediately."

Boredom is not a bad thing. It's just what happens. In recovery, we have to work against our impulses to make life very complicated.

This extends even to long-term sobriety. Many women have to continue to make conscious choices to keep their lives uncomplicated after many years of recovery. This is not something that changes quickly. Women who have been sober four to nine years often talk about the difficulty of continuing a life of honesty, humility and action, which are essential in the recovery from compulsions.

There are many activities that lesbians need to relearn in recovery. The following information is written with sexual recovery in mind, since it is so rarely talked about. This process may be transferred to many other types of activities, so try to apply this information to other areas of your recovery as well.

Sex changes for many women in recovery. I did a survey in 1984 at a conference for recovering lesbian alcoholics and co-dependents. Ninety-five percent of the 287 recovering alcoholics/addicts answering the survey said that their sex life changed when they became clean and sober. Often what that change means is: no sex, no how, no way, with nobody. Most (62 percent) went through a period of celibacy during the first year. Recovering addicts are often terrified of sex because they have never had sex except while on drugs of one sort or another.

Many women in recovery haven't been sexual for a long time. If this is so for you, and you want to be sexual, you'll have to reteach yourself. You'll have to be willing to be sexual, even if your alcoholic family taught you to be scared, even if you don't have information, even if you've never done it this way before. You probably learned how to do things while under the influence of drugs—like pick up women in bars—that you'll feel very shy about doing sober. You may feel a lot of pain at losing that self who was so easily sexual, so easily able to let go of inhibitions.

Your opportunity now is to get to know this new, sober self. Begin a love affair with yourself. I recommend that women in recovery start with masturbation. Pick up where you left off—at age thirteen, or whenever you started using drugs. Learn to know your own responses again. Then practice being intimate with another person.

Taking it slowly—with yourself, and with another person—may sound ridiculous. You may be thinking, "Who, me? Start at the beginning? Are you kidding?"

I'm not kidding. All of us want to be comfortable and excited about sex. We want it to be natural and easy, just like in the movies. But this isn't the movies. The truth is, you may need to go very slowly in order to take care of your new, sober self who in fact feels very unsure and afraid.

Be willing to talk about sex with your other recovering friends. I mean details: fingers, vaginas, boredom, excitement, turn-on. Imagine this teenager who's loose with her other teenaged buddies, and they're being sexual with each other, and they're telling each other all about their sexual adventures.

Be willing to tell the truth. For some of us, telling the truth is a new experience, and we have no idea how to do it. And to tell the truth about sex? Yikes! One of the areas of telling the truth that impacts our sexual relationships and those of our community is whether we are at risk for AIDS, and whether we are using safe sex. This adds a whole new level of honesty to any sexual relationship.

Those of us who were raised in alcoholic homes were taught that it's better to get bored with sex and stop having it than to try to talk about it or do anything to change it. That's certainly what I was taught. No one said it verbally, but the message came through. Rather than discuss sex, or love, or intimacy, we would argue about things like who was on the *Merv Griffin Show*.

"I'm sure it wasn't Arlene Dahl. Do you think it was Arlene Dahl, JoAnn?"

"I don't even know who Arlene Dahl is, Mom."

"Well, I don't think it was her on *Merv Griffin*. I don't know who it was, but it was not Arlene Dahl."

This is life in an alcoholic family.

So if sex is boring, the last thing you probably want to do is tell your partner. You'd probably much rather create a commotion over dog food or *Merv Griffin*. But the reality is, your partner already knows that the sex is boring. She is probably bored too. If you talk about it, then you give yourselves the opportunity to make it interesting.

When we begin to tell the truth, we have no idea how things will evolve. We may withdraw, or we may initiate the deepest conversation we've ever had with our lover. She may react with her own fear, or with compassion, or with nonchalance. Truth can turn boredom into something very interesting. All that's required is that we be willing to risk experiencing something new and unpredictable.

Telling the truth about boredom is just a beginning. Eventually you'll learn to tell her that you like anal sex. Or that you like oral sex. You'll learn to tell your partner you're a former intravenous drug user, and therefore need to use safe sex practices to protect her from AIDS. You'll learn to tell her you feel terrified of sober sex. Or that you feel attracted to her. She may not tell you all of her sexual truths, but you will still benefit by revealing some of yours. You don't have to say everything at once; practice revealing a little bit at a time. You may be amazed to find that the earth does not stop turning.

It's particularly difficult to ask for what we want in sex because we're not supposed to talk about sex in the first place. We're not even supposed to be having sex. We're certainly never supposed to act as if sex is as normal as going to the laundromat. If you or your partner are in recovery, and someone wants to change the things you do sexually, watch out. Remember what it was like when I wanted to go to the restaurant instead of shopping for groceries?

So what do you do? What if she's slobbering on your clitoris and you hate it? How about just telling her, "Please don't slobber on my clitoris"? I had a therapist once who said, "You can be scared and still do what you need to do." It was an amazing concept to me at the time. I used to think that if you were scared you had to stop. That's what I had been taught: you get scared, you stop in your tracks, you survey the situation, you figure out how to get out of it.

The reality is, you can be scared and still ask somebody out on a date. You can be scared and still be sexual with your partner. You can be scared and still masturbate. You can be scared when you ask for what you need in sex. You can be scared and say, "You know what? I like to use a vibrator because it gets me more excited." Or you can say, "That kind of pressure on my clitoris isn't hard enough." Or "I don't like you to touch my clitoris. It's too sensitive and it freaks me out." Usually we just give the message nonverbally instead, scooting our bodies around on the bed, trying to avoid her fingers or tongue. The problem with this technique is that your lover may end up feeling like you don't like her, or don't want to have sex with her at all.

Try saying, "I'm scooting around like this because you're touching my clitoris directly and it's too much." Imagine the relief for your partner if you told her that. Imagine the relief for you to not have to worry, "Is she going to touch me that way? And how am I going to have to scoot tonight?"

Often a co-dependent person has never experienced sexual pleasure for herself—only through pleasing another person. So when she decides to put her own needs first, she may find herself at a loss, especially in bed. How can she tell her lover not to touch her that way, or not to make love to her at all, if she can't even pass by a hitchhiker? I still have to give myself a little pep talk before I say, "Please don't put that finger that you had in my asshole into my vagina. Bad infections can start that way." Sometimes I tell a lover I don't like the way she's touching me, and her feelings get hurt. That's enough to make me stop wanting to have sex for a long time. But I keep telling the truth, and keep honoring my own needs, because the only other alternative is to go back to my old co-dependent behaviors in which I took care of everyone else and neglected myself. I'd rather feel scared and healthy than numb and addicted.

While other people in recovery are trying desperately to get sexual feelings back, the sex addict is trying to curb her sexual appetite. She has to learn she is worthwhile even if she is not having sex. She has to stop proving she is a good lover. She has to learn she can be loved without flirting, can be appreciated out of bed.

Like other addicts, the sex addict must learn to love herself. Some sex addicts decide to be celibate for a while. Others decide to refrain only from the particular form of sex that had become compulsive for them: masturbation, pornography, one-night stands. Not having sex can be very difficult and can bring up great wells of sadness, anger and fear. This may be very surprising.

The sex addict's task is to explore what purpose sex has served for her. Has it been a way of avoiding feelings? Has it helped her feel important or loved? By being honest with herself about the role sex has played in her life, and by abstaining from sex for as long as she deems appropriate, the sex addict can eventually have sex again without having her self-worth depend on it. As with other forms of recovery, the process may be a long one.

Sober sex is quite thrilling. You can remember her name. You remember what you did the night before. You remember how the two of you got into bed together. You know what you like about how you make love together. You didn't throw up in her car. You don't wake up with a headache or a sense of regret and dread. These are only a few of the benefits of sober sex.

In sobriety, you have more of an opportunity to enjoy the sensations in your body, and your particular connection with this woman. You are able to feel her skin, and feel her touching your skin. You can actually remember how she likes to have you stimulate her body. You can tell her what you want done to your body. You don't have to pretend anymore. You don't have to pretend that this sex will fill either of you up.

You can feel happy, sad, scared and angry, all at the same time or in rapid succession. The important aspect of sober sex is that you are being your real self, maybe for the first time. This new self may feel like a pretender, but that person you became under the influence was the fake.

Sober sex offers an opportunity to have a real experience with a real other person, to let in your real feelings, to accept her attention. You can do it for a short period if that is all you can handle. You can go on all night if that feels right. This is a time when you can open up with the intimate touch of another woman, and allow your hidden, magical, true self to blossom.

Recovery from addiction is a process that lasts a lifetime. The most important part of recovery is the abstinence. In itself, this is a challenge. To go beyond that and reclaim one's emotional and sexual health can be even more difficult, especially in a culture that encourages us to anesthetize ourselves and lie to ourselves and each other. Sex in recovery is bound to become easier and less scary. Recovery is about the ability to change your life, and you can change your sex life as well.

When you're relearning how to be sexual while in recovery, be gentle with yourself. Love the little girl who probably didn't learn that it's okay to make mistakes and be needy, and tell the teenager that her sexual energy is welcome now. Practice being sexual with yourself and with someone you trust. Try doing things differently, even if it's frightening. Tell the truth about how you feel and what you want. The possibilities are endless. We can feel the love inside. We can have access to that life force of sexuality, and we can be sober. We can be free of wanting to get out of wherever we are. It can be a thrilling experience. Just try it. Just try it for five minutes at a time.

After Incest: The Road to Recovery

So long as little children are allowed to suffer there is no true love in this world.

—ISADORA DUNCAN

Children are such precious beings, I can't imagine how adults could hurt them. How could anyone take advantage of a tiny person, so young and so vulnerable? I wonder how an adult who is responsible for the survival of a child can jeopardize the well-being of that child with sexual abuse. And how can a very little, innocent being survive the onslaught of sexual violence? How can a heart survive such abuse?

Incest is staggering to contemplate. If you were sexually abused as a child, you're not alone. Childhood sexual abuse has occurred throughout the ages in every part of the world, every class, and every racial group. The stories range from being sexually abused by a relative one time to being raped by a father every night for years. Situations vary from everyone in the family being part of the abuse to no one knowing but the child and the abuser. The memories vary from being quite vivid to being only a hazy remembrance of degradation. Many women believe that, since they survived, they couldn't have had it so bad.

At a recent workshop for incest survivors, I asked the women to arrange themselves in a semi-circle, with the chair on one end of the circle representing the worst story of abuse, the chair on the other end representing no real story, and each chair in between representing a step on the continuum. Three quarters of the women in the room arranged themselves in positions ranging from no real story to a story in the middle. One woman bravely sat in the worst story seat. A few other women were sprinkled along the section reserved for middle stories to bad stories. It was not surprising, but it was heartbreaking to see these women describe the abuse in their lives as really not much at all. If what happened to them were happening again in the life of a child they knew today, they would undoubtedly call the police; yet many applied a different standard for the child they once were and the suffering she experienced.

In my survey of 1566 lesbians, 38 percent said they had experienced childhood sexual abuse, either from a family member or a stranger, before the age of eighteen. In her book, *The Secret Trauma* (New York: Basic Books, 1986), Diana Russell reports the same statistic—38 percent—from her random sample of 930 women.

Though my survey was not a random sample, I think it's interesting that the two statistics match exactly. It leads me to believe that lesbians are *not* more likely to have suffered childhood sexual abuse than the general population. This is especially important because lesbian survivors often hear, "Oh, you're an incest survivor? That's why you're a lesbian."

You may have even said to yourself, "If that man hadn't raped me, I wouldn't be a lesbian." Childhood sexual abuse may have had a profound effect on you, but in most cases, that's not why you're a lesbian. If that were true, all of those women in Diana Russell's study—38 percent of all women—would be lesbians.

If almost 40 percent of lesbians are incest survivors, then at some point in her life, almost every lesbian will be affected by childhood sexual abuse. As a lesbian, if you weren't abused yourself, you're very likely to come across a partner who was. That's why talking about childhood sexual abuse and incest is so important in the lesbian community. Heterosexual women are less likely to have partners who were sexually abused as children, since only about 25 percent of boys are sexually abused. (Kepler, Victoria. *One In Four: Handling Child Sexual Abuse.* 1982. Reprint. Wooster, Ohio: Social Interest Press, 1984.)

Let me make a brief aside about terminology. Lately the word 'survivor' has frequently replaced the word 'victim' in reference to women who experienced incest. Many women like to call themselves survivors as an affirmation of what they have accomplished since the violence was perpetrated. They've been through an intense, awful experience, and here they are walking around, working a job, raising children. Other women, after all, have not survived—they were killed or later killed themselves. Survivors like to feel powerful in the aftermath of a situation in which they felt powerless.

Yet the truth is, many women still feel like victims. Some survivors get very elitist. "I've worked on this, and I'm a survivor, and you shouldn't be a victim." But I think it's important not to make those women feel wrong for identifying more with the word 'victim' than 'survivor.'

The women in my survey identified the perpetrators of their abuse as follows: father (34 percent); older male relative (30 percent); male stranger (20 percent); sibling (20 percent); mother (8 percent); male lover/partner of mother (7 percent); female stranger (2 percent); older female relative (2 percent); same age female relative (1 percent); female lover/partner of mother (1 percent). Keep in mind that people could answer yes in more than one category, so the numbers don't add up to 100 percent. Some women were abused by both women and men.

I also asked when the abuse happened, again allowing room for women to answer yes in more than one category. Thirty-two percent of the women said they were under five years old when they were molested. Sixty-six percent of them were between the ages of five and ten. Fifty-five percent said they were abused between the ages of eleven and fifteen. Twenty-three percent were between the ages of sixteen and eighteen.

The age at which the abuse happened is an important part of the information gleaned in my survey. Many women feel they were responsible for the abuse that was perpetrated against them. Partly, this is developmental. When we are children we believe we are omnipotent, all powerful. That is why, for instance, children often feel they are responsible for the divorce of their parents. Children believe they are the center of the universe. If that universe includes sexual abuse, they believe they are responsible for that as well. Children at these young ages *cannot* be responsible for the abuse. They have no power; they are not capable of creating situations of violence and assault.

Even for teenagers who found that sexual abuse was a way to get some attention, there is still no excuse for sexual abuse being perpetrated against them. Adults need to be in control of their impulses; children and adolescents are not responsible for keeping the grown-ups under control. No matter what traditional psychoanalysts say about the Oedipal complex and young girls wanting sexual attention from their fathers, fathers have no right to violate and abuse their daughters. No adult has the right to be sexual with children.

I also asked women in my survey how often the abuse happened. Nineteen percent of the respondents said that the abuse happened one time. Thirty-three percent said that it happened "a few times." Twenty-five percent said that it happened "several times." Twenty-three percent said that it happened frequently.

These numbers may help you feel less isolated. No one likes to think that she's the only one whose father raped her every night of the week, or that she's the only one who feels traumatized by a single incident. Whether your abuse was frequent or infrequent, there are other women who had similar experiences.

I also learned that there is a correlation between early sexual abuse and adult rape. Twenty-seven percent of the women who were sexually abused under the age of eighteen were also raped as adults. Only eight percent of the women who were not abused as children were raped as adults. That's a major difference.

Russell had similar findings in her research. She reported that 65 percent of incest survivors were raped by non-family members after the age of fourteen, while 36 percent of those women who were not incest survivors were raped after the age of fourteen. (Other research has been done on why women who have been sexually abused in childhood have a high incidence of victimization later in life. Finkelhor and Browne. "The Traumatic Impact of Childhood Sexual Abuse: A Conceptualization." *American Journal of Orthopsychiatry* 55, no. 4: 1985.)

Before you jump to conclusions and say, "See? That proves I'm wrong, I'm bad, I'm dirty," let me say that these numbers do *not* mean that you are responsible for the sexual violence either as an adult or a child. Judging from my private practice, I think there's a higher rate of adult trauma among those abused as children because we treat ourselves as grown-ups the way we were treated as children. For instance, children who grew up in alcoholic homes are more likely to become alcoholic, because they learned to cope with life by drinking. (There may also be genetic factors, but certainly some of the behavior is learned.) If you were sexually abused as a child, you were not adequately taken care of. You were not taught that you could ask for or receive protection from the adults around you. Because you did not experience safety, you didn't learn that you could set boundaries and limits. You didn't know that you could say no. You didn't know that you had a right to protect yourself. Those of us who grew up in dysfunctional homes don't believe that we have very fundamental rights. Growing up with this internalized hatred, the incest survivor tends to believe that she is not worthy of protection or, in extreme cases, that she deserves to be sexually abused. Of course, no woman deserves to be abused sexually or in any other way.

Some women have learned how to 'leave' their bodies when in dangerous situations. They go 'dead,' can't feel anything, and can't think; they certainly have no ability to protect themselves when in these situations. Many women report watching their own sexual abuse as if from somewhere else in the room. It's as though their real selves floated out of their bodies and watched what was taking place from a safe distance. Others report coming out of a fog sometime long after the abuse took place and not remembering anything. Our minds are endlessly creative when we need to survive trauma.

Sometimes, an incest survivor comes to believe that her only valuable asset is her body. She may then put herself in situations in which she is again vulnerable to sexual assault, seeking love or a sense of self-worth through sexual abuse. This is an unconscious attraction for what is familiar—not fulfilling, just familiar.

I don't know all the reasons for an increased incidence of adult assault, but, in any case, you weren't responsible for either the early abuse or for the rape. There is nothing a woman can do to deserve rape or abuse. Women tend to believe that any trauma they suffer is their own fault, and the world tends to support that view. After all, this lets all men off the hook. There is nothing a person can do that justifies another human hurting them.

Women who have suffered, and continue to suffer, sexual trauma can break out of the cycle. It is not easy. This phenomenon is similar to the vicious cycle in which women who are physically abused often find themselves. One must begin by admitting that abuse is taking place. The next step is to use behavioral modification programs to stop your part of the abuse cycle, learning how to judge a situation as potentially dangerous, learning how to say no, learning how to leave. Once you have those tools, you can work with a therapist to help increase your self-esteem. This takes a good deal of effort, and sometimes takes a long time. Don't give up. You are worth it. You deserve safety and well-being.

You do not have to heal from childhood sexual abuse alone. You are joined by 40 percent of the women around you. There is a tremendous bond in numbers. You are not dirty, bad, or unsalvageable. Just because this is your history, just because you feel you have no tools for survival, does not mean you have to give up on that precious self inside you. Even if you do not find yourself precious, others will. You can find a circle of women who are willing to support you through the process of change.

Many incest survivors have a hard time reconciling that sexual trauma could have even happened to them. Often, women completely repress the memories for years. I was recently talking with Cassandra Dills, a social worker, who works with incested children through Child Protective Services of San Mateo County, California. She has found that even being identified by social services does not guarantee that children will stay aware of the incest. In Dills' experience, children who do remember the sexual trauma are those who have been in group or individual therapy dealing specifically with the incest at the time of its discovery. Even when a child and her family go through having the abuse reported, if the child has not had therapy at that time, within one year she will have completely repressed the memory of the sexual assault. So if you're having difficulty remembering exactly what happened many years ago, you might be comforted to know that this phenomenon is common.

Recovering memory is not easy. I have often worked with women for two years in therapy before they begin to remember their sexual abuse. We all work hard at protecting our parents or the grown-ups who raised us. Our work now is to uncover that system of protection. The underlying fear is that if we no longer protect our parents, then we will have to accept that the abuse really took place, and that realization will increase our sense of worthlessness. We must deal with the fact that our parents did not protect us as children. We must deal with our anger and hatred of people who have abused and neglected us. This is not easy for any of us.

Peeling away this layer of protection is a delicate process. You may find that you need to do this so slowly that it seems as though your feet are stuck in concrete. Take as long as you need to; there is no race. It will probably help to be in a survivors' group or in a therapy situation, to have support for this child who fears revelation. Take seriously any memory you have. You can also use the information in your dreams and visions. Your memories will come slowly. Eventually they will come more clearly. The more you believe yourself, the stronger the memories will be. Support your child within. Act as if a small child is coming to you with this information. Would you shrug this child off and act as though she were making this up? Of course you would not. Children don't have the ability to make up stories like these.

Remember that adults can, do, and indeed have done anything and everything to children; the culture does little to stop them.

It is essential that this information be used toward healing, not despair. For this reason, therapy with a counselor who is knowledge- able about sexual assault can be helpful. Your counselor should be able to help you turn the information into grist for lessons, not fuel for self-hatred.

Trust is a major issue for incest survivors. There is usually a great sense of having been betrayed both by the perpetrator of the violence, and also by the other parent, who didn't offer enough protection. Many clients have said to me, "My father would come into my room every night," or "My mother would touch my breasts and genitals with everyone in the family standing right there," or "My mother would drop me off at my grandfather's house. I found out recently that my grandfather had molested my mother too, yet she left me in his care." Some clients have told me that their brothers had sex with them; when they told their parents, the parents didn't do anything.

"Don't bother us," they said. "It's just child's play. No big deal."

Many mothers claim ignorance of their child's assault. I can see why it's difficult for women to believe that their mothers didn't know what was going on. I have a five-year-old and I always know where he is. When he comes home from somebody else's care, I know if he's upset. Even if I lived in a mansion, I would know if someone were in my child's bedroom at night. It may be very painful to come to terms with the fact that a family member didn't protect you.

Think of a child you know. Imagine someone sexually abusing that child, and the other adult in the house not taking care of her. The only logical response would be for the other adult to say, "You can't do that anymore, and in fact, you fucker, I'm leaving you, and I'm taking the baby!" But most moms, dads, or other family members in charge didn't do that. Some of these caretakers had been sexually abused as children themselves. If they were women, they had been oppressed by a culture that told them they were worthless, powerless and necessarily dependent on men.

They were disabled by numerous addictions as well that helped them to live in a realm of denial.

I've heard many women say, "I'm sure it's my fault. My father wasn't that bad." "My aunt couldn't have done that to me. I must have done something wrong." Or they say, "I liked it. It was the only love and affection I got. I initiated it, so I'm responsible."

If you have friends who are mothers, you can ask them, "Could your kid say no to sexual innuendos or advances from somebody she knows and trusts?" You may be amazed to find out that there's no way a child could say no under those circumstances. Moms complain a lot about kids saying no, but the truth is, a kid can't say no unless someone is willing to listen to no. Children kick and scream a lot, but you can always overpower them, either verbally or physically.

I have heard stories along the lines of, "I said no and then my uncle stopped." There are those rare cases. Even so, the perpetrator stopped only because he was willing to. It wasn't because the kid had power. Kids don't have power. When a child is abused in her own home, she has no power to change that reality unless an adult decides to do so.

There is no way you could have behaved that would have made you deserve sexual abuse. Children deserve the protection of the adults around them. They deserve to know that they are safe with their parents and the adults their parents invite into the home. They have a right to be treated with loving respect. They need to be taught that they have a right not to be touched in ways that make them feel uncomfortable.

Think about how children will eat anything. When a baby is tiny, you have to teach her not to put poisonous or dangerous things into her mouth. You have to teach children not to touch hot stoves. You have to teach children how to cross the street safely. You have to watch children playing near water. Children are helpless little beings who have to learn absolutely everything. They don't know what to eat; they don't know what to touch; they don't know what to expect of the world. They are completely dependent on the grown-ups around them to teach them about the world. The trust children develop is directly dependent on the trustworthiness of the adults around them.

Women who enjoyed the sexual abuse speak of it in many ways: "My body betrayed me. I would get sexually aroused, and I hated myself and him for it." "I often felt turned on when he came into the room." "I still get excited about incest fantasies. I think that's sick."

These are common reactions. Women who have been raped are often similarly disturbed by the fact that their bodies were aroused. Our bodies respond on a level that has little to do with intellect.

Keep in mind that most of the pornography in this country is based on the subjugation of women. Many of us have learned to link subjugation and arousal in our subconscious. Thus, a woman's own domination may feel erotic to her, though in fact she does not wish to be dominated or abused. Even if you did like the abuse, or did initiate it, you still had a right to get love and affection another way.

Girls who have been abused often confuse violence and sex, or love and sex. They sometimes grow up to be women who avoid sex because they associate it with degradation and shame. Or they may grow up to be women who have a lot of sex, because that is the only way they can feel they're worthwhile and loved. It is a rare incest survivor who has no residual effects in her adult sex life from the early trauma. It's devastating to have one's first experience of sex be at a very young age, with an adult. It can lead to all sorts of confusion, pain and self-hatred. The early trauma also affects the survivor's ability to be intimate on nonsexual levels. If your trust has been betrayed at an early age, it can be difficult to trust again.

An incest survivor may experience times of great intimacy; then, feeling out of control, she may pull away. Non-incest survivors do this too, but the incest survivor's fear of betrayal makes intimacy particularly difficult. Yet in my survey, women who were abused as children reported being as satisfied with their sex lives as those who weren't.

When comparing the number of times in a month childhood sexual abuse survivors masturbate or have partner sex with those who were not abuse survivors, the numbers are almost identical.

This information offers hope for incest survivors, especially those who are not currently having sex with themselves or others. As more healing takes place, your sex life can be as satisfying and as frequent as that of those women with no abuse in their history.

This information also helps survivors to not blame all sexual dysfunction on the sexual abuse. Though we will always be the survivors of abuse, many of our problems as women and as lesbians are universal.

Many sexual abuse survivors received the message, verbally or nonverbally, that they should deny their tender feelings, their child selves. "Take that kid away from here," one of your parents may have said to the other. One of the major ways to heal sexual abuse is to honor the inner child with a broken heart. Imagine holding her on your lap, creating a safe environment for her.

When people start to uncover their hurt little child, they often immerse themselves in her sorrow and despair. That's a valuable beginning, but at a certain point it's important to see that inner child as someone who is inside of you, not who you are. The child is only a part of you. She may be suffering, but you have suffered enough. Try to love her instead of suffering with her.

This can be difficult to do. When we have friends or relatives who are chronically or even terminally ill, it's difficult to say to ourselves, "I get to have fun, even though so-and-so is sick or dying." It's doubly hard to do this when we discover that the person who is sick, needy, or dying is inside of us. But we need to keep living our lives.

It's possible to take care of your adult self without abandoning your little girl in the process. Often when women remember where the abuse took place, they realize that they 'left' their little girl in that house when they moved away. They were so ashamed and guilty that they left her in the place where the crime was committed.

This is not to say that you're wrong if you can't handle your little girl's despair and anguish right now. No one taught you how to do this. But you can eventually learn to find your little girl, comfort her, bring her home, and still live a joyous life.

To start healing your inner child, find out how old she was when the abuse first happened. If you don't know her age, ask yourself: was she in school yet? Could she write? Could she multiply? Could she add? Those are the kinds of questions that will help you sort out how old you were.

If you feel like she's still stuck back in that house where the abuse happened, you can drive by, if you're close enough, or you can just drive by in your mind. You can imagine talking to her. If it's too difficult for you to bring her home to where you live today, you can say to her, "You know what? I'm preparing a home for you. I'm preparing a place for you to come and live and be safe with me."

You don't need to do this alone. It may not be easy or even appropriate for your partner to help you through this very intimate time of reclaiming your little girl. But you can ask a friend to sit with you while you talk to your little girl and listen to what she has to say. In some towns, there are Twelve Step programs for people who have been sexually abused as children. There are also therapists who deal with childhood sexual abuse. Before you meet with a therapist, ask her over the phone, "Do you have experience with adults who were sexually abused as children? What do you know about it?" Then be wary if she says, "Oh, yes, I can do that. I can do anything. I specialize in 75 things."

I say 'she' because I'm always hesitant to send a survivor of childhood sexual abuse to a male therapist. By all means, do not go to a male therapist because someone told you, "You'd better go work out your issues with men." If you want to know the right thing for you to do now, imagine a five-year-old doing it. Imagine saying to a five-year-old, "Well, you've been raped by your father, and I think you should work your problem out with him, so I'm going to send you to a male therapist." Would you do that? If you have been sexually abused by a woman, then should you go to a male therapist? I feel reluctant to send any sexual abuse survivor to a male therapist, but it's important for you to do what feels right for you.

In the process of healing, a new reality sets in. You have a child within you who has had a very difficult childhood. You have an adult in the present who wants to live a more full life. Your adult life is still significantly affected by your childhood. The little child within needs loving energy; she needs care that she has not previously been given. In fact, we must now take over where our parents or foster families left off. We must take over where the authorities, school systems and relatives left off. Your child needs further guidance toward self-loving and increased self-esteem.

You've got a serious case of fostercare on your hands. You've got a child inside you who needs to be reparented, who does not know what it's like to feel safe. You're in charge of creating safety for that child. This may seem like an impossible task. However, it is possible to recover from severely damaged ability to trust. It is possible to take the wisdom you have as an adult and to share it with the child who was so hurt. You have an opportunity to turn your life around. It takes patience, not something children from dysfunctional homes have much experience with. This is an opportunity to turn the home you live in today into one that functions fully for the child and the adult.

I suggest that you get yourself a baby doll who you can hold, rock and take care of. I mentioned this in a previous chapter, but it's especially important for incest survivors. Make her a 'room' of her own that no one goes into without knocking. When a woman has a real baby, strangers often want to rock her, pinch her face, kiss her. Now, with your baby doll, you can protect her. You can say, "Hey, this is my baby. I'm in charge of this little being. No, you can't do that."

Many survivors of childhood sexual abuse experience memories of the abuse or vague, uncomfortable feelings during sex. When that happens, your little kid has awakened; she's scared, and she needs you to stop. When our actual sons or daughters wake up when we're having sex, and they're freaked out, we don't say, "Just wait until I'm finished." Nor do we say, "Come on in, join the fun." We get up and take care of them, no matter how upset we are that things have been interrupted. That's what you need to do for that little girl who wakes up inside of you and freaks out. Stop the sex between the adults, because one of you has turned into a kid. Find your baby doll, rock her, calm her down, tell her that she's safe, that you're the one having sex, not her. Try to differentiate between you and your kid.

If you have a partner who has a difficult time tolerating the stopping and starting, some negotiating needs to take place. You have a right to take care of your inner child and nurture that little self. That may mean that you're sexual with your partner less frequently, and it may mean that you're sexual only with yourself until you can get through this. The most important thing is that you take care of your little girl as well as you can.

Women trying to heal their past seem to benefit most from a combination of supportive therapeutic techniques. These can include individual or group therapy, hypnotherapy, weekend workshops, self-help groups, reading about other women's experiences and quiet meditation.

It is important to go at your own pace. Sometimes people say, "Let's do intensive therapy. Let's do intensive weekends. Let's do group. Let's do it five nights a week." But that can be overwhelming. If you try to heal too quickly, the result can be increased pain and self-hatred. Do not take this journey lightly. Do not rush. Your childhood will always be there to explore.

The truth is, you are perfect. You deserve love for simply breathing. You don't have to do anything. You don't have to jump through hoops. You don't have to get good grades. You don't have to make a lot of money. You don't have to bring home somebody Mom would think is acceptable. You deserve love because you're here.

How can a survivor of childhood sexual abuse be perfect? It's hard to conceive of because we've been taught by the culture that sexual abuse is dirty, awful, bad. Then we've been taught in supposedly supportive therapy sessions that it's devastating, shameful and debilitating.

The more you love your little girl within, the more you'll see her perfection. And the more you love her, the less pain you'll feel. Tell her that you'll help her feel loved and protected and safe. Make it a promise.

Nurture your adult self as well. You might set aside time for the inner child each day, and devote the rest of the day to your adult needs: work, socializing, sex, or whatever. Try to have fun now, as an adult; try to play, be light, and have a loving, easy time. It's okay not to be working on healing your child all the time, and it's okay to have more fun than your parents ever did. Enjoying your adult responsibilities and privileges is just as important as healing the child within.

Partners of Incest Survivors

*No person could save
another.*

—JOYCE CAROL OATES

Since there is a high incidence of childhood sexual abuse among
women, there's almost a 40 percent chance of becoming lovers with an
incest survivor. Partners of incest survivors are frequently frustrated
because incest almost always interferes with a woman's ability to be
intimate.

If you are the partner of an incest survivor, you are in the
unfortunate role of being yet another family member who has sex with
the survivor. Though you are not a perpetrator of violence, your
partner may consciously or unconsciously confuse you with her previous abusers. No wonder intimacy is difficult.

The starting point for the partner of an incest survivor is to
acknowledge the truth. Your lover actually was abused. It actually
affects every day of her life. It shaped who she has become.

Accepting reality is not only tough for partners of incest
survivors—it's tough for everyone. Denial is a cornerstone of our
culture. We ignore the fact that nuclear war could annihilate us all. We
don't trust politicians, yet we keep electing them. When we are in a
couple, we ignore each other's drug and alcohol problems; we overlook

class and race differences; we don't talk about body size. We are fearful of going to the source of the issues that we symbolically act out through arguments about what kind of bread to buy or when to pay the bills. This is particularly true for couples who have incest in the background of one or both of the women. More often than not, we don't want to deal with the impact this has on the relationship.

Many women have said to me, "I didn't know she was a survivor of childhood sexual abuse when I met her. Now she's found out in therapy, and here I am again with another abuse survivor. She's the third one, and I swore I'd never be with an incest survivor again."

I don't know why you got involved with another survivor of childhood sexual abuse. Call it magic. If you've done this many times and are feeling overwhelmed, clearly there's information for you in this; there's a lesson to be learned. In any case, it's important that the blame not be put on the survivor. She's been blamed all of her life, either by other people or by herself.

Remember that no one hates the fact that she was sexually assaulted as much as she hates it. No one is ashamed of it like she is. Remember that she did not create this background to hurt you. You are the one who chose her as a partner, and that is your responsibility.

If you are a survivor yourself and your partner is as well, the recovery process can be difficult because there can be a competitive edge: "I'm over that. Why don't you get over that?" Or "I can have sex. Why can't you have sex? What's the big deal?"

When two survivors are together, the abuse can become the focus of the relationship: "We're so close because these awful things happened to us." It's important to remember the other reasons you chose each other. You're not together just because someone else can understand what you're going through. You're together for many reasons besides the abuse.

Whether you were sexually abused as a child or not, it can be difficult to face the pain of someone whose childhood was devastating. It's frightening to be around people who are in pain.

I was in an airport recently, and there was a group of about twenty people of all ages in wheelchairs. It's hard to ignore twenty wheelchairs rolling through an airport. But that's what people were doing. They were looking up at the ceiling. They were looking out the windows. They were trying to find an airplane to look at. We can't stand pain and we can't stand our own discomfort. We don't want to hear about indwelling catheters, radiation treatments, psychiatric medications, or eating disorders. It's too hard to hear.

So if your partner is an incest survivor, you have her pain to deal with. You can't just ignore her, like wheelchairs in airports. Whether she lives with you or not, her pain influences your life. Naturally, you get resentful. It's unpopular to say, "It's such a drag! I hate that she's an incest survivor!" But of course you hate it. Who wouldn't hate it?

If you are a mother or have spent time co-parenting a child, you know how difficult it is not to lose your patience when your child makes a mess or is loud or whiny or needy. This is hard enough for mothers, but when we didn't choose to have the child, it's especially challenging to let them take up as much space as kids naturally do. Mothers have been programmed for centuries that they have to do that, but non-mothers are not programmed that way.

If you're with a survivor of childhood sexual abuse, it's as if your partner has a needy child inside her. While this is true for all of us—as I've said before, we all have a needy child within—the incest survivor's pain is usually very deep. For you to allow that injured child to take up space in your relationship can be very difficult. I believe it takes a special gift for someone to make room for her partner's pained little child, and to stay attentive while that child gets taken care of.

Often there's an unspoken battle: whoever is in the most pain wins. If someone had a worse childhood than you had, she gets to be in therapy and support groups. She gets to receive the most sympathy. She's the one who needs to be 'fixed.'

Assure your own internal little kid—your needy self—that regardless of who suffered the most, she gets to be Number One for you. Promise her you won't abandon her in your efforts to support your partner. She needs to know that it's okay for her to take up space, and to have your undying love and attention. She doesn't want to share that with anybody, and she shouldn't have to. Sometimes partners of incest survivors need to reactivate their primal self-protection mechanisms.

My five-year-old is an only child, and every once in a while he says to me, "Now, all these clothes are mine, right?"

"Right."

"And all these toys are mine, right?"

"Right."

I don't wear his clothes or play with his toys, but he just has to check it out. Once we're adults, we try to hide these feelings, but they're still there.

The other day somebody said to me, "My lover is so stubborn. She wants everything her way."

I said, "Who doesn't?"

But as a partner of an incest survivor, you may be feeling left out. Nowadays, incest survivors have their own support groups, their own therapists, their own books. I have heard of one support group for partners of incest survivors in San Francisco, but few other cities have them.

I encourage you to start your own groups. Your particular challenges are very important, and you need sympathy and support. The survivor in your life cannot be expected to be extremely understanding. Other women in your position are much more able to do this.

You might be saying to yourself, "I'm not the one who's in pain. I didn't have the terrible childhood. My parents were sort of weird and rude, but it wasn't that bad."

Even if the biggest trauma in your life was that Mom took you to kindergarten and left you there, it's helpful to honor your own brokenhearted little girl. I tell incest survivors to make a shrine to their little girl, and I think it's a good idea for partners too. Get pictures of yourself as a child, and put them in a special place where you can look at them every day. Would you be willing to give your child a kiss every day? Would you be willing to let your kid be important and valuable, even if the incest survivor in your life has a kid who is in tremendous pain?

This is so important for partners of incest survivors because they put themselves in the position of being the adult in the relationship, over and over again. It's not even the incest survivors who ask their partners to be the adult. In fact, many incest survivors complain that their partners are critical of them and treat them as if they are children. It's the partner herself who takes on this role. One of the results is that the partner doesn't confront or heal her own little kid with a broken heart.

You may feel like there is no room for your little kid. That's probably what you were taught when you were growing up: "You're doing okay? Great. I've got to work with your brother here who's failing. You're Mommy's little helper."

If you were that kid in the family, it's not surprising that you've teamed up with someone who seems more needy. You're recreating your experience of childhood.

Often I hear partners say, "We can't afford for both of us to be in therapy, and she needs it more." The incest survivor gets to be in pain. The incest survivor gets to be vulnerable. The incest survivor gets to be able to say her feelings.

Now is the time to put your little kid first, even if the other little kid in the house needs help. The good news is, you only have to take care of the child (or children) inside you. It's hard to do only that, and not to do the childcare for someone else, especially since as women, we have been taught that everyone comes before us.

A bigger problem exists for women who have actual children: children who run around the house; children who need us to pick them up from school because they got sick; children who are sixteen and want to drive our on-its-last-tires car; children who throw fits and cry and get excited. These kids need our support and loving attention. These kids are our priority. Sometimes we mothers have to put the little child within aside and take care of those children outside of us. Probably our biggest test is to determine when our children outside of us need our attention more than the children inside of us.

If you've been trying to parent your lover's inner child instead of your own, it's not a horrible thing you're doing. You're probably very good at it. I'm just suggesting that you'd be better off directing that loving energy toward your own broken-hearted little child inside. We recognize pain in others because we share the pain ourselves. So when you find yourself hurting along with your incested partner, you may find it valuable to acknowledge the fear and abandonment you felt as a child. If you focus all your energy on your partner, your own inner child will be abandoned and betrayed one more time. Your lover may even learn from your example. Showing her how you take care of your own little kid may be the greatest gift you can give her.

There are many ways to take care of that little child within. One way is to acknowledge how much you hate the fact that you have to deal with your partner's incest. Your partner is usually not the one who can listen to this sentiment. Take your comments to a friend, a therapist, a support group. This is a good example of how to take care of your own child and at the same time respect your partner's child. There is room for both.

If your lover starts acting broken-hearted, the best thing you can do for that child inside her is to go to your own inner child and see what she needs. You may be surprised to find out that your own child is in just as much pain as your lover's. In contrast to the homes we grew up in, now there can be enough room to accommodate all the injured children. We don't have to take the kid who's in the worst shape and heal her first, then take care of the next kid.

Caring for someone else at the expense of one's own needs seems to be one of the major reasons why partners of incest survivors leave their relationships. The resentment builds, the sadness builds, and the pain in the house multiplies from so much ignoring and denying. What it comes down to is this: if you don't take care of yourself, you're not going to be able to stick around.

You may be saying to yourself, "I don't know why I should stay in this relationship. This is such a big hassle, and I can't see any end to it, and I'm not getting what I need, so why should I stick this out?"

We want a rule book that tells us what we should do, but there are no rules here. You can go find someone who's not an incest survivor, or you can stay and try to change things within the relationship, or you may just go pick out another survivor. There isn't any formula. There's no right way to do it. It's up to you.

Sometimes leaving is the thing to do. We often have a belief that if we don't stay in a relationship for 25 years, it doesn't count. If we're not together for the rest of our lives, then the relationship is fucked and awful. "See? Aren't lesbians weird?" But the truth is, many couples, both straight and gay, are not staying together for their whole lives anymore. We're in a difficult transitional time period, because we're living with the ideas and myths of the people before us who believed that couples should stay together for life.

That's why we say, "You've been together 30 years? I've never met a couple who's been together 30 years!" It's a very hard thing to pull off these days. This is not to discourage you if you're in the throes of a young relationship. I'm not saying this to predict disaster. I'm just saying what's so.

Most of us explore, learn new things, change and eventually decide to be with other people or by ourselves. This does not make us bad people. This is just part of living in these times.

Do keep in mind that we live in a culture that teaches us: if it hurts, get out. If it's hard, don't be there. I've heard many people say, "My parents didn't have to struggle with their relationship, so I figure that if I have to struggle with my relationship, then it's not right."

I say to them, "Do you want to have your parents' relationship?"

We don't want to have our parents' unconsciousness, and we don't want conscious living to be so painful. Consciousness is sometimes painful. It's also sometimes wonderful. We tend to forget that life can be joyful and easy.

In any given day, there are some moments that are difficult and painful, and some that are joyful and easy. But we forget the easy ones. We take those times for granted. Someone says, "How was your day?" And we say, "It was a real drag. I got a flat tire." But what about all the other moments? Why are our days defined by the one thing that made them difficult?

We also tend to define our relationships by what is bad in them rather than by what we love about them. We tend to talk about how our lover made us upset rather than about the ways she made us happy.

What if you were willing to stay in this relationship, accepting the reality that in fact she is a survivor of childhood sexual abuse? What if you were able to do this and still be joyful? You could look at it as an opportunity to learn a lot about how to take care of your little kid. What you're often watching in the survivor is her struggle to stop ignoring or suppressing her own inner child. Naturally, in this process of watching her, you'll begin to be aware of your own child and your own pain. It is an opportunity for you to see what you do with your own little kid. You'll notice how infrequently you pay attention to your own child. You'll see how much you hate or at least are bothered by your child inside.

Often our silent contract with our partner is: "I will take care of you if I get to feel superior." That's what I've done with lovers in my own life. I hate to admit this, but it's true: I've chosen partners with the silent contract, "You can be the needy one if I get to take care of you emotionally, which proves I'm better." Those are the kinds of unspoken deals we make. It's not that we consciously figure out who's in more pain than we are, then go hang out with them to prove that we had happy childhoods or worked harder in therapy. But that's one of the payoffs. We get to feel that we're healthy by comparison.

You shouldn't have to have had a terrible childhood in order to get some attention now. In other words, you deserve love now, as an adult, no matter what kind of childhood you had.

Consider what might happen if you changed your deal with your lover to this: "I'll take care of my kid. That's my gift to this relationship." You may think it's only fair to add, "And you take care of your kid, okay?" But it doesn't work like that. She won't necessarily take care of her kid. How or if she takes care of her kid is her business. The best you can do is take care of your own.

This is especially crucial if you're an incest survivor as well and you think you're further along in your healing process than your partner. You may want to help her because you've been through it. But she'll change in her own time.

The other night I was watching *Hoosiers*, an exciting basketball movie, with two friends. Everybody in the theater was screaming and yelling, but the people in front of us kept turning around and giving us dirty looks. We were having such fun being rowdy that it was hard for us to honor them and stop what we were doing. We tried; during the quiet parts, we got quiet. But it was hard for me to change for just a moment what I wanted to do and the way I wanted to do it. I wanted the people in front of me to change—to be playful and excited and to quit being so uptight. There, at the movie theater, the stakes were very low. I didn't know those people, and I'll probably never see them again. Still, I wanted them to change to be more like me.

When we're in a relationship, it's even more of a challenge. We each want our lover to change. We want her to not leave hair in the bathroom sink. We want her to act right—right, of course, as determined by our definitions. We want her to be sexual when we want to be sexual. We want her to be quiet when we want her to. We want her to be happy when we want her to. We want her to work when we want her to and not work when we want her to.

To your little child inside, the need you have may appear to be a matter of life or death. Your little child within may feel that if your lover doesn't do what you ask, something very bad will happen. Rationally, you may know that if a friend went against your wishes the way your lover just has, it would not feel like a serious matter. Remember, though, that we also have parts of us operating as little tiny beings. To a little kid, her balloon flying off into the sky is a serious matter. And when the little kids inside us are in charge, we find it difficult to compromise.

The little kids inside us are also saying, "What if Mom or Dad finds out? We could be in a lot of trouble." So when your lover doesn't hang up her clothes, or doesn't stop to buy groceries on the way home, you may have a little voice inside that says, "Mom's gonna yell." Instead of recognizing that, we start thinking our lover is a jerk or doesn't care about us. When we pay attention, we find that it's our parents talking and our little kid being afraid.

That's when it's important for you to separate your little girl inside from your adult. An adult can compromise on differences. An adult can keep her mouth shut. An adult can take care of the kid who is her responsibility. An adult can help the little kid within to separate her needs from those of her parents.

We also have parents within. When it's your lover's week to do the dishes, and she doesn't do them, and when this would be fight number one million about dishes in the sink, you can talk with the parents in your head. You can let them know that you believe in doing the dishes daily. You can let them know that you can't help it that your lover doesn't understand simple priorities in life. You can let them know that she grew up in a different house. You can have this conversation every morning with your parents in your mind. Silently, between them and you; you don't even need to involve your lover. This really has nothing to do with her.

Once you practice this with the little things (that break up relationships), you can do them with the bigger things as well. You can do this with the differences you and your lover have over therapy, how fast she's dealing with her incest, how often you have sex. You can use this rather simple tool and build on it. Write letters to the parents in your mind. Call your real parents and talk with them about it. Talk to your siblings about how they react to their lovers. Get some concrete, loving information for your child.

Once you've learned to interrupt your automatic responses to the parents in your head, you can begin to evaluate those rules on your own. Is it really that important to have the dishes clean every day? Next to world hunger, how important is it?

Once we start caring for our own child within instead of trying to get someone else's child within to act the way we want her to, life gets easier. Relationships run smoother. What I'm suggesting is that you let your kid come live with you. Bring her in from the storm. Let your partner take care of her own kid, however she can. Her fight with her parents within is no less painful, no less time-consuming and no less intense than yours. You don't get to control her kid, but you can put your own home in order.

By the time we are adults, we have usually learned to make our relationships look good to the outside world. I'm sure you watched your parents act normal in front of company and then start a fight after the guests left. I'm sure you have learned how to be polite to your lover in front of others and then, on the way home, immediately become rude.

Paradoxically, we often express more intimacy in public than in private. When we are around others, there is a stress taken off our relationships. We often have more ease in communicating with one another. You may feel comfortable expressing physical affection among friends, while in private the implications are too frightening. After all, you can't have sex in public.

Lesbian relationships in which one or more partners are incest survivors often contain a fair amount of this public intimacy. When in public, the partners talk and touch; when separated, the partners avidly call each other on the phone. But when they are alone, they turn on the television and watch it silently.

This is especially common if there is repressed anger and sorrow in the relationship. If you, as the partner, have not been clear about your sadness or anger in dealing with your lover's incest, the need for separation when you are in private will increase.

To create or recreate intimacy and sexual sharing in your private relationship, start by spending a part of each day telling your partner something important to you. Open up in some way—simple talks at the dinner table, not late-night marathons. Allow intimacy to begin in small, non-threatening ways.

Because the survivor often associates sex with abuse, she may be ambivalent about being sexual, even with a loving partner. Needless to say, this can be frustrating for you as her partner. If this is your situation, try not to take her sexual ambivalence personally. This is not easy, because most women blame themselves for the reactions of others. Partners often blame themselves for problems that manifest in the present, but were actually created in the survivor's childhood.

If your partner is frequently unwilling to have sex, you may end up feeling like a letch. You may begin to believe that you have an unusual need for sex. But there is nothing outrageous about wanting sex in a lover relationship. Most people expect sex with a lover.

The incest survivor may feel a tremendous need to control the physical part of the relationship. If this is creating turmoil in your relationship, it is important to begin to feel like you're on the same team. I offer many suggestions about this in my first book, *Lesbian Sex*.

However, the sexual problems in your relationship may not be simply because your partner is an incest survivor. That's a handy excuse, and it lets you experience yourself as the healthy one, the one who would be having a satisfying sexual relationship if it weren't for her. You also get to feel like a sympathetic, patient mate. "You are so good to stay with her even if she won't have sex with you," friends may say.

If you suspect that some of this might be true for you, investigate your past sexual liaisons. Did you have sex? Were you interested? Was there some reason in those relationships that sex was not active?

Your sex life is still in your hands. Your partner may be the one who has flashbacks, says no, or stops and starts the action, but you are participating. You may feel exasperated, yet you stay. This is neither right nor wrong, but it is important to remember that you are part of the process, not just an innocent bystander.

Also keep in mind that you have a right to have sexual feelings and to ask for sex. The longer you go without sex, the trickier this becomes, since you may become frustrated and angry. Yet it's crucial that you approach her respectfully and lovingly, or she will not feel safe enough to comply. This is where acceptance of reality comes in. She has, after all, had sex against her will, and she will understandably be reluctant to have sex except under the safest of circumstances.

If the issue has become particularly sensitive, you might want to make your needs known in a counseling session. This way, you will have a third party to help you communicate and compromise.

You might not realize that it's really okay to make demands. You can say you want sex, you can say how often you want sex, you can say what kind of sex you want. You may not get your needs met, but you'll never know until you ask, and the process of asserting your needs can do wonders for your self-esteem.

In my research, I found that women who were sexually abused in childhood are not different from the women who were not abused in childhood. Both groups have similar sexual functioning. They each have the same satisfaction with sex, they masturbate the same amount each month, and they have the same amount of partner sex in a month. This information provides hope for you as the partner of a survivor. As she heals, your partner's sexual functioning will probably change.

It is possible for the partners of sexual abuse survivors to have sex and intimacy within the relationship. It may not be easy, but it is possible. Don't allow her pain to stop you from experiencing your own feelings and your own needs.

I also suggest that you and your partner let go of the myth that it's because of her incest that you have the sort of relationship you do. You are more than a partner of an incest survivor; she is more than an incest survivor. Think of it this way: you're not just in a couple but in a blended family. Each of you is an adult and each of you has one or several children running around inside. Take care of your own child first, and you may find your partnership flourishing beyond what you'd dreamed possible.

Research on the Lives and Sex Practices of Some Lesbians

There is no more effective medicine to apply to feverish public sentiment than figures.

—IDA TARBELL

What do lesbians do in bed? Are we satisfied? How often do we have sex? These are some of the questions I asked 1566 lesbians in a written survey. (A copy of the questionnaire appears at the end of this chapter.) Most of the questionnaires were handed out at lectures and workshops I gave on lesbian sexuality throughout the United States and Canada from 1985 to 1987. The questionnaire was purposely short to enable women to answer it in a few minutes before they left my workshops.

In addition to my talks and workshops, I also distributed questionnaires through lesbian resource centers in different cities, including Anchorage, Detroit and Seattle. Some were distributed via advertisements in women's newspapers throughout the country. Many were distributed by lesbians who had been at the lectures and volunteered to disseminate them in their home towns. There are over 134 towns and cities throughout the United States and Canada represented in this study.

We need to look at statistics in a way that reflects a political understanding—by looking at the size of the sample, who is in the sample, what exactly the sample says. As women, we have been consistently hurt by statistics prepared by white males who want to pontificate on who we are and what is wrong with us. When researching ourselves, we must always try to be responsible to the community and not draw incorrect inferences. We must learn to use the numbers as guidelines, not something with which to criticize ourselves or explain our lesbianism. We need to keep saying who we are to anyone who will listen. This report is offered to give you some information that may be valuable.

These findings cannot be generalized to the entire lesbian community. The age, race, class and education of the respondents was *not* similar to the population as a whole. This is not a random sampling of lesbians. Because lesbians are oppressed by the majority culture, it is difficult to locate those who do not show up at public events. A random sample of lesbians is virtually impossible to obtain at this time.

However, the information here is still significant. For the population this study covers, the numbers seem to be internally consistent. We started by analyzing the results of 200 of the surveys. Then we added another 250, then another 300, and so on. *There was never any significant change in the percentages.* This was exciting, because it means that at least for this population, these figures seem to reflect the real experience of lesbians.

SELF-DESCRIPTION REPORT

The first section of the survey asked respondents for a description of themselves. The results show which lesbians are represented in the survey. This could also generate discussion about who is visible in the community and why.

The women who responded represented a limited age range.

SELF DESCRIPTION

Age of Respondents:

10%	*Under twenty-five*
22%	*Twenty-five to twenty-nine*
47%	*Thirty to thirty-nine*
18%	*Forty to forty-nine*
3%	*Fifty to fifty-nine*
1%	*Over sixty*

Only 10 percent were under twenty-five and only 1 percent were over sixty; 22 percent were twenty-five to twenty-nine; 47 percent were thirty to thirty-nine; 18 percent were forty to forty-nine; 3 percent were fifty to fifty-nine.

When asked to describe the class in which they were raised, respondents predominantly indicated a middle-class background. Forty-one percent considered themselves from the middle class, although all economic classes were represented (6 percent working class; 25 percent lower middle class; 24 percent upper middle class; 2 percent upper class; 2 percent mixed class). In a major oversight, no question was asked about the respondents' *current* class identification. However, the class of origin is usually more significant when discussing the impact class has on one's life.

The responding group was overwhelmingly Caucasian (92 percent), although other racial groups were included: 3 percent Black; 2 percent Hispanic; 2 percent Native American; 1 percent Asian/Pacific Islander.

Most of the above numbers differ from the distributions in the population of the United States as a whole, raising a number of questions. One must wonder about the outreach in the lesbian communities where my lectures and work

Class of Origin of Respondents:

6%	Working class
25%	Lower middle
41%	Middle
24%	Upper middle
2%	Upper
2%	Mixed

Race of Respondents:

92%	Caucasian
3%	Black
2%	Hispanic
2%	Native American
1%	Asian/Pacific Islander

shops were held. Because I am a white, middle-class, thirty-nine-year-old woman, does my work attract women from very similar backgrounds? What other kinds of outreach can be done to attract the community as a whole? How else can questionnaires be distributed to the groups that do not regularly attend my functions? Some women cannot afford my workshops, others may feel therapy is not relevant in their lives. Racism, ageism and classism are all factors that contribute to this bias. Homophobia is a factor as well. The majority of the women who responded to the questionnaire had to be willing to go to a lecture given by a lesbian on lesbian sex. This narrows the population of respondents considerably.

The distributions which were similar to the population of the U.S. as a whole were those regarding religious upbringing. There were slightly more Jewish women answering this questionnaire and slightly fewer Fundamentalist Christians compared to the general population. The distribution was as follows: 37 percent Protestant; 23 percent Catholic; 12 percent Jewish; 9 percent No religion in their background; 6 percent Fundamentalist Christian; 1 percent Mormon; and 8 percent Other.

This sample reported that 12 percent of the respondents were differently abled. Of these, 56 per-

Religious Background of Respondents:

37%	Protestant
27%	Catholic
12%	Jewish
9%	No religious background
8%	Other
6%	Fundamentalist Christian
1%	Mormon

cent became disabled after the age of fifteen, 30 percent became disabled in childhood and 14 percent were disabled at birth. It is not clear whether this number accurately reflects the numbers of lesbians who are physically challenged, since many public activities are still not fully accessible. Most of the places in which I worked during the distribution of this questionnaire were in fact accessible to wheelchairs, the deaf, the blind and the environmentally allergic. However, there were still times when the needs of disabled women were not served fully. In addition, sometimes the accessibility was not advertised. Finally, one must acknowledge the isolation common to the disabled, and the often limited outreach of the lesbian community towards those lesbians. This is not intended as criticism of any of the women who worked on the events I spoke at over the years, only as a prodding for all of us to continue to question our prejudices in our efforts to unite our communities.

The level of education of the women in my survey differed from the population of women as a whole in the United States. The majority were college graduates (38 percent) or advanced degree holders (32 percent). Twenty-six percent had attended some college; four percent had a high school education only. In the general popula-

Age of Onset of Being Differently Abled (12% of Respondents):

14% At birth
30% In childhood
56% After age fifteen

Education Level of Respondents:

38% College graduates
32% Advanced degrees
26% Some college
4%   High school or less

tion, only 13 percent of women over twenty-five have college or advanced degrees. This comparison does raise the question of why more lesbians (70 percent) might have completed higher education. Is it because they are not dependent on men for their livelihood? Does it imply that they are less likely than their heterosexual counterparts to interrupt their college education to pursue a relationship and have children? Or does it simply suggest that participating in a workshop or attending a lecture is more comfortable for those women who have been in school many years?

The final question in the self-description section asked how long these women have identified as lesbians. (A client of mine recently had an anniversary party for her twentieth year as a lesbian. She and her lover put name tags on each woman stating how long they had been lesbians. They added up the numbers and had several hundred years worth of lesbian identity, wisdom, sex and culture represented in that home. What a wonderful thought!) In this survey, 25 percent said they had identified as lesbians for fewer than five years; 31 percent five to ten years; 31 percent ten to twenty years; and 13 percent over twenty years. If we add up these statistics, we have at least 17,000 years of lesbian experience responding to this questionnaire!

Years Respondents Identified as Lesbians:

25%	Less than five years
31%	Five to ten years
31%	Ten to twenty years
13%	Over twenty years

BACKGROUND FACTORS

The second part of the survey asked respondents questions that might have an influence on their sex lives. They were asked questions about their childhood, the influence of religion, the incidence of sexual abuse, and the presence of substance abuse in the home in which they were raised. There were also questions regarding the incidence of assault and sexual abuse as adults and the use of chemical substances in their lives today.

Organized religion has done a great deal to oppress lesbians. We have been told that we will go to hell, that we are sinners, that we are dooming ourselves to a life of evil. We have been told that we can only save ourselves by going straight or being abstinent from sex with a woman. No wonder many lesbians have little to do with religion. It certainly has been distorted by the men who control it. It is painful for many lesbians to be told that they cannot partake in the religion of their heritage because of their sexual orientation. This is often what keeps lesbians from coming out to their families. They are afraid of the religious judgments that might substantiate their parents' rejection.

In this survey, 63 percent of the lesbians felt they had experienced 'little,' 'some,' or 'average' religious influence. For 31 percent

BACKGROUND FACTORS

Influence of Religious Upbringing on Respondents:

63% Little to average
31% Very strong
6% All-encompassing

the influence was 'quite strong,' and for 6 percent it was 'all-encompassing.' The latter two groups may find their sex lives significantly influenced by their religion. They may find it difficult to reconcile their sexual preference with the teachings they learned at an early age.

Childhood sexual abuse was experienced by 38 percent of the respondents. This statistic is the same as that described by Diana Russell in her research on a random sample of 930 females (*The Secret Trauma: Incest in the Lives of Girls and Women*. New York: Basic Books, 1986). She found that 38 percent were survivors of sexual abuse under the age of eighteen. The fact that these statistics are identical helps to lay to rest the mythology that women become lesbians because they have had negative experiences with men. What *is* true is that many women have negative experiences with men. What is also true is that not all childhood sexual abuse is perpetrated by men.

In my survey, the women who were sexually abused experienced that abuse at the following ages: 31 percent under age five; 65 percent age five to ten; 56 percent age eleven to fifteen; and 23 percent age sixteen to eighteen.

The frequency of the sexual abuse was: 21 percent once; 37 percent a few times; 28 percent sev-

38% of Respondents Were Sexually Abused as Children
12% were Unsure

Age at Which Childhood Sexual Abuse Occurred:

31%	Under five
65%	Five to ten
56%	Eleven to fifteen
23%	Sixteen to eighteen

eral times; 26 percent frequently.
These numbers add up to more
than 100 percent because many of
the women were abused by more
than one person. The question of
frequency of abuse is often discussed in survivor groups. Women
who have had one instance of
childhood sexual abuse often feel
they have no reason to be traumatized when they compare themselves to women who experienced
frequent abuse. But trauma is
trauma, regardless of the experience of others. We each, after all,
have to reconcile our own past. No
matter how frequent, the trauma
affected our sense of self, safety
and boundaries. These become
issues for abuse survivors later in
life. Survivors often feel unsafe
when they are being sexual; and
they have distorted boundaries
when it comes to intimacy. However, we will see later in this survey
that the current sexual experience
of these women is heartening and
perhaps surprising.

Several other issues con-
nected to childhood sexual abuse
survivors were researched. They
include: sex of the perpetrator;
relationship of perpetrator to the
respondent; survivor's satisfaction
with current sex life; frequency of
masturbation and partner sex for
survivors; and relationships
between childhood abuse, chemical
addiction, and adult sexual abuse.

Frequency of Childhood Sexual Abuse:

21% Once
37% A few times
28% Several times
26% Frequently

Let us begin with the sex of the perpetrators. The number of male perpetrators was much higher than that of female perpetrators. That women do perpetrate sexual abuse, even though it is at a much lower frequency than men, is often difficult for lesbians to accept. This disbelief often makes lesbians who have been abused by a female unwilling to tell other lesbians about that abuse. It's important for all of us to acknowledge that some women do sexually abuse chidren.

The perpetrators were identified as follows: 35 percent father; 30 percent older male relative; 20 percent male stranger; 20 percent sibling; 10 percent male family friend; 9 percent male employer or co-worker; 8 percent male acquaintance; 8 percent mother; 7 percent male lover/partner of mother; 6 percent not remembered; 5 percent doctor; 5 percent neighborhood boys; 3 percent same age male relative; 2 percent local businessman; 2 percent grandmother; 2 percent grandfather; 2 percent female stranger; 1 percent older female relative; 1 percent same age female relative. Perpetrators reported by 1 percent of those abused as children were: landlord, male teacher, church leader, priest, female lover/partner of mother. Again, some respondents reported more than one perpetrator, so the

Perpetrators of Childhood Sexual Abuse:

35%	Father
20%	Older male relative
20%	Sibling
10%	Male family friend
10%	Others
9%	Male co-worker
8%	Mother
7%	Male partner of mother
6%	Don't remember
5%	Neighborhood boys
3%	Same age male relative
2%	Female stranger
2%	Grandparent (male or female)
1%	Female lover of mother
1%	Older female relative
1%	Same age female relative

numbers add up to over 100 percent.

As is obvious, many people take advantage of girls sexually. While the incidence of father/daughter incest was high, many women were molested by someone other than their father. Whoever the perpetrator was, and however infrequent the abuse, each survivor experienced some form of the denial, pain, and abandonment connected with childhood sexual abuse.

Perhaps the most universal concern when we are talking about sex, intimacy and loving is the impact childhood sexual abuse has on women's ability to trust anyone in an intimate situation. The reality is that we all live in a culture that does not adequately protect children or women; we have to learn to take care of ourselves. If a woman grew up in a household in which she was sexually abused, she learned almost nothing from the adults about protecting herself. This has to affect her trust and her ability to be intimate, as well as her ability to choose partners. This little child must be healed.

The questionnaire also investigated assault and sexual abuse in the adult lives of the respondents. When asked if they were abused as adults, the women reported the following kinds of assaults: 49 percent verbal harassment; 26 percent physical harassment; 16 percent

Adult Assault and Sexual Abuse:

49%	Experienced verbal harrassment
26%	Physical harassment
16%	Rape
9%	Beating

rape; and 9 percent physical beating. The FBI reports that one in
three women will be raped within
her lifetime (Boston Women's
Health Collective. *The New Our
Bodies, Ourselves,* revised ed. Old
Tappan, New Jersey: Simon and
Schuster, 1984). The percentage in
this survey is much lower. Part of
the discrepancy is because these
women have not lived their entire
lifetimes. In fact, most of the
women in this study are under the
age of forty. Another reason the
questionnaire results show a lower
incidence of rape may be that most
rape is committed by someone
known to the victim; perhaps since
lesbians are less likely to relate
sexually to men, they are less likely
to know someone of the opposite
sex to rape them. It may be that
many lesbians are less likely to follow societal proscriptions about
how women should act and dress,
and thus are able to protect themselves both because they are less
invested in what men think of
them than heterosexual women
and because they may be dressed in
a style that equips them to run or
protect themselves in other ways.

Though the difference in the
rate of rape between the lesbians in
this group and women in the population as a whole is significant,
there is really no sure way to know
why. I offer these suggestions in
the hopes of further study.

In investigating adult abuse, I compared women who had been sexually abused as children to those who had not. I found that of the women who had been abused as children, 40 percent were physically beaten or raped as adults. Of the women who reported no childhood sexual abuse, 14 percent were physically beaten or raped as adults. The difference between these two groups is very large, clearly showing that women who suffered abuse as children are more likely to suffer abuse as adults. Diana Russell (*The Secret Trauma*) found that women who had been sexually abused in childhood were three times as likely to be physically abused or raped as adults. Some possible explanations are discussed in the chapter on incest.

When the women in my study who had experienced adult abuse were asked who perpetrated this violence, they reported: 53 percent male stranger; 21 percent male lover/friend; 13 percent female lover/friend; 10 percent other than these categories; 9 percent male relative; 9 percent male husband/mate; 4 percent female mate; 2 percent female stranger; 1 percent female relative. Remember this does not add up to 100 percent because some of the women suffered abuse by more than one perpetrator. What is striking about these reports is that

Correlation of Childhood and Adult Abuse:

Survivors of Childhood Sexual Abuse Experienced Abuse as Adults:

26%	Rape
14%	Physical battering

Respondents With No Childhood Sexual Abuse Experienced Abuse as Adults:

8%	Rape
6%	Physical battering

Perpetrators of Adult Abuse:

53%	Male stranger
21%	Male lover/friend
13%	Female lover/friend
10%	Other
9%	Male relative
9%	Male mate/husband
4%	Female mate
2%	Female stranger
1%	Female relative

over half the assaults were committed by close relations.

It is very important that readers, researchers, clinicians and educators do not use any of these statistics to blame victims. Women are not responsible for physical abuse and rape. No woman should have to fear walking the streets or being in her own home—where most rapes occur. No matter what the circumstances, no one has the right to perpetrate violence on a woman. This is true even if the woman is part of a vicious cycle in a battering relationship. While she can learn ways to not participate in her own destruction, we must always hold the perpetrator responsible for physical abuse.

In looking at these statistics, it becomes clear that both men and women commit abuse. There have been volumes published on the reasons why men perpetrate violence upon women. There is documentation on men's fear of women and on their compulsion to dominate, as well as on women's socialization into passivity. American culture has institutionalized violence against women. More than five times as much violence by men than women was reported in this study.

However, 17 percent of the women in my study reported abuse by a female 'mate,' 'lover,' or friend. This seems an appropriate and safe place to briefly discuss the issue of lesbian violence.

Over 500 women attended a day-long forum held in San Francisco in 1987 to address lesbian violence, but denial about woman-to-woman violence is still prevalent in our community. We find it hard to believe that women can engage in the very behavior we so condemn in men. Because of homophobia, we are reluctant to acknowledge problems within our own subculture. We long to be part of a community that's better and more harmonious than the heterosexual world. In the face of real oppression, it is hard to tolerate diversity and difference among ourselves.

The reality is that we are all more diverse than we like to acknowledge, and the problem of battering and rape does exist between women. To help combat this problem, we must begin to tell one another the truth, divulging the secrets we have maintained. In the Twelve Step programs, there is a phrase, "We are only as sick as our secrets." Bringing the secrets into the open immediately creates a forum for healing. Lesbians who speak out about their abusive and battering relationships will find others who understand and others who have found help.

I believe that in any survey of lesbians it is important to seek information about substance abuse. Another researcher reports a 30 percent incidence of alcohol addiction in the lesbian and gay male community (Rofes, Eric. *I Thought People Like That Killed Themselves.* San Francisco: Grey Fox Press, 1983). The impact of this level of addiction on the lesbian community needs to be explored, and was studied in many ways in this survey.

The first question concerned growing up in an alcoholic home. Thirty-seven percent said they were raised in an alcoholic family, and another 11 percent were unsure. Fifty-three percent were not from alcoholic homes. The incidence of alcoholism in the American population as a whole varies according to different studies. *The New Our Bodies, Ourselves* reports that 12 percent of the population is alcoholic. A recent Gallup Poll reported that 30 percent of American families feel alcohol is a serious problem in their home life.

My study shows a higher level of alcoholism among the respondents' families than in the population as a whole. Since denial is such a major component of any discussion of substance abuse, people often do not admit when they are alcoholic and are reluctant to name family members as well.

It's possible that we report a higher level of family alcoholism here because there is such a high incidence of recovery (29%) in the

Respondents Who Were Raised In Alcoholic Families:

37%	Were
11%	Unsure
53%	Were not

population studied. Lesbians who
are more informed about substance
abuse are less likely to deny that
their parents were alcoholic. I'm
also fairly certain that alcoholism
is also underestimated in the population as a whole.

When asked about their current use of chemical substances,
the respondents reported: 2 percent were presently addicted; 3
percent were heavy users; 51 percent were casual users; 15 percent
never used chemicals; and 29 percent had been addicted to chemicals and were now clean and sober.

It is important to remember
that this is a self-reporting questionnaire. I believe that the statistics in the first two categories are
low because of the respondents'
denial about abuse. Other studies
show that addiction is high in the
population in general and in the
lesbian community as well. That so
many women in this study are in
recovery from substance abuse is
heartening information, and an
indication that drug and alcohol
use is prevalent among lesbians.
Because I work with and am
involved in the recovery community, it is also likely that my lectures
attract women in recovery from
addictions.

Using these statistics, I looked
at correlations between current
substance abuse, family substance
abuse and sexual abuse of children
and adults. There were many
interesting results.

**Respondents' Current Use
of Chemical Substances:**

51%	*Casual users*
29%	*Recovering addicts*
15%	*Never used*
3%	*Heavy users*
2%	*Currently addicted*

Current substance abuse and family alcoholism were strongly correlated. Fifty-seven percent of the respondents who considered themselves in recovery from addiction or currently addicted were raised in alcoholic/addict homes. Only 27 percent of women who did not see themselves as abusers grew up in alcoholic/addict homes. Many researchers are trying to find a genetic link to substance abuse. Whatever the reasons, environmental or genetic, these statistics support the theory that alcoholism and drug addiction is a family disease.

When I looked at the incidence of childhood sexual abuse in alcoholic families, the statistics showed an extremely high correlation. Fifty percent of the women raised in alcoholic homes had a history of childhood sexual abuse. This contrasts with 32 percent of those raised in nonalcoholic homes. Of course, the numbers in either group represent a high level of abuse, but the fact that half of the respondents raised in alcoholic homes were sexually abused in childhood is a truly significant statistic.

I also compared the relationship between childhood sexual abuse and the respondents' use of substances. Of those who are currently addicted to chemicals or who are in recovery, 49 percent reported childhood sexual abuse,

Correlation of Respondents Raised In Alcoholic Families with Respondents' Current Substance Abuse:

57% *Addicts and recovering addicts were raised in alcoholic homes*

27% *Non-addicts were raised in alcoholic homes*

Correlation of Childhood Sexual Abuse and Alcoholic Families:

50% *Respondents in alcoholic homes were sexually abused as children*

32% *Respondents in non-alcoholic homes were sexually abused as children*

with another 16 percent unsure. Those reporting no current or past chemical addiction had a 34 percent incidence of childhood sexual abuse, with another 10 percent unsure. These numbers show a correlation between adult substance abuse and childhood sexual abuse. It is possible that more women become addicted to chemicals in order to stop the devastating feelings caused by childhood sexual abuse.

When I compared the relationship between adult rape and the current use of chemicals, the results were interesting. The sample as a whole reported a 16 percent incidence of rape as adults. Eleven percent of those who never use chemicals had been raped; 13 percent of casual users; 14 percent of those who are currently addicted to chemicals; and 18 percent of those who heavily use chemicals. Twenty-four percent of those who were previously addicted to chemicals reported that they had been raped.

According to these statistics, the incidence of rape increases significantly with any increase in the use of chemicals. Lesbians who were previously addicted and are now clean and sober reported twice the incidence of rape as those lesbians who have never used chemicals. Interestingly, those who identified themselves as heavy users or currently addicted

Correlation of Respondents' Current Substance Abuse with Childhood Sexual Abuse:

49%	Current or recovering addicts were sexually abused in childhood
34%	Non-addicts were sexually abused in childhood
16%	Current or recovering addicts unsure about childhood sexual abuse
10%	Non-addicts unsure about childhood sexual abuse

Correlation of Incidence of Rape as Adults (16% of Respondents) and Level of Substance Abuse:

11%	Respondents who never used chemicals were raped
13%	Respondents who casually used chemicals were raped
14%	Respondents who are currently addicted were raped
18%	Respondents who heavily use were raped
24%	Respondents who are recovering addicts were raped

reported fewer rapes than did recovering addicts. There's no clear information about why this is true. It's possible that women who are currently clean and sober are better able to remember their histories and are more willing to be honest about sexual assault than women who are still using (and who report fewer rapes). It's also possible that substance abuse leads to impaired judgment, both of how safe a situation is and of how to take appropriate action. I'm not implying that women cause their own rapes. It is important, however, that we all be aware that heavy substance abuse certainly increases the degree to which one is at risk.

CURRENT SEXUAL ACTIVITIES

Now for the good part. The third section of the survey consisted of a series of detailed questions about current sexual activities. The responses were then cross-tabulated to provide more detailed information about the sexual activities of specific groups of lesbians.

The first question asked how respondents identified in terms of current relationships. Twenty-six percent were single; 12 percent were casually involved with friends; and 62 percent were coupled. While there have been many complaints by single lesbians that they are discriminated against

CURRENT SEXUAL ACTIVITY

Current Relationships:

62%	Coupled
26%	Single
12%	Casually Involved

in a subculture dominated by couples, these numbers show that
though a majority of this sample
identify as couples, nearly 40 percent do not identify in this way.

I was also interested in how
long the women had identified
with their current status. Most of
the women had been in their current situation fewer than three
years, no matter which category
they were in. Eighty-one percent of
the single respondents were single
for three years or less. Eleven percent were single four to eight years.
Eight percent of them were single
for nine or more years. Virtually all
(95 percent) of those who were
casually involved had been in that
situation three years or less. Four
percent were casually involved
four to eight years. Only one percent had been casually involved for
more than nine years. Sixty-nine
percent of all the couples in the
survey were together three or
fewer years. Twenty-four percent
of the couples were together four
to eight years. Seven percent
reported being in a couple for more
than nine years.

The majority of these
respondents had not been single,
casually involved, or coupled for
long. This does not mean that the
women hadn't previously been in
another category or even in their
current category more than once; it
simply means that this group had
not been involved in their current

Length of Time In Current Situation

Single:
81%	Fewer than three years
11%	Four to eight years
8%	Nine or more years

Casually Involved:
95%	Fewer than three years
4%	Four to eight years
1%	Nine or more years

Coupled:
69%	Fewer than three years
24%	Four to eight years
7%	Nine or more years

situation for long. We can specu-
late about the reasons for this, but
it is important that we not use this
information against ourselves. We
live in a fast-paced world in which
very little lasts long. A 'lifetime
guarantee' on products or services
in most states is only legally bind-
ing for seven years. Half of all
heterosexual marriages end in
divorce. The reason that we have
short relationships is not necessarily because we are lesbians, but
rather because we live in a rapidly
changing world. Our bonding
often cannot withstand the strain.

The next series of questions
concerned specific sexual practices.
We have so little information
about what lesbians actually do
sexually and how we feel about it
that this was an exciting part of the
survey. When queried about celibacy, most respondents (78 percent) replied that they had been
celibate at some point in their
lives. The length of celibate periods had varied: 57 percent had
remained celibate less than a year;
35 percent for one to five years; 8
percent for six or more years.
When asked if this had been a
choice, 35 percent answered "yes,"
and another 48 percent answered
"sort of." In this study, celibacy
appears to have been primarily a
voluntary choice, although 17 percent of the respondents were celibate involuntarily.

*78% had been celibate at
some time*

Duration:
57%   Less than one year
35%   One to five years
8%   Six or more years

Was it by choice:
35%   Yes
48%   Sort of
17%   No

Reason:
21%   Lover left
17%   Stress
13%   It felt good
10%   Abuse memories
9%   Addiction recovery
3%   Illness
3%   Motherhood

For those lesbians who had been celibate, the reasons given for the celibate period were: 21 percent no lover; 17 percent stress; 13 percent felt good; 10 percent sexual abuse memories; 9 percent recovering from substance abuse; 8 percent spiritual practice; 6 percent partner wanted celibacy; 5 percent personal growth; 5 percent no desire; 5 percent fear of sex; 3 percent illness; 3 percent motherhood; 2 percent anger at lover; and 1 percent political reasons.

Almost everyone in this sample masturbated (89 percent). This statistic compares to a report on 1844 women (of all sexual orientations), 82 percent of whom masturbated (Hite, Sher. *The Hite Report: A Nationwide Study of Female Sexuality*. New York: Dell Publishing, 1976). The percentage of lesbians who masturbated remained remarkably similar, no matter what the woman's situation: 92 percent of the single women masturbate; 92 percent of the casually involved women; and 88 percent of the coupled women.

Most of the women who did not masturbate had been in a coupled relationship for fewer than three years. This may indicate that sex is so frequent early in a relationship that partnered women do not have time to masturbate; that they romanticize sex with their partner and do not want

89% Masturbate

92%	of single women masturbate
92%	of those casually involved
88%	of those in couples

to have sex alone; or that lesbians believe they shouldn't masturbate when they are in a couple.

Paradoxically, it is also true that those who masturbate most often in all three groups have been in their current situation fewer than three years. It's possible that women who are having frequent partner sex want to have more sexual stimulation, including masturbation. Newly single women, used to partner sex, may be having more sex with themselves to replace the former stimulation. The possibilities suggested by this data are as numerous as the women answering the questionnaire.

When asked how they masturbated, the sample revealed the following: 58 percent use hands; 24 percent use a vibrator; 8 percent practice tribadism; 6 percent engage in other activities. If we could know in detail how each lesbian masturbates—using what fantasies, strokes, timing—we could certainly learn a great deal about lesbian sex.

When asked how often they masturbated in a month, the respondents reported as follows: 10 percent masturbated less than once; 7 percent once; 38 percent two to five times; 22 percent six to ten times; 15 percent ten to twenty times; 8 percent over twenty times. "Ah, 10 percent of us masturbate less than once a month! Yeah, I'm not weird or crazy or bad! I just

Method of Masturbation:

58%	By hand
24%	With a vibrator
8%	Tribadism
6%	Other

Frequency of Masturbation:

10%	Less than once a month
7%	Once a month
38%	Two to five times a month
22%	Six to ten times a month
15%	Ten to twenty times a month
8%	More than twenty times a month

don't masturbate." These statistics can show each of us that there are other lesbians like ourselves.

The big question followed: "How often do you have sex with a partner in a month?" I call this the big question because it is most frequently asked when I am speaking about lesbian sexuality. We have a lot of cultural support for this obsession. We count everything in this culture: our money, our weapons, our friends, our paper clips. How often we have sex with another person in a month is no exception. Why do we need to count at all? Really, who cares? What matters is, are you having good sex, adequate sex? Is it enough for you? If you're having no partner sex, is that okay with you? Try to be aware of your reactions to your own sex life when reading the information throughout this text.

Everyone answering this survey was asked about frequency of partner sex, including single, casually involved and coupled women. In a typical month, lesbians in this study reported having sex with a partner: 12 percent never; 19 percent once or less; 35 percent two to five times; 20 percent six to ten times; 14 percent eleven or more times.

Many women reading this will be relieved—twelve percent of lesbians you know are having no partner sex in a month; if you are

Frequency of Partner Sex (in a typical month):

12%	Never have sex
19%	Have sex once or fewer times
35%	Two to five times a month
20%	Six to ten times a month
14%	Eleven or more times a month

part of that group, you are not bad, wrong, or inadequate. In fact, one third of lesbians in this survey were having sex with a partner once or less a month. Really, not much. The largest percentage of the women were having sex two to five times a month. There is no way to know if this was usually twice a month, or as often as five times a month.

The respondents were asked another 'big' question: "Do you have orgasms?" The results showed that 86 percent of the women orgasm with masturbation, and 81 percent with a partner. There are a significant number of women who do not orgasm. With masturbation, 6 percent answered that they never orgasm; 8 percent said they only orgasm occasionally. With partner sex, 6 percent reported they never orgasm; 13 percent said they do occasionally. 'Occasional' was self-defined in the study. Some women who listed themselves in this category probably have had orgasms a few times in their whole lives. Perhaps others have orgasms only when they least expect it. Others probably listed themselves in this category because they do not orgasm as often as they would like. It is important that you do not use this information about orgasm to criticize yourself or your partner. You are not alone—there are always other lesbians who share your experience.

Orgasms:

86%	Orgasm with masturbation
81%	Orgasm with a partner
13%	Occasionally orgasm with a partner
8%	Occasionally orgasm with masturbation
6%	Never orgasm with masturbation
6%	Never orgasm with a partner

The respondents were then asked to report their satisfaction with their sex lives, whether or not they were having partner sex. The ratings they gave were: 16 percent not at all satisfied; 24 percent somewhat satisfied; 8 percent passably satisfied; 38 percent fairly well satisfied; 14 percent completely satisfied.

Regardless of whether the women were coupled or single, they became less satisfied with their sexual lives as time went on. The single, casually involved and coupled women all had sex (either through masturbation or partner sex) less frequently the longer they were in their current situation. Coupled women often assume casually involved women are having more sex than those who are in couples; conversely, single women assume coupled women are having more sex. In this sample, there were no significant differences between the two groups.

It is difficult to tell exactly what makes someone satisfied with her sex life. When asked why respondents were dissatisfied with their sex lives, the following reasons were given: 21 percent relationship problems; 20 percent celibacy; 12 percent orgasmic problems; 10 percent partner not sexually compatible; 1 percent unacceptable sex practice; 36 percent other.

Satisfaction with Current Sex Life:

16%	Not at all satisfied
24%	Somewhat satisfied
8%	Passably satisfied
38%	Fairly well satisfied
14%	Completely satisfied

The 'other' category in this question yielded many replies. Some of them included: no sexual desire; self-hatred; fear of sex; coming out and feeling awkward; can't talk about own needs; incest background of self or partner; heterosexual acting out by partner; sexual initiation by partner uncomfortable; no lover; unrequited love; stress in other areas; physical pain; emotional pain. These numbers do not show how frequency affects satisfaction, nor whether for some women sex may become less frequent simply out of boredom.

I was interested to find that for couples, the incidence of partner sex decreased the most after the first year. This is usually the time when limerence is lost— limerence being the state of infatuation or being 'in love.' The frequency of sex then decreased significantly again after the second year. In subsequent years, partner sex decreased at a slower rate, but did continue to decrease. However, most couples reported that satisfaction with their sex lives decreased only after the first year. After that, the satisfaction stayed relatively the same no matter how long the relationship continued. It seems likely that a coupled lesbian remains satisfied with her sex life when she is satisfied with the relationship. In fact, the most common reason women gave for dissatisfac-

Reasons for Dissatisfaction with Current Sex Life:

21%	Relationship problems
20%	Celibacy
12%	Orgasmic problems
10%	Partner incompatibility
37%	Other reasons

tion with sex was relationship problems. Even with infrequent sex, it seems possible that a woman remains satisfied with her sex life because she feels loved. However, since many lesbians will leave a relationship because of a sexual attraction or liaison with someone new, do we in fact deny our sexual needs while in a relationship because love or companionship is more important? It may also simply be difficult for lesbians to admit to themselves and to others that they are dissatisfied. In further research, it would be interesting to ask women what makes sex satisfying for them, rather than focusing on dissatisfaction.

When thinking about satisfaction, it's important to remember that most of the lesbians in this survey had been in their current situations (single, casually involved, coupled) for fewer than three years. Does this imply that as sex became less satisfying, the women moved out of their situation—that single women looked for a partner, partnered women became single or became attached to a new partner, when they were no longer having satisfying sex? Does this mean that those who were casually involved with a sex partner eventually became coupled with that woman or broke off relations? No matter how many questionnaires were analyzed, the statistics did not change significantly, so it seems likely that lesbians generally do not stay in their situations for long. It would be illuminating to talk frankly in our communities about staying in long-term situations and about the reasons we decide to change.

Often what lesbians need most is information and permission to help them create a sex life that is exciting and satisfying. There is more discussion of this in the chapter, "Fanning the Flames." Each woman needs to consider how important sex is for her. Often it is too scary, and there is not enough motivation to create more sex in an existing relationship. But we each need to decide for ourselves about satisfaction and frequency, rather than trying to have sex as often as others.

My belief is that lesbians are more tied to the emotional impact of their relationships than they are to sex. After working with lesbians for a dozen years, I believe the quality of a relationship is the reason lesbians became coupled or uncoupled. The quality of a woman's relationship to herself is the greatest motivator for remaining single. Women who have casual involvements do so from a position of liking loving connections; usually either the casually involved woman or her partner is unwilling to be coupled. When choosing whether to be single, casually involved, or coupled, lesbians are

more invested in how they are loving and being loved (both themselves and with another woman)
than they are in sex *per se*.

Because we are all so quick to
make ourselves unique and others
different, I thought it would be
interesting to look at several
groups of women to see if indeed
we are so different. I considered
the questions of how often women
masturbated, how often they had
partner sex, and how satisfied they
were with their current sex life. I
did cross-correlations for the physically challenged, different age
groups, and survivors of childhood
sexual abuse, and then compared
them to the sample as a whole. In
most cases, there were virtually no
differences in sexual practice.
Graphs at the end of this chapter,
will illustrate these cross-
correlations. They can be used to
identify where differences do
occur.

It may be surprising that
women of all ages, varying abilities
and childhood sexual abuse experiences have very similar sex lives.
While this survey cannot general-
ize to all lesbians, it can certainly be
used as a basis for discussing the
sexual practices in our different
communities.

ACTUAL SEXUAL ACTIVITY

The last section of the questionnaire asked lesbians specifically what their current sexual

activities were: what they do to their sex partners, and what their partners do to them. All percentages in these sections were calculated using those who answered that they 'usually,' 'frequently' or 'always' did these practices. Those who 'never' or 'occasionally' did these practices were not counted in the percentages.

Perhaps the most poignant aspect of this survey is the question of whether or not lesbians hold hands. When asked if they held hands, 80 percent reported they did. When asked if they held hands in public, only 27 percent said they did. This is a statement about the oppression of lesbians in our culture. Heterosexuals assume they have the right to hold hands with their partner in public; most lesbians do not. This is symbolic of what we have to do to create a sex life. We have to keep hidden all of what we do; we fear reprisal if we are demonstrative in public. The majority of lesbians in this survey keep private even the most innocuous of acts, holding hands. This strains the flow of loving, sexual feelings.

The respondents' sexual activities were varied, some predictable and some not. The following is a partial listing. The most common activities were: 96 percent hugging; 92 percent snuggling; 91 percent kissing; 90 percent holding body to body; 89 percent masturbation; 87 percent being naked with partner; 80 percent holding hands. The activities done by over 50 percent of the group were: 76 percent french kissing; 70 percent petting; 64 percent necking; 52 percent kissing all over body.

Activities experienced by 11 to 40 percent of the group were: 39 percent fantasizing about sex with others; 32 percent fantasizing during sex; 30 percent massaging partner naked; 30 percent taking baths with partner; 29 percent blowing in ears; 27 percent holding hands in public; 23 percent fantasizing practices that they would never do; 23 percent reading erotic literature; 15 percent being naked with others; 14 percent having sex after fight with partner; and 11 percent looking at pornography.

A smaller, but still relevant, group of women regularly had: 8 percent psychic experiences during sex; 6 percent sex standing up; 6 percent sucking toes; 3 percent going to pornographic movies; 3 percent sex with men; 2 percent sex with more than one woman; 2 percent sex in public places; 1 percent sex for money; 1 percent group sex with both sexes; 1 percent sex with animals.

The following activities were gleaned from the 'other' category. They are listed without percentage points since so few women filled in the 'other' category that the results would probably misrepresent real

'Usual,' 'Frequent,' or 'Constant' Sexual Practices of All Respondents:

96%	Hug
92%	Snuggle
91%	Kiss
90%	Hold body to body
89%	Masturbate
87%	Are naked with partner
80%	Hold hands
76%	French kiss
70%	Pet
64%	Neck
52%	Kiss all over body
39%	Fantasize about sex with others
32%	Fantasize during sex
30%	Give massages naked
30%	Take baths together
29%	Blow in ears
27%	Hold hands in public
23%	Fantasize about practices they would not do
23%	Read erotic literature
15%	Being naked with others
14%	Have sex after fighting
11%	Look at pornography
8%	Have psychic experiences during sex
6%	Have sex standing up
6%	Suck toes
3%	Watch pornographic movies
3%	Have sex with men
2%	Have group sex with women
2%	Have sex in public places
1%	Have sex for money
1%	Have group sex with both sexes
1%	Have sex with animals

practice. This does not necessarily mean these activities are rarely done; it simply shows that I didn't think of everything when preparing the questions.

The activities the women reported were: sex in unusual places; vibrators and dildoes; sadomasochism; tickling; biting; tribadism; fisting; anal sex; licking; sucking; mutual oral sex; ejaculating with stimulus; tongue in ears; smelling underarms and between legs; dressing up; taking showers together; swimming; eating sensually; playing; fantasies about being male; exhibitionism; entering partner from the rear; lying on top of partner; dressing in leather.

Twelve percent of those answering 'other' listed sadomasochism as part of their sexual activity. Some women may find this shocking, while others may feel this percentage is too low and not representative of the women they know. There's no way to know if this number is high, perhaps because those doing S/M are more likely to attend a lecture on lesbian sex; or if this number is too low, since there were no direct questions about S/M anywhere on the questionnaire. We won't know the answer until someone else does another survey. Go for it.

Some of the practices listed may be disturbing, while others may be familiar. I think all of us expect that most lesbians hug, snuggle and kiss. I have to admit I had my prejudices when I put together the list. I thought *every-one* kissed.

There are many women who fantasize during sex and more who fantasize about someone else while having sex. Have you ever felt guilty about your fantasies, especially when fantasizing about someone other than your partner? Well, join the human race: 40 percent of us do. Another interesting point is that many women fantasized about sexual activity they would never actually want to do. Fantasy is perfect because you can imagine anything you want.

The age-old controversy about who is *really* a lesbian gets heated up when we see a survey in which lesbians (those who did not identify as lesbians were removed from the sample) admit they have sex with men. Others say they have sex for money. This may be the first time you learned that lesbians have sex with men or work as prostitutes. Women have been judged and made to fit narrow definitions for eons. I believe each lesbian has the right to engage in any sexual practice that is not harmful to herself or others.

To me, the most exciting aspect of this section is the varied ways we have sex, and the new ideas we can get from this list. We can use our bodies however we want, and we can participate with other women in whatever body play we both want.

I then asked women to list what they actually do with their partners and what their partners do to them. Most respondents thought they did more, sexually, to their partner than their partner did to them. This raises some interesting questions. Do lesbians perceive their sex practices as giving more than they get? Is receiving more difficult than giving? Do we feel shy about reporting exactly what we do with each other?

Respondents also believed their partners were less monogamous than they were. Since many couples answered the questionnaire, it is unlikely that such a large disparity exists. Perhaps we perceive ourselves as more loyal or do not consider our own outside sexual activities as breaking monogamy. Perhaps we fear our partners are more likely to betray us than they are in reality.

When reading this part of the survey, it's important to keep in mind that respondents may do different activities to a partner than they want done to themselves. Lesbians listed the following things they did to partners: 95 percent touch breasts; 92 percent kiss breasts; 88 percent are monogamous; 83 percent lick breasts; 83 percent put fingers in vagina; 71 percent do oral sex to their partners; 56 percent put their

Activities Respondents Do to Their Partners:

95%	Touch breasts
92%	Kiss breasts
88%	Are monogamous
83%	Lick breasts
83%	Put fingers in vagina
71%	Have oral sex
56%	Put tongue in vagina
55%	Masturbate partner
51%	Nurse on breasts
21%	Talk 'dirty'
16%	Use vibrator
14%	Put fingers in anus
9%	Put dildo in vagina
9%	Are nonmonogamous
8%	Act out fantasies
8%	Put tongue around anus
6%	Put whole hand in vagina
5%	Have sex when they don't want to
5%	Spank
4%	Practice bondage
2%	Do water sports
1%	Use dildo in anus
1%	Put whole hand in anus

tongues inside vagina; 55 percent masturbate partner; 51 percent 'nurse' on breasts; 21 percent talk 'dirty'; 16 percent use vibrator; 14 percent put fingers inside anus; 9 percent put dildo in vagina; 9 percent are nonmonogamous; 8 percent act out fantasies; 8 percent put tongue around anus; 6 percent put whole hand in vagina; 5 percent have sex when they don't want to; 5 percent spank; 4 percent practice bondage; 2 percent engage in water sports; 1 percent use dildo in anus; 1 percent put whole hand in anus. (We need to note that some respondents may have used 'water sports' to describe any water play, not knowing 'water sports' usually refers to urinating on each other.)

Respondents reported that their partners did the following to them: 90 percent touch breasts; 86 percent kiss breasts; 83 percent are monogamous; 80 percent put fingers in vagina; 76 percent lick breasts; 67 percent perform oral sex; 54 percent put tongue inside vagina; 54 percent masturbate them; 46 percent 'nurse' on breasts; 22 percent talk 'dirty'; 15 percent use vibrator; 13 percent of partners are nonmonogamous; 11 percent put fingers inside anus; 10 percent use dildo in vagina; 10 percent act out fantasies; 8 percent put whole hand in vagina; 6 percent put tongue around anus; 5 percent have sex when they don't want to; 5 percent spank; 5 percent engage

Activities Partners Do to Respondents:

90%	Touch breasts
86%	Kiss breasts
83%	Are monogamous
80%	Put fingers in vagina
76%	Lick breasts
67%	Have oral sex
54%	Put tongue in vagina
54%	Masturbate partner
46%	Nurse on breasts
22%	Talk 'dirty'
15%	Use vibrator
13%	Are nonmonogamous
11%	Put fingers in anus
10%	Put dildo in vagina
10%	Act out fantasies
10%	Put whole hand in vagina
6%	Put tongue around anus
5%	Have sex when they don't want to
5%	Spank
5%	Practice bondage
5%	Do water sports
2%	Put whole hand in anus
1%	Use dildo in anus

in water sports (again, remember this may be an unclear category); 5 percent practice bondage; 2 percent put whole hand in anus; and 1 percent use dildo in anus. As can be seen, with a few exceptions (notably nonmonogamy), the percentage points in this section were slightly lower than those in the first section.

One of the most important uses of this survey is to learn what we really do when we are having sex. Not what we tell others we do, not what we wish we did, but what we actually do. This is important because it helps to correct myths about lesbian sex and encourages telling the truth.

See if you are willing to tell your friends about what you do during masturbation or partner sex. You and your friends, or you and your partner, might discuss this list to see which activities you prefer and which you would like to try.

Some statistics may be surprising to many lesbians. It's a common assumption that lesbians have oral sex, but 29 percent of these women did not perform oral sex on their partners, and 33 percent of the respondents had partners who did not perform oral sex on them. Many women will read this and be greatly relieved—one third of lesbians do not go down on each other. When I talk about this statistic before audiences, they make hissing sounds and laugh. When I point out how large one third of the audience is, they don't want to believe that that many lesbians don't have oral sex.

Notice your own prejudices when reading this information. You probably have many preconceived notions about how lesbians have sex. The value of this survey is that it reflects lesbian experience. We need to allow ourselves the freedom to tell the truth about our sex lives.

As a final question, I asked lesbians how they felt about sex. Four percent said they hated it, 87 percent said they loved it, and 9 percent didn't answer. If I asked these same women today, I might get a different response. If you are a lesbian who hates sex, it may be a relief to you that you are not alone. Some of us feel this way, even though we have been taught that we are not allowed to have these feelings.

This survey should be used to empower each and every one of us. It is a tool to help with our self-loving, our excitement, our interest and our understanding of our lesbianism.

There is much more to investigate. Hopefully, this information will stimulate discussion, research and communication about sex. As we become less oppressed by a homophobic culture, we will be more able to gather information

Feelings About Sex:

87%	Love It
4%	Hate It
9%	Didn't respond

from our community and share it with the world.

The current AIDS crisis has greatly affected the self-esteem and sexual lives of lesbians in this culture. The quickly changing face of AIDS is evident in that there is not a single question about AIDS or safe sex on this survey. When I began distributing it in 1984, we didn't know that lesbians were at risk. Now we know better, and in a subsequent survey, the topic of safe sex and AIDS must be addressed.

The more we understand lesbian sexuality, the better able we will be to love ourselves and each other. There is something so magical and precious about women being sexual with themselves and with each other. We have much nurturing, tenderness and love to share.

Yes, many of us have difficulty with masturbation, partner sex, commitment, and so on. The exciting part is that we are changing. We are learning more about loving, healing and honesty. What other community consistently works at creating room for the differently abled? What other community has taken themselves to task about childcare? What other community has come in such numbers to recovery? What other community examines difficult issues like racism, S/M and battering? What other community has searched for a better way in such earnest?

There is something so lovely, so giving about women. We are the healers of battered women; we are the healers of abused children; we even participate now in healing men with AIDS. Who would have thought ten years ago that so many lesbians would have rallied around men in their time of need? We are so magical.

That magic is nowhere better expressed than in our sexuality with ourselves and other women. We deserve that special love, that healing, that deep, satisfying touch. May we support each other to have loving, exciting sex. We are lucky to be lesbians.

May our passion grow strong and free.

Length of Time in Relationship and Satisfaction with Sex Life

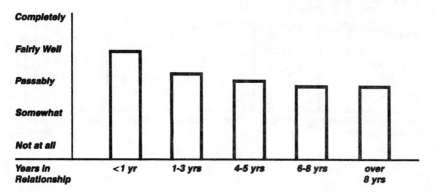

Frequency of Sex with Partner by Length of Time in Relationship

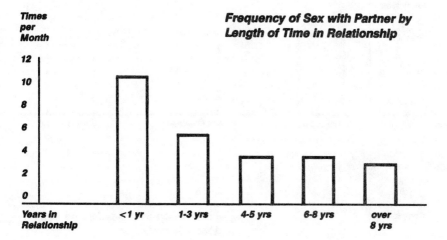

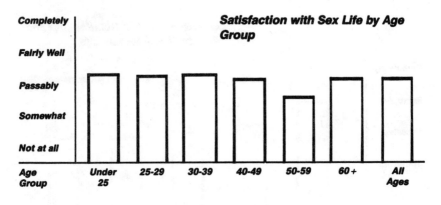

Satisfaction with Sex Life by Age Group

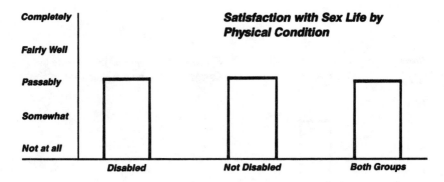

Satisfaction with Sex Life by Physical Condition

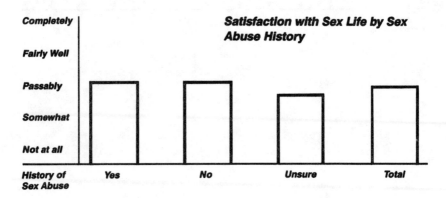

Satisfaction with Sex Life by Sex Abuse History

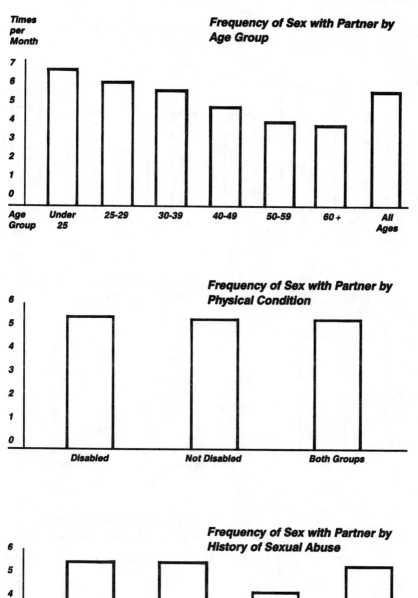

Frequency of Sex with Partner by Age Group

Times per Month

Age Group: Under 25, 25-29, 30-39, 40-49, 50-59, 60+, All Ages

Frequency of Sex with Partner by Physical Condition

Disabled, Not Disabled, Both Groups

Frequency of Sex with Partner by History of Sexual Abuse

History of Sex Abuse: Yes, No, Unsure, Total

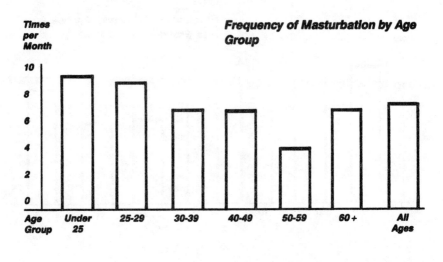

Times per Month

Frequency of Masturbation by Age Group

Age Group: Under 25, 25-29, 30-39, 40-49, 50-59, 60+, All Ages

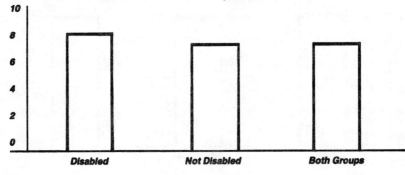

Frequency of Masturbation by Physical Condition

Disabled, Not Disabled, Both Groups

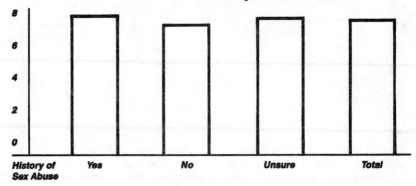

Frequency of Masturbation by History of Sexual Abuse

History of Sex Abuse: Yes, No, Unsure, Total

Appendix: Questionnaire

LESBIAN SEXUAL EXPERIENCES

This has been prepared by JoAnn Loulan, a lesbian who is the author of *Lesbian Sex*, a book for lesbians about sex. I want to give lesbians information about lesbian sex lives. The best way to do this is to ask lesbians themselves. If you are willing, please fill out this questionnaire and return it at the end of this event or mail it to me.

PART A. SELF DESCRIPTION
Are you a lesbian?

yes	not sure	no

(If yes), for how many years has lesbianism been your orientation?

Under 1	1-3	3-5
5-10	10-20	over 20

What is your age?

Under 25	25-29	30-39
40-49	50-59	Over 60

What economic class were you raised in?

lower	lower middle	middle
upper middle	upper	mixed

Ethnic designation:

Black	Caucasian	Hispanic
Asian/Pacific Islander	Native American	

What religion were you raised in?

Catholic	Jewish	Protestant
Fundamental	Mormon (LDS)	Other
Protestant	None	

Are you disabled?

yes   no

(If yes), at what age did you become disabled?

at birth	birth-5	5-10
10-15	15-21	over 21

(If yes), what is the nature of your disability?

paraplegic	quadraplegic	post-polio
diabetic	food allergies	hearing impaired
vision impaired	life-threatening illness	heart disease
amputee	ostomy	mental illness
hidden disability	not listed (please name)	visible disability not listed (please name)

What kind of educational background do you have?

high school or less   some college or technical   college degree
post grad degree

PART B. BACKGROUND FACTORS

How strong was the religious influence in your upbringing?

not at all	somewhat	average
quite strong	all encompassing	

Does your pre-adult personal herstory include any incidence of sexual abuse?

yes   no   unsure

If unsure, please comment as to what your remembrance is:

(If yes), how often did this abuse take place?

once   a few times   several times
frequently

(If yes), who was the perpetrator? (Mark all that apply)

father	mother	sibling
older male relative	same age male relative	older female relative
same age female relative	male lover/husband of	female lover/partner of
male stranger	mother	mother
female stranger	other (specify)	

(If yes), what age(s) were you at the time of the abuse?

under 5   5-10   11-15
16-18

Please list the degree to which you have experienced sexual abuse as an adult.
(Mark all that apply)

not at all	verbal harassment	physical harassment
physical beating	rape	

If this was your experience, who was the perpetrator(s)?

male stranger	female stranger	male relative
female relative	male lover/friend	female lover/friend
male husband/mate	female mate	other (specify)

Were you raised in an alcoholic/addict home?

yes	not sure	no

Please describe your present status with regard to use/abuse of chemical substances:

presently addicted	addicted in past,	casual user
heavy user	currently clean and sober	never used

PART C. SEXUAL EXPERIENCES

Are you presently:

single	casually involved with a sexual friend	in a couple

How many years have you been in the above arrangement?

under 1	1-3	4-5
6-8	9-15	over 15

Have you ever been celibate (no sex with a partner)?

yes	no

(If yes), what is the longest period of time you have been celibate?

under six mos.	six mos.-1 yr.	1-3 yrs.
3-5 yrs.	6-8 yrs.	9-15 yrs.
over 15 yrs.		

(If yes), was it a choice?

yes	sort of	no

(If yes), what was the reason(s) for celibacy?

felt good	motherhood	recovering from
illness	spiritual practice	substance abuse
stress	my lover left	sexual abuse memories
other		

Do you masturbate?

yes	sort of	no

(If yes), how often per month?

| less than once | once | 2-5 |
| 6-10 | 10-20 | over 20 |

(If yes), how do you usually masturbate?

| hands | vibrator | rubbing clitoris on some- |
| other (specify) | | thing (tribadism) |

During a typical month, how often do you have sex with another person?

never	less than once	once
2-5	6-10	10-20
over 20		

If you use/have used chemical substances, how would you generally describe your sexual experiences when under the influence?

| fantastic | good | okay |
| unsatisfactory | awful | |

How would you generally describe your sexual experience when not under the influence of chemical substances?

| fantastic | good | okay |
| unsatisfactory | awful | |

In general, how are you satisfied with your sex life?

| not at all | somewhat | passable |
| fairly well | completely | |

If you are dissatisfied, why are you?

celibacy	relationship problems	partner not sexually
sex practices not	orgasmic problems	compatible
acceptable	other (specify)	

PART D. ACTUAL SEXUAL ACTIVITY

Section 1: Please mark one number that indicates your activity.

1 = never   2 = occasionally   3 = usually   4 = frequently   5 = always

Holding hands	Holding hands in public	Kissing
French kissing	Blowing in ears	Necking
Petting	Kissing all over body	Being naked w/partner
Being naked with others	Holding body to body	Holding naked
Taking baths with	Massage naked	Sex with more than one
partner	Masturbate	woman
Sex with men	Sucking toes	Hugging
Fantasize about sex with	Fantasize about practices	Read erotic literature
others	would never do	Go to pornographic
Look at pornography	Snuggle	movies
Fantasize during sex	Group sex w/both sexes	

Have sex after fight with partner

Orgasmic with masturbation

Sex standing up

Other practice (specify):

Sex with animals

Orgasmic with partner

Never orgasmic

Hate sex

Sex in public places

Psychic experiences during sex

Orgasmic occasionally

Love sex

Sex for money

What city and state do you live in

What is the population of your city

Where did you receive this questionnaire

Section 2: Please mark number that fits for each column.

1 = never   2 = occasionally   3 = usually   4 = frequently   5 = always

You do to a partner:

Touch breasts

Use vibrator

Put tongue inside vagina

Put fingers inside anus

Put whole hand in anus

Non-orgasmic

Oral sex

Act out fantasies

Nonmonogamous

Kiss breasts

Masturbate

Use dildo in vagina

Use dildo in anus

Orgasmic

Bondage

'Nursing' on breast

Have sex when don't want to

Lick breasts

Put fingers in vagina

Put tongue around anus

Put whole hand in vagina

Water sports

Spanking

Talk 'dirty'

Monogamous

Partner does to you:

Touch breasts

Use vibrator

Put tongue inside vagina

Put fingers inside anus

Put whole hand in anus

Non-orgasmic

Oral sex

Act out fantasies

Nonmonogamous

Kiss breasts

Masturbate

Use dildo in vagina

Use dildo in anus

Orgasmic

Bondage

'Nursing' on breast

Have sex when don't want to

Lick breasts

Put fingers in vagina

Put tongue around anus

Put whole hand in vagina

Water sports

Spanking

Talk 'dirty'

Monogamous

Please describe any other activities:

JoAnn Loulan is a psychotherapist, sex educator and author specializing in the sexual and emotional concerns of lesbians. JoAnn is nationally recognized as a pioneer in the field of counseling lesbians about issues that undermine their sex lives, relationships and self-esteem. JoAnn's experience includes teaching courses on human sexuality to health professionals at the University of California/San Francisco Medical School. She has presented research on lesbian sex practices to such groups as the American Psychological Association, American Women in Psychology, the International Transactional Analysis Association and the National Gay & Lesbian Health Conference, and to groups of recovering addicts and their families. JoAnn presents lectures, lesbian sex community workshops and training seminars for mental health professionals throughout the U.S. and Canada. She is a licensed Marriage, Family & Child Counselor with a private practice in Palo Alto, California. JoAnn's published works, including *Lesbian Sex* and *Period*, have sold over 80,000 copies.

Photo: Irene Young

LOULAN PRODUCTIONS presents "The Lesbian Sexuality Lecture Series," a collection of JoAnn Loulan's lectures on cassette tapes. The following titles will be released Fall 1987:

#1 "Lesbians, CEBV, AIDS & Safe Sex"
55 minutes, $9.95 retail
#2 "Incest Survivors"
"Partners of Incest Survivors"
90 minutes, $12.95 retail
#3 "Fanning the Flames for Couples"
"Healing the Child Within"
90 minutes, $12.95 retail

To order, please include $.75 each P/H, CA residents also add 7% sales tax, and mail to: Loulan Productions, 1450 6th St., Berkeley, CA 94710. (415) 525-7979. Credit cards accepted; please include Visa or Mastercard number, expiration date, and signature. Please indicate whether you'd like to be added to JoAnn's mailing list to receive info on further tape releases and lecture tours.

◙spinsters | *aunt lute* ▣

Spinsters/Aunt Lute Book Company was founded in 1986 through the merger of two successful feminist publishing businesses, Aunt Lute Book Company, formerly of Iowa City (founded 1982) and Spinsters Ink of San Francisco (founded 1978). A consolidation in the best sense of the word, this merger has strengthened our ability to produce vital books for diverse women's communities in the years to come.

Our commitment is to publishing works that are beyond the scope of mainstream commercial publishers: books that don't just name crucial issues in women's lives, but go on to encourage change and growth, to make all of our lives more possible.

Though Spinsters/Aunt Lute is a growing, energetic company, there is little margin in publishing to meet overhead and production expenses. We survive only through the generosity of our readers. So, we want to thank those of you who have further supported Spinsters/Aunt Lute—with donations, with subscriber monies, or with low and high interest loans. It is that additional economic support that helps us bring out exciting new books.

Please write to us for information about our unique investment and contribution opportunities.

If you would like further information about the books, notecards and journals we produce, write for a free catalogue.

Spinsters/Aunt Lute
P. O. Box 410687
San Francisco, CA 94141